IMAGES
of America

PEMBROKE
1905–2005

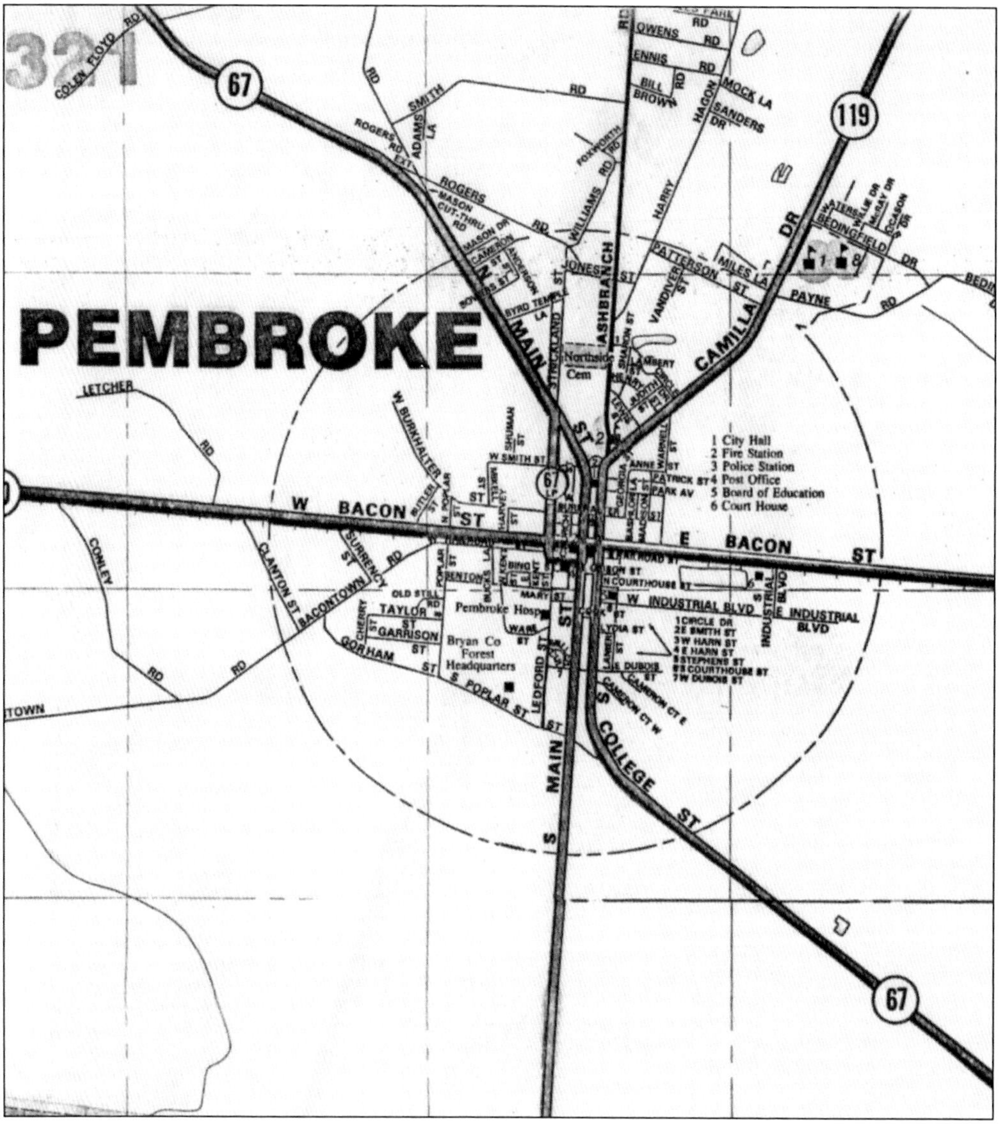

This map depicts the current Pembroke area as of 2004.

IMAGES of America

PEMBROKE 1905–2005

Pembroke Centennial Committee

ARCADIA PUBLISHING

ISBN 978-0-7385-1798-8

Published by Arcadia Publishing
Charleston, South Carolina

Printed in the United States of America

Library of Congress Catalog Card Number: 2005920889

For all general information contact Arcadia Publishing at:
Telephone 843-853-2070
Fax 843-853-0044
E-mail sales@arcadiapublishing.com
For customer service and orders:
Toll-Free 1-888-313-2665

Visit us on the internet at www.arcadiapublishing.com

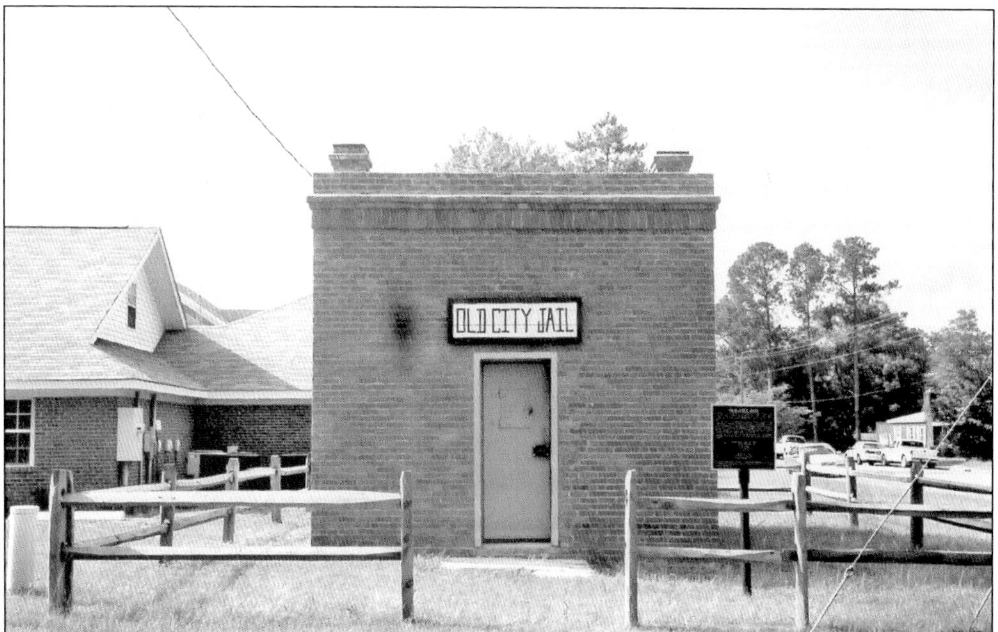

The old city jail was built in 1912. A one-room building, it was dismantled and shipped by wagon and then reassembled in Pembroke in 1938. Inside the old jail is an 1897 two-unit cell that was purchased from the Bryan County seat in Clyde, Georgia. It remained in operation until the 1950s. In 2003, it was restored by Pembroke City Council as a historic site.

CONTENTS

Acknowledgments

The Pembroke Centennial Committee was organized in June 2004 to plan activities in celebration of Pembroke's first 100 years. Additionally, plans were made for the publication of centennial calendars, note cards, and a pictorial history book about Pembroke. The Centennial Committee has worked diligently; among the activities planned are a parade, arts and crafts booths, a community choir, and food booths. And it's a must that we include old-time train rides through downtown Pembroke! A special guest speaker will be on hand to commemorate the occasion.

The Centennial Book Committee wholeheartedly expresses their gratitude to all those individuals who so graciously shared their photographs, as well as their memories. This book could not have happened without the support, interest, and talents of our many contributors. A special thank you goes to George and Jan Hendrix for sharing many of the photographs included. The following people also shared their photographs and memories and/or worked directly with the Book Committee to compile all of the information: Pat Marlotte, Earline Geiger, Freddie Drexel Lee, Glenda Hendry Carter, Paul Weinberger of the Pembroke Library, Teresa Zimmerman, Louise Bunch, Charlene Williams, Mayor Judy Cook, and Barbara Nelson Lanier, attorney for the City of Pembroke. If we have omitted anyone, we sincerely apologize and do appreciate your help in our endeavor.

Disclaimer

The size restrictions for this book (128 pages and no more than 240 images) have meant that many worthy photographs had to be excluded. Some were too light or too dark to include. We have tried to be as accurate as possible. The various sources used to document names, places and dates include, but are not limited to, *The Pembroke Journal*, Bryan County Clerk's Office records, and the personal knowledge of those mentioned above. Our sincere thanks and appreciation goes to Mr. Buddy Sullivan, author of *From Beautiful Zion to Red Bird Creek*, for permission to use his work as a reference. Additionally, we are indebted to the people of Bryan County, Georgia, for their outstanding work on *The History of Bryan County 1793–1985*, which we referred to many times. We apologize for any errors and ask that you notify us so that they may be corrected in our files.

INTRODUCTION

Pembroke came by its name from a prominent citizen of the late 19th century, Judge Pembroke Williams. As was true for so many small towns of the rural South, Pembroke's inception was dependent upon the railroad. It was one of the lucky sites, inasmuch as the "train stopped there." Its sister town, Ellabell, was not so lucky when the train passed her by. According to historians, Pembroke came into existence when the Savannah and Western Railroad extended its line from Meldrim, Georgia, to a point 32 miles west of Savannah. Indeed, a most interesting fact is that the first resident of Pembroke worked for the railroad. When a boxcar was switched off, he began living in it, and that is how the story began. This gentleman's name was M. E. Carter, and he became Pembroke's first section-master.

The railroad's importance stemmed from the fact that Pembroke, as well as other small rural towns during the late 19th century, was a large producer of naval stores as well as lumber. By the late 1890s, permanent buildings of a substantial nature were being constructed, and by the early 20th century, Pembroke became the commercial and business center of Bryan County. The little town was incorporated August 23, 1905, by an act of the Georgia General Assembly. It is evident that the forefathers were interested in education, because on December 5, 1905, a bond referendum was called to approve the issuance of $8,000 in bonds for the purpose of building Pembroke's first school. This school was the Bryan Normal Institute. In 1919, it was sold to the Bryan County Board of Education for $4,000, with the stipulation that there would always be a high school in the city of Pembroke. Education is still a high priority throughout Bryan County.

Pembroke encompasses approximately eight square miles of land and is located at the intersection of Highway 280, Highway 67, and Highway 119. The railroad tracks run through the middle of town parallel to Highway 280. There are many old buildings built in the 1930s with beautiful motifs along this section of highway. One such building housed the Tos Theatre, now planned for renovation, where many of the residents of Pembroke and surrounding areas spent many enjoyable Saturdays and, if they were lucky, weekdays as well.

Next door to the theatre was the drugstore, where there were wonderful treats such as ice cream cones piled high, comic books, and small tables and chairs where you could sit and enjoy not only the delights sold in the store, but friendships as well. Many Saturday afternoons in Pembroke were spent sitting in cars parked on Main Street "people watching." It was a quieter, more peaceful time, even though everyone had just come through the Depression.

Other businesses in Pembroke were a grocery, dry goods store, hardware store, and a bank, as well as doctors' and lawyers' offices. Some of the loveliest buildings housed the various denominations of churches.

Throughout the years, Pembroke has grown. The population of Pembroke, as well as the population of surrounding areas, has contributed to the growth of the town itself. In recent years, under the excellent leadership of the mayor and councilmen, numerous activities bring many people to the town. The annual Christmas parade has become a favorite, as well as the Balloon Fest. The local school system has earned an exceptional reputation, and along with extracurricular activities has enticed people to move to Pembroke and Bryan County.

Pembroke is a town that combines the beauty of its antiquity with the excitement of its growth. It is, in many ways, an anomaly, in that when you "drive through Pembroke" you have a wonderful sense of its past and all those wonderful memories; however, they are mingled with the present and all its activities that denote growth. Local residents consider themselves very lucky to live in Pembroke, Georgia!

We hope you will enjoy this book of Pembroke's past and present.

Incorporation of the Town of Pembroke—No. 549

An Act to incorporate the town of Pembroke, in the county of Bryan, State of Georgia; to define the corporate limits thereof; to provide for a mayor and councilmen and other officers; to prescribe their duties; to provide municipal government of said town; to confer certain powers and privileges on same; to provide for the enacting of all necessary ordinances; to provide for penalties for the violation of the same; to authorize and empower the mayor and council to issue bonds for the purpose of building school buildings and equipping the same, and for other purposes.

Section 1. Be it enacted by the General Assembly of the State of Georgia, and it is hereby enacted by the authority of the same, that the town of Pembroke, in county of Bryan, be, and the same is, hereby declared to be incorporated under the name and style of the City of Pembroke, and shall be entitled to sue and be sued, plead and be impleaded, purchase and hold real estate, necessary to enable the mayor and council of the said city of Pembroke to the better discharge of their duties, and needful for the good order, government and welfare of said town, and by said name also shall have perpetual succession.

Section 2. Be it further enacted by the authority aforesaid, that the corporate limits of said city of Pembroke shall extend in every direction the distance of one mile from the depot, or warehouse of the S.A.L. railway as now situated.

Section 3. Be it further enacted, that the municipal authorities of said city shall be a mayor and five councilmen, who are hereby constituted a body corporate for said city of Pembroke and by that name, and that W. J. Strickland is hereby constituted and appointed mayor for said city, and R. S. Burgess, M. A. Gibson, James B. Moyd, Julius Morgan, and C. C. Moyd, all of said city, be, and they are hereby constituted and appointed councilmen of said councilmen of said city, the mayor and councilmen to hold their respective offices.

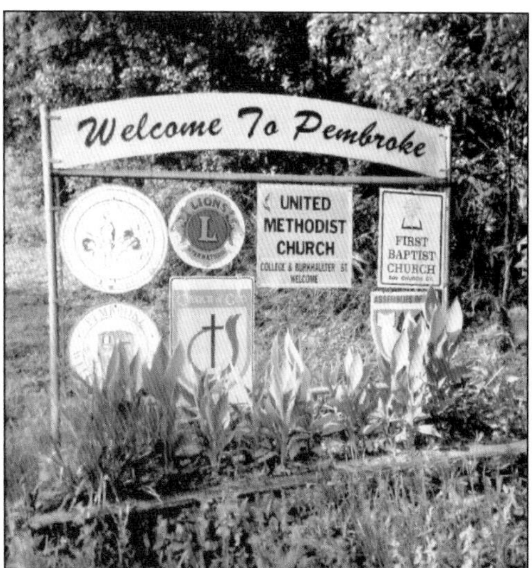

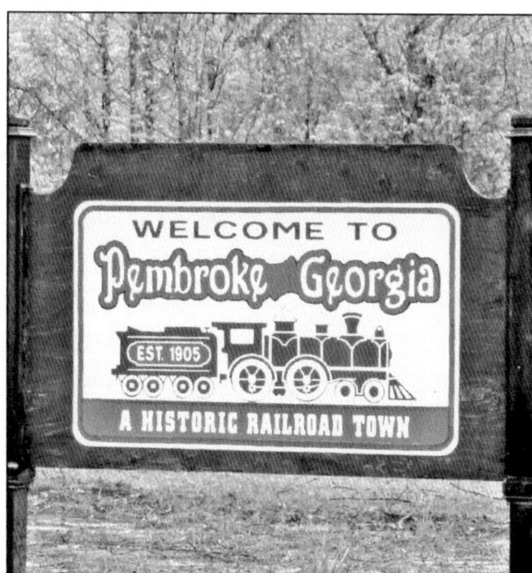

(Above left) This "Welcome to Pembroke" sign was erected by the Lion's Club.
(Above right) A sign erected on Highway 280 East shows the entrance into Pembroke, "A Historic Railroad Town." A duplicate sign is located on Highway 67. In 1996, the City purchased these signs to be erected on various roads leading into the city.

One

Pembroke Then and Now

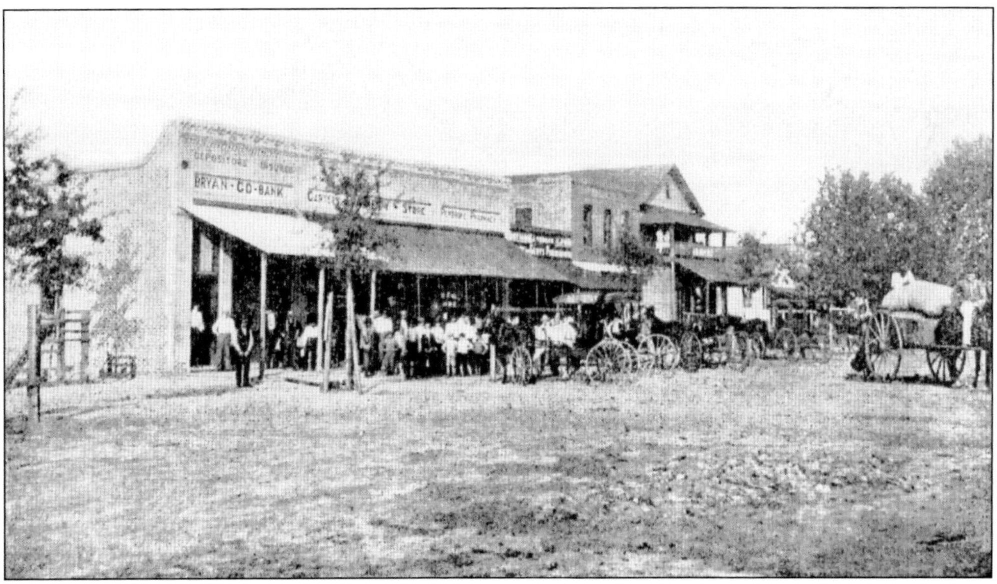

In this early view of Pembroke, Railroad Street is pictured looking east, showing Bryan County Bank, Carter's Variety Store, and Pembroke Pharmacy c. 1890. The Bryan County Bank was chartered on August 12, 1903, and the incorporators were M. E. Carter, J. B. Moyd, P. J. Burkhalter, and B. F. Burnette. The Bryan County Bank was the first bank established in Pembroke.

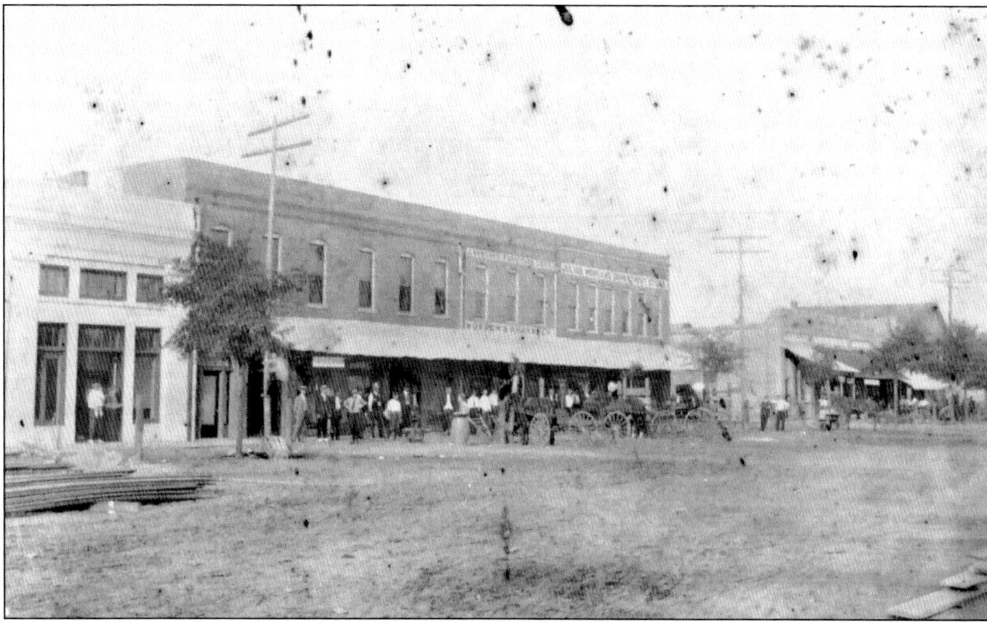

Pembroke's Main Street is seen in earlier times. Many small towns such as Pembroke were established in the early 20th century, and Pembroke came into being when the Savannah and Western Railroads extended its line from Meldrim, Georgia, to a point 32 miles west of Savannah.

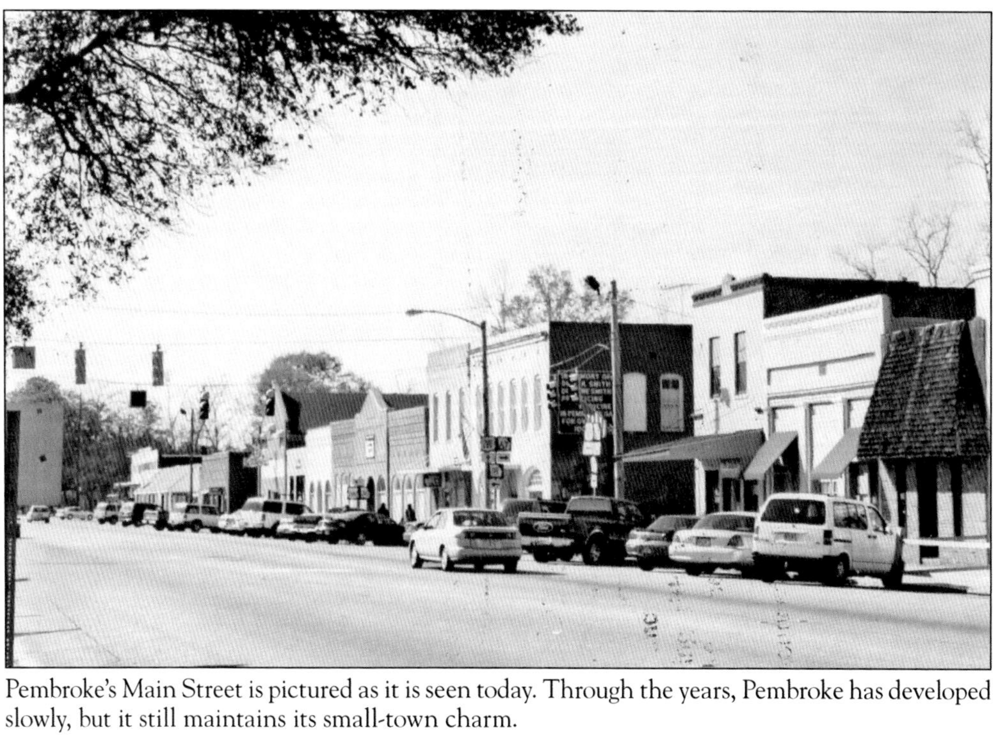

Pembroke's Main Street is pictured as it is seen today. Through the years, Pembroke has developed slowly, but it still maintains its small-town charm.

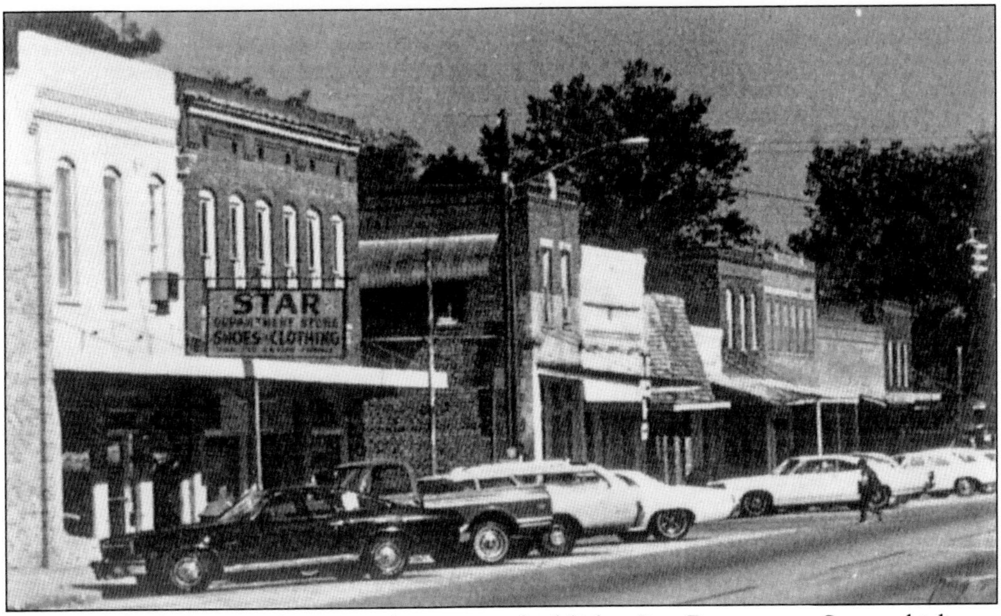

In this photograph from the 1960s, the marquee highlights Star Department Store, which was one of the few dry goods stores in the community.

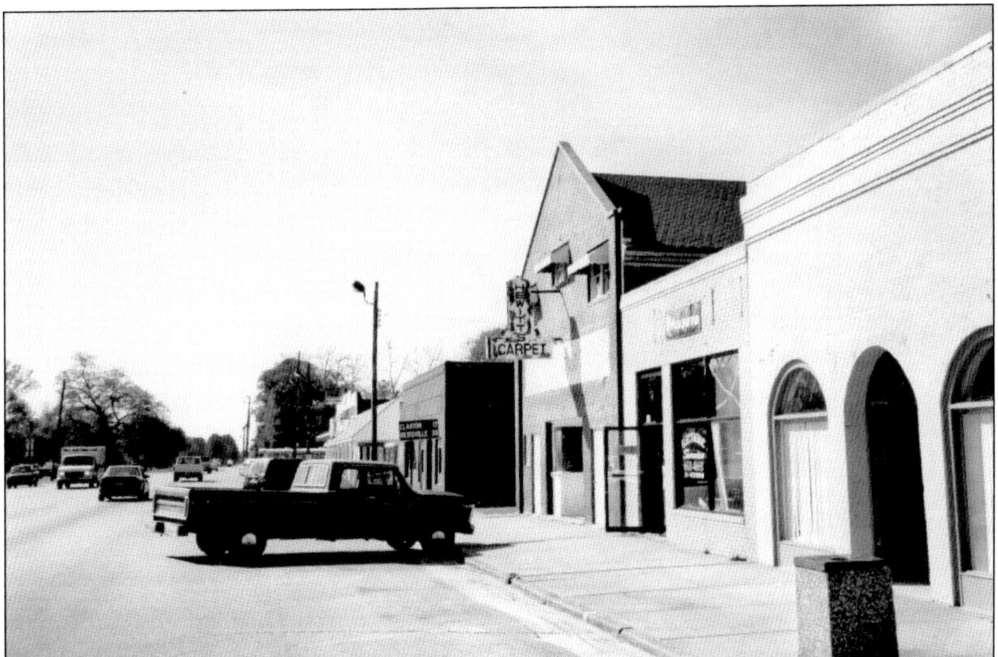

Another modern photograph depicts Pembroke as it is today. Pembroke is still thriving as Bryan County's seat and looks forward to continued growth.

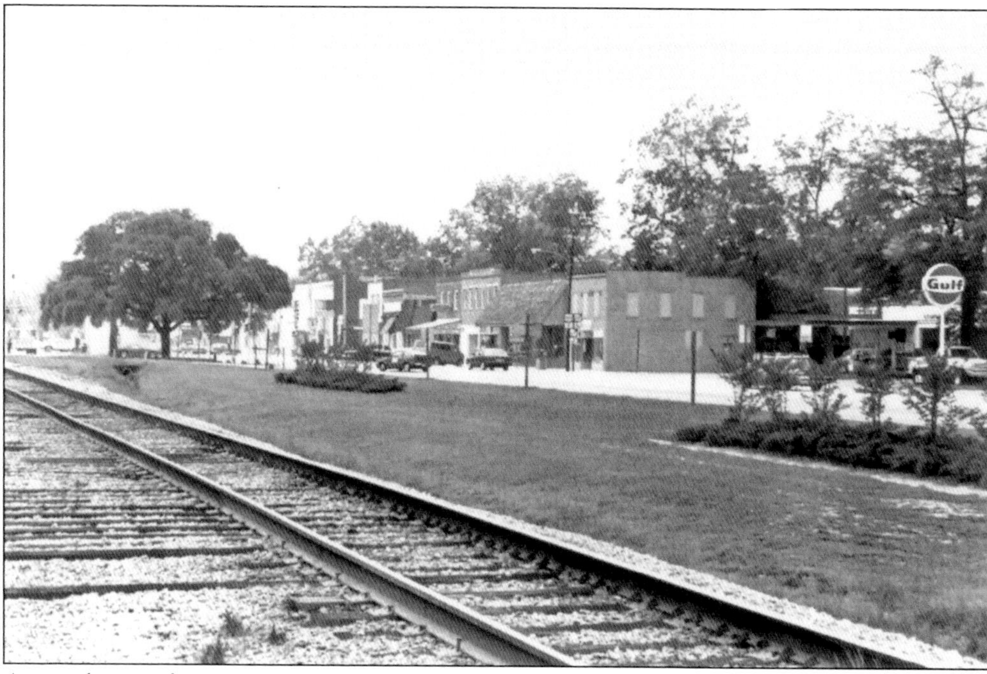

As was the case for many towns established during this time period, the railroad was the heartbeat of the community, and many houses sprang up on different sites.

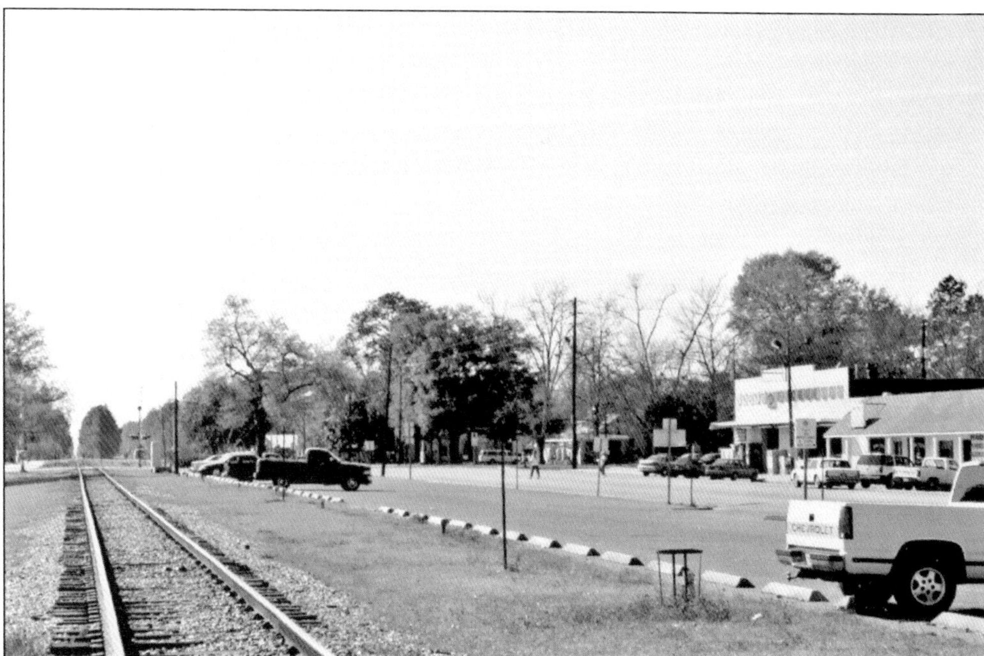

The new railroad no longer offers passenger service, but it is still actively used to ship merchandise throughout Georgia and beyond.

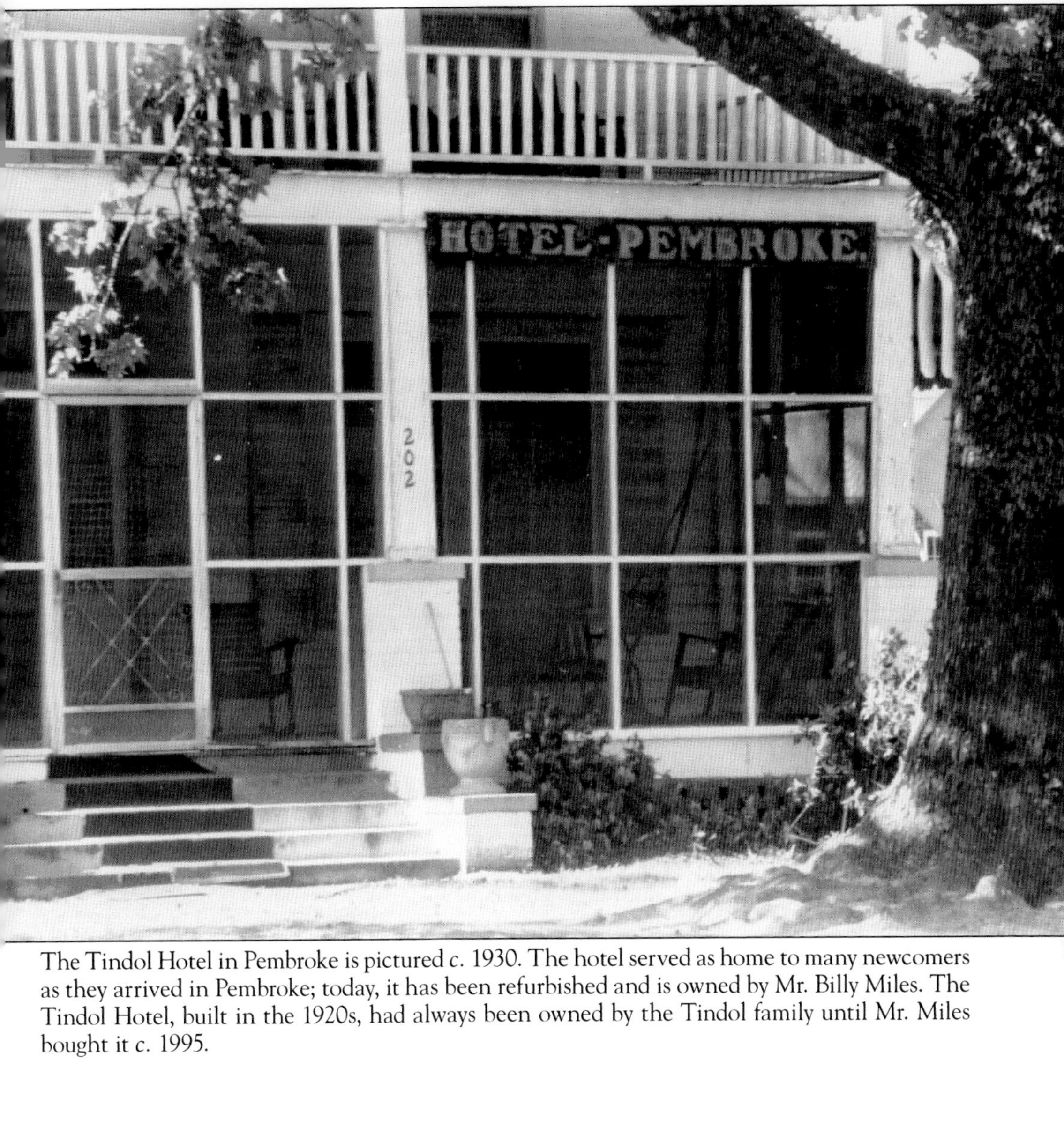

The Tindol Hotel in Pembroke is pictured *c.* 1930. The hotel served as home to many newcomers as they arrived in Pembroke; today, it has been refurbished and is owned by Mr. Billy Miles. The Tindol Hotel, built in the 1920s, had always been owned by the Tindol family until Mr. Miles bought it *c.* 1995.

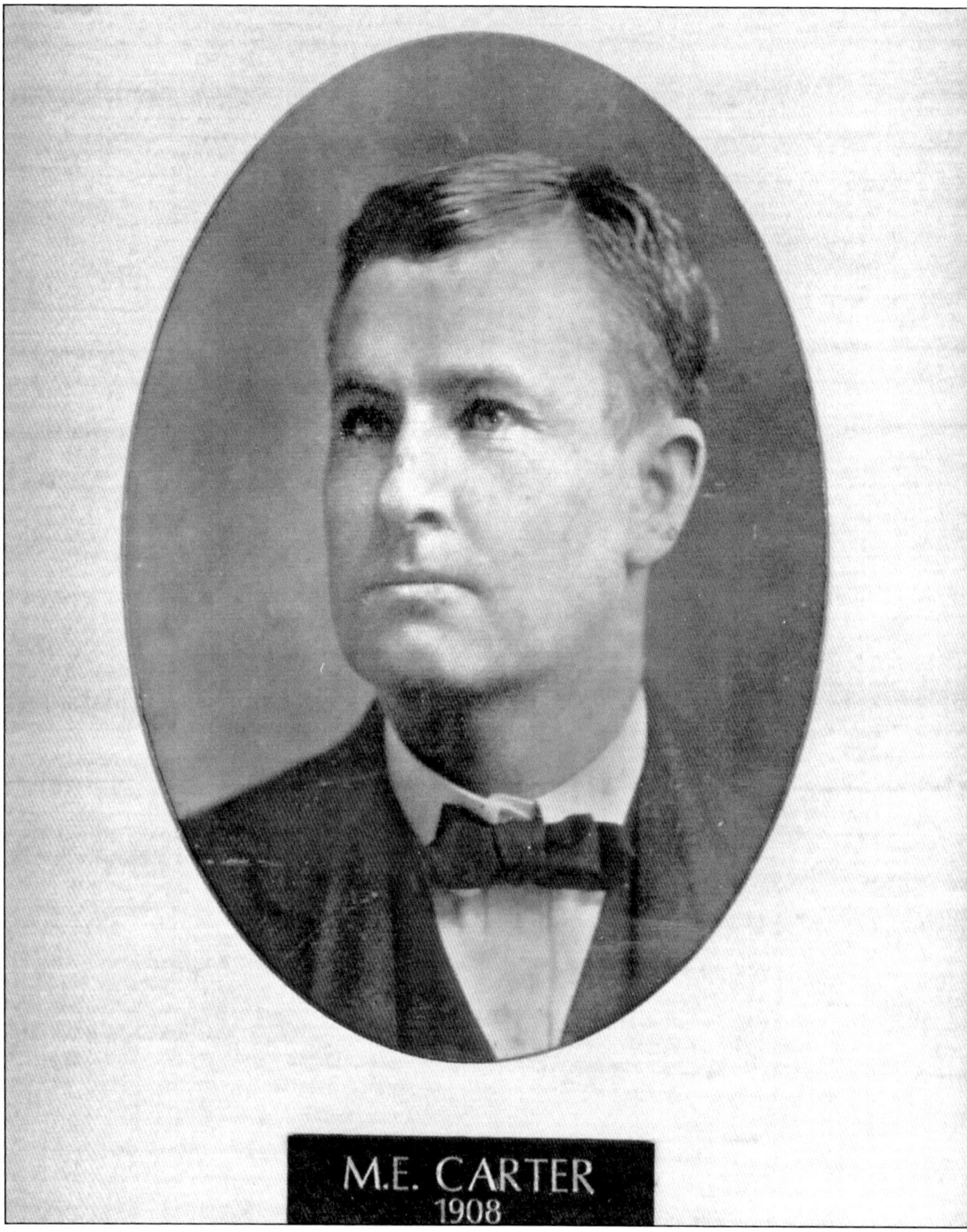

M. E. Carter was a member of the railroad construction crew, and when a boxcar was switched off he lived in it, thus becoming Pembroke's first "resident."

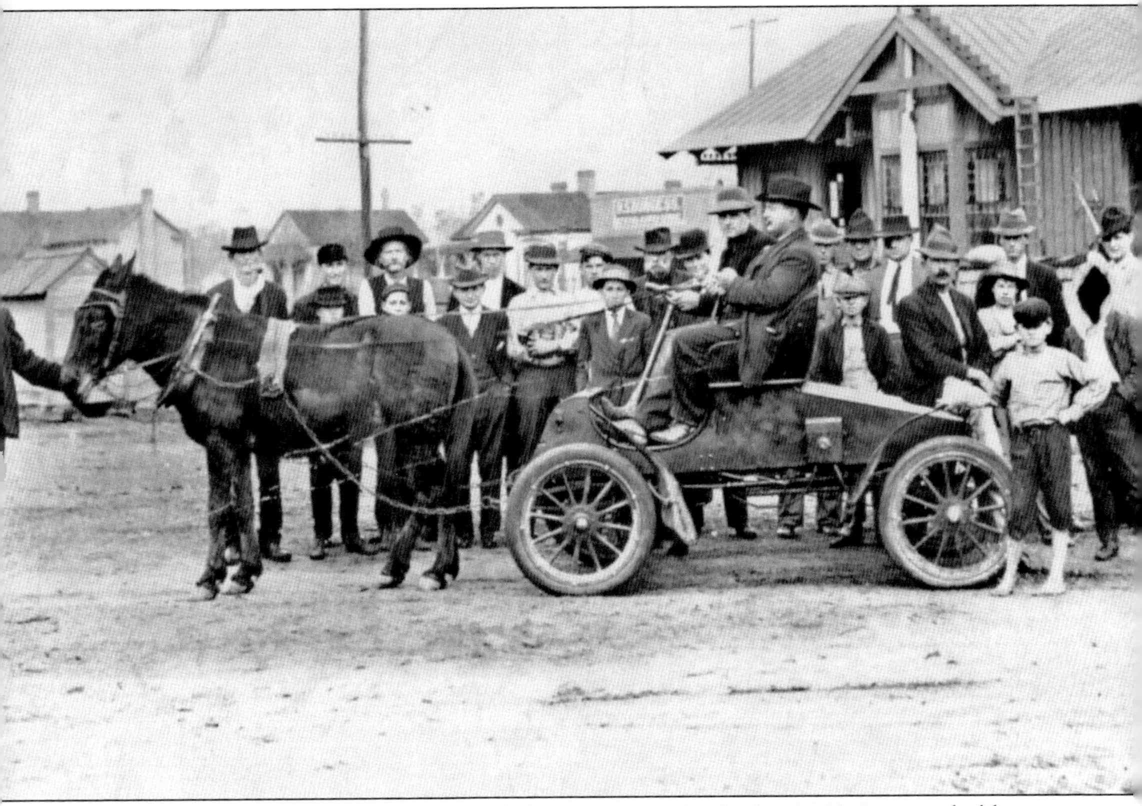

In this photograph of one of the first automobiles to come to Pembroke, M. E. Carter is holding the mule, which had probably just pulled his car into town. Mr. Carter was the publisher of the *Pembroke Enterprise* newspaper. Sitting in the car are Fred Grimes and Pete Wolf. Included in this *c.* 1907 photograph are Jim Purcell, Jim Leonard, Roy Carter, Ira Futch, "Uncle" Ben Bacon, Steve Purvis, Louis Purlmutt, and H. A. Griffith, who was depot agent at the time this picture was taken.

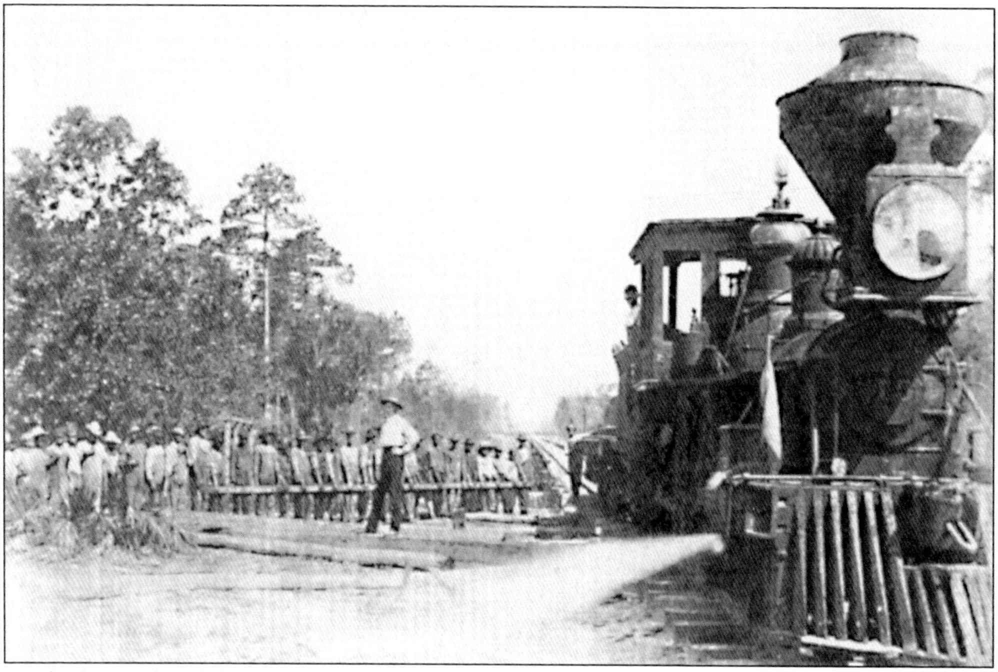

Pembroke's railroad development in the 1890s is depicted in this photograph of an engine and railroad cars of that era.

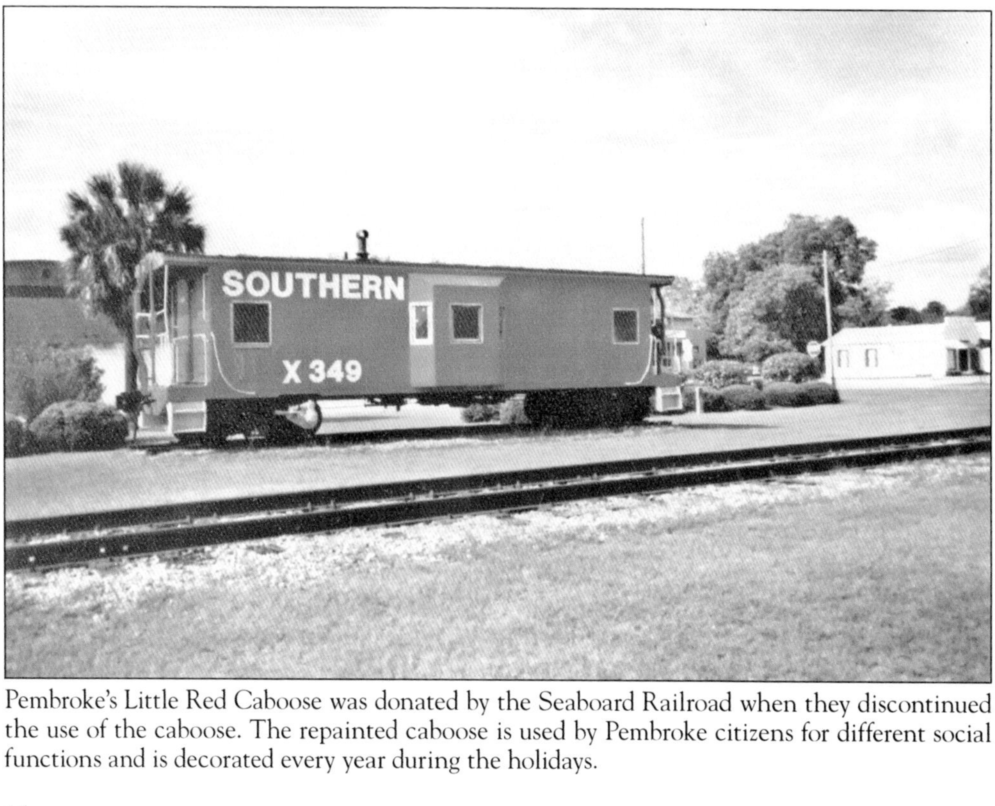

Pembroke's Little Red Caboose was donated by the Seaboard Railroad when they discontinued the use of the caboose. The repainted caboose is used by Pembroke citizens for different social functions and is decorated every year during the holidays.

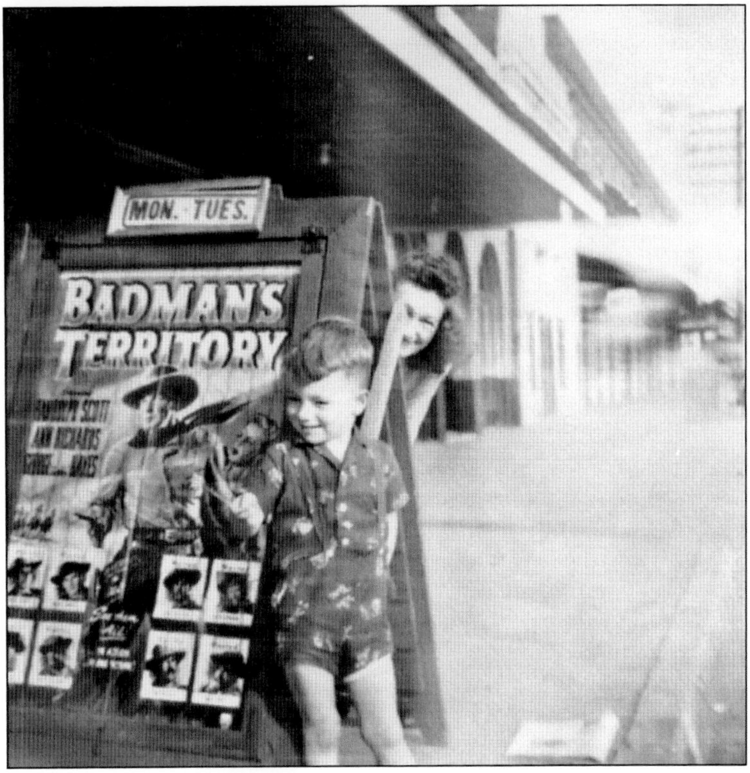

When this 1940s photograph of the entrance to the Old Tos Theatre was taken, the movie playing was a western entitled *Badman's Territory*. Peering from behind the marquee is Margie Bacon Nolan.

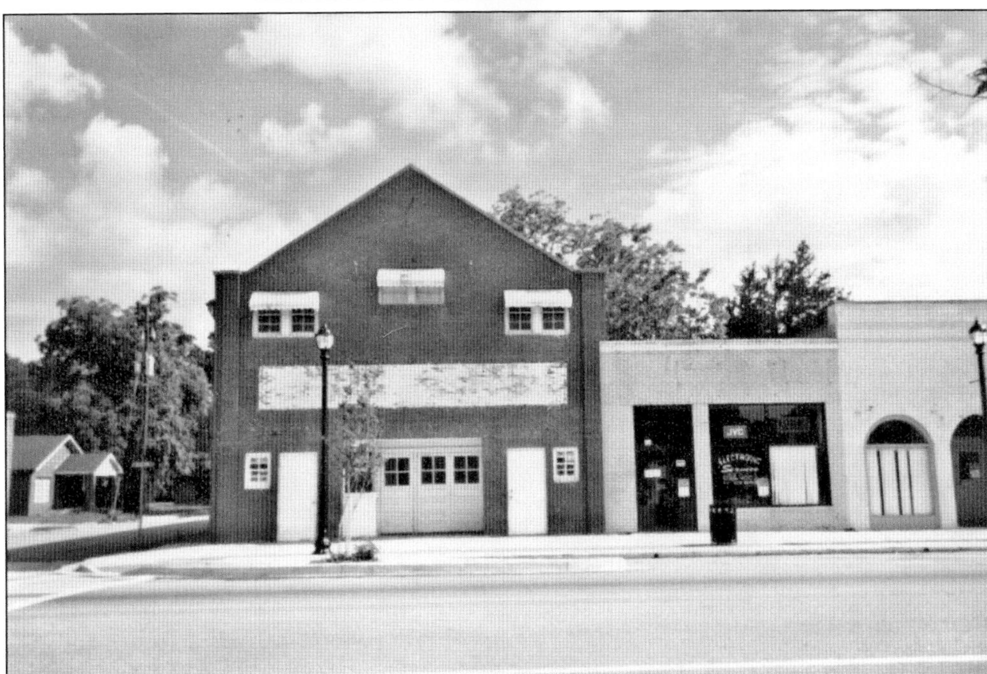

Old Tos Theatre was built by S. G. Tos of Claxton, Georgia, in September 1938. The old theatre provided entertainment for many families in the area. It closed in the 1970s. Plans for the old theatre include renovating it for use as a cultural arts center.

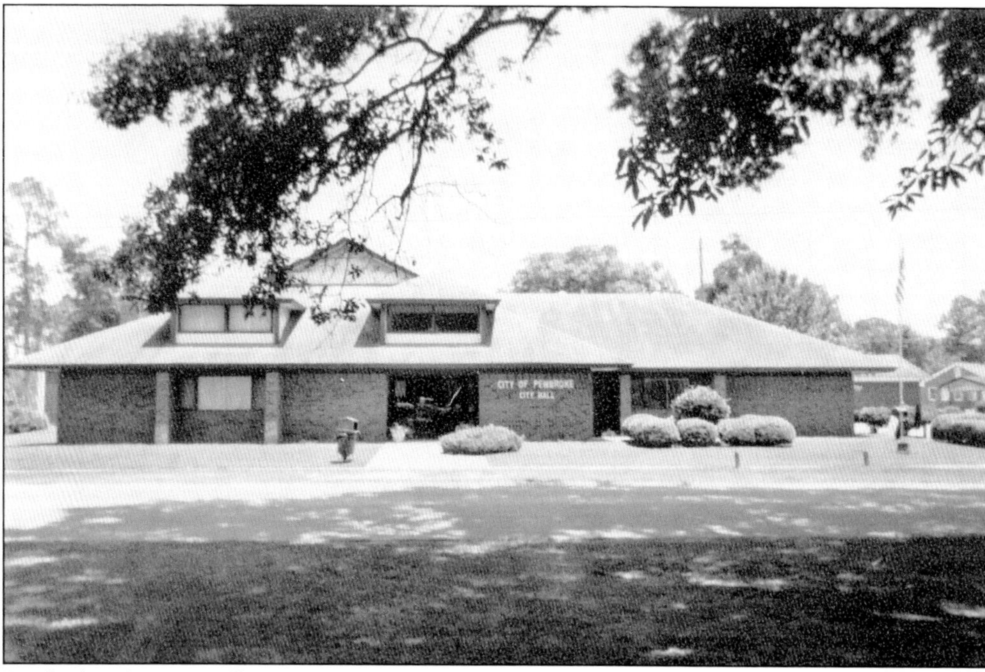

Pembroke's first city offices were constructed in 1977. Prior to that time, city business had been transacted in stores. A federal grant financing approximately 78 percent of the cost enabled the city hall to be constructed.

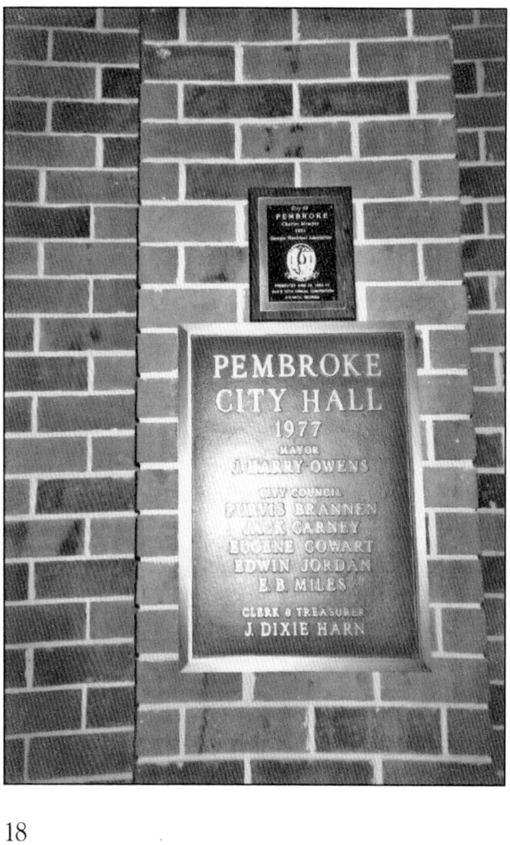

This plaque located at city hall shows the names of Mayor J. Harry Owens, council members Purvis Brannen, Jack Carney, Eugene Cowart, Edwin Jordan, and E. B. Miles, and clerk and treasurer J. Dixie Harn, Pembroke's elected officials in 1977, in commemoration of the new facility.

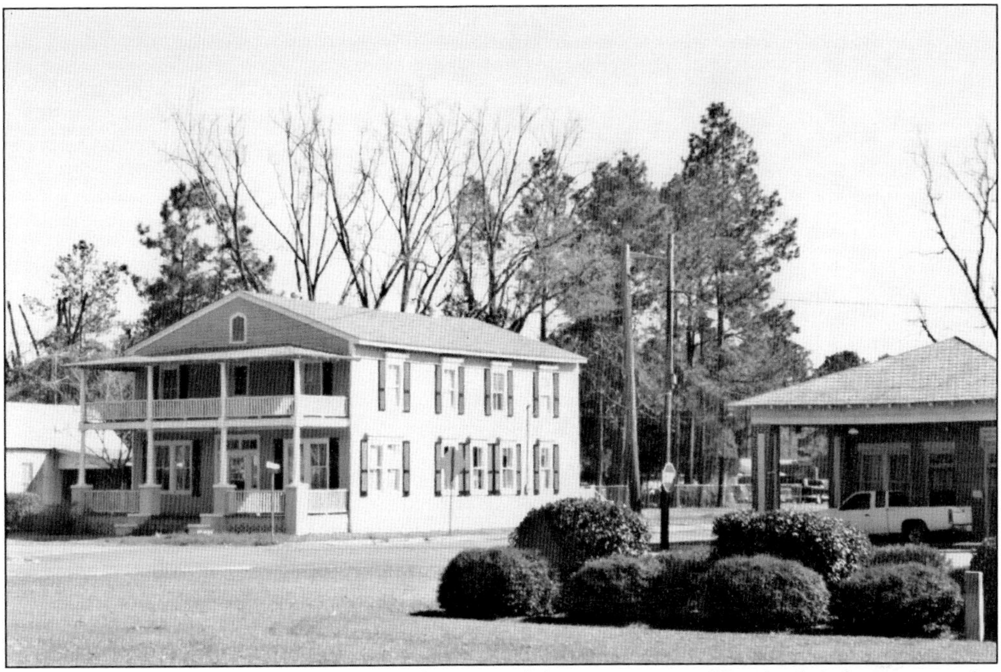

The Tindol Hotel, sporting a new coat of paint and shutters, is one of Pembroke's finest examples of early-1920s architecture.

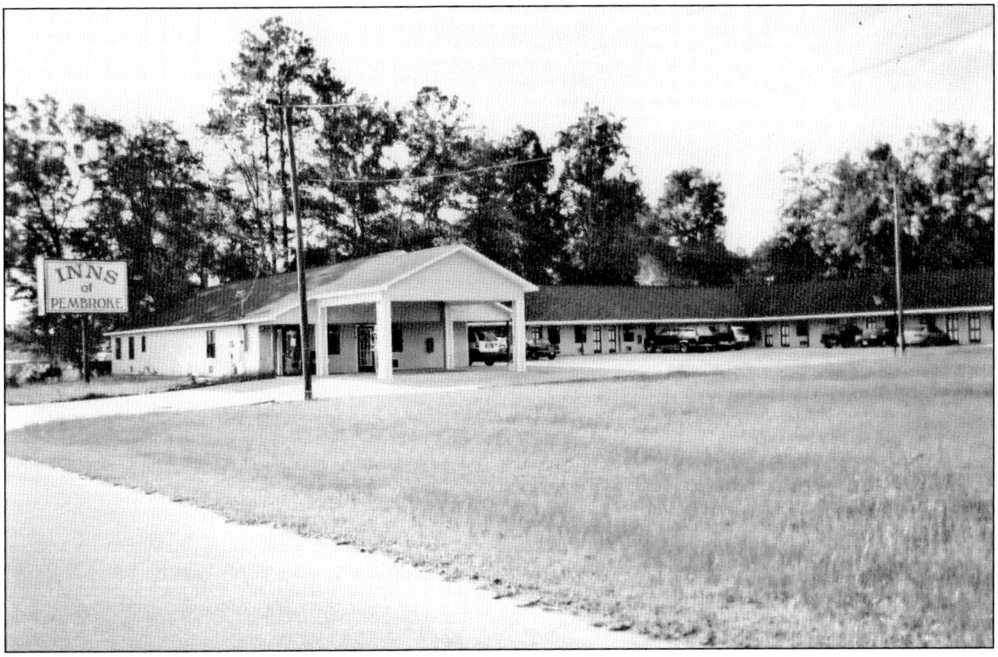

The Inns of Pembroke at 160 East Railroad Street is the only modern motel providing accommodations in Pembroke at the present date. It is also the only motel between Clapton, Georgia, and Chatham County along Highway 280. Built in 1998, it has 19 rooms.

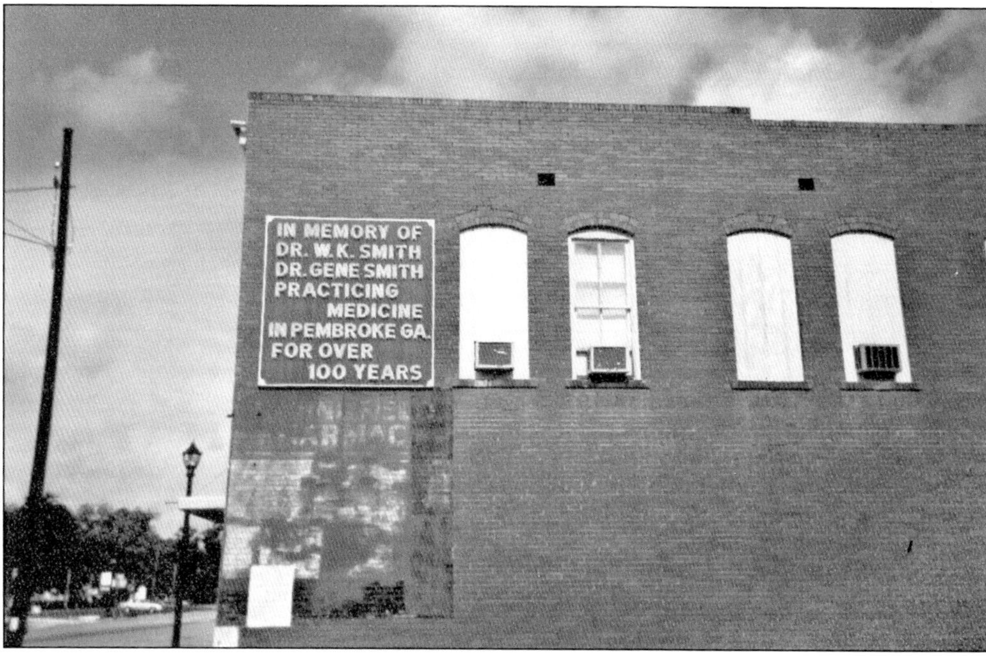

The Julius Morgan Building also represents early architecture of Pembroke. A sign located on the building designates 100-plus years of practicing medicine by Drs. W. K. and Eugene Smith. Dr. W. K. Smith and his son, Eugene, were both general practitioners in Pembroke. Dr. W. K. Smith attended Georgia Medical College, and his son earned degrees from Mercer University and the University of Georgia.

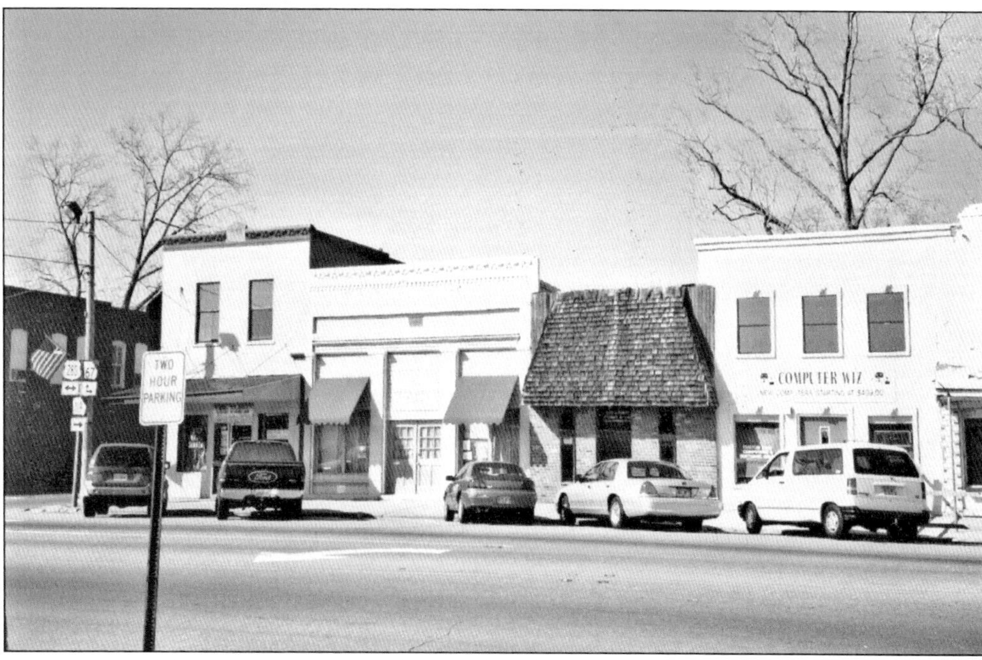

Main Street Pembroke of today shows the same buildings as yesteryear. These historical buildings are now occupied by Pembroke Finance Company, *Bryan County Times*, Georgia Farm Bureau Insurance Company, and Computer Wiz.

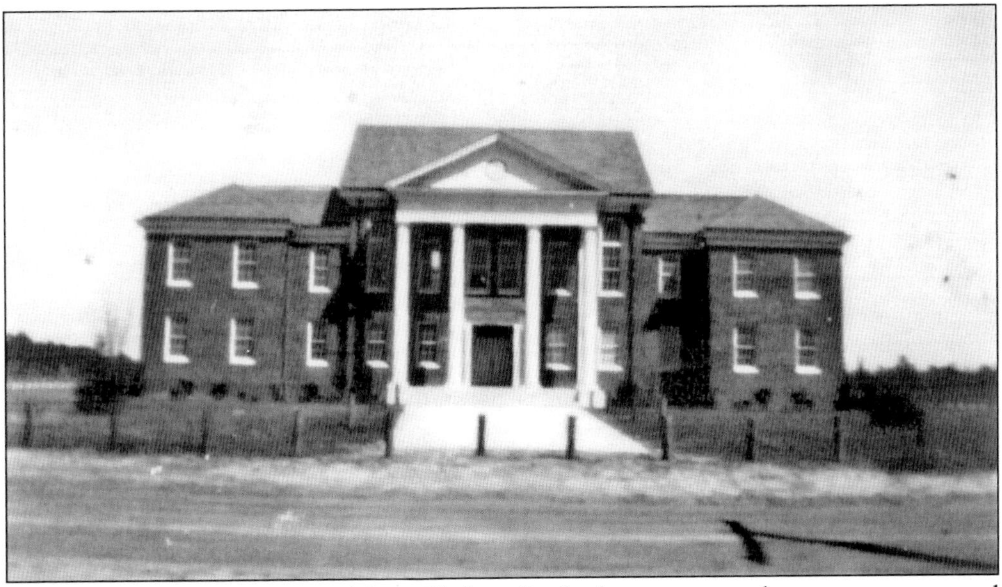

After the county seat was moved from Clyde to Pembroke, a new courthouse was constructed in 1938.

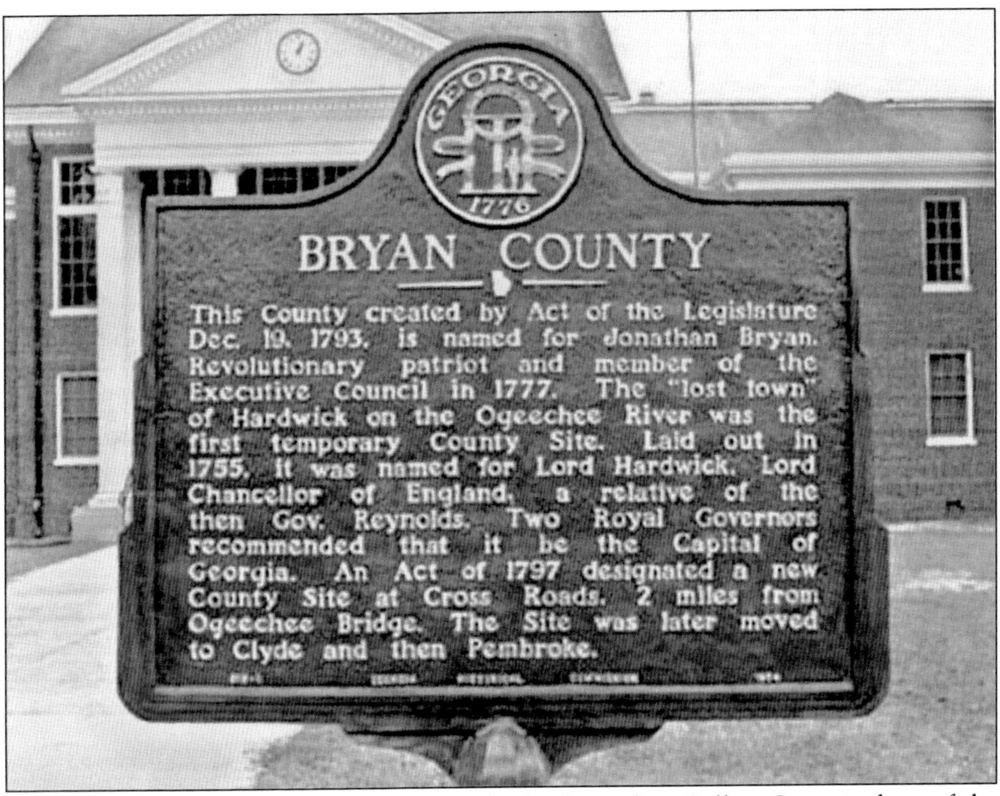

This Bryan County historical plaque in Pembroke, located on College Street in front of the county courthouse, designates the history and formation of the county.

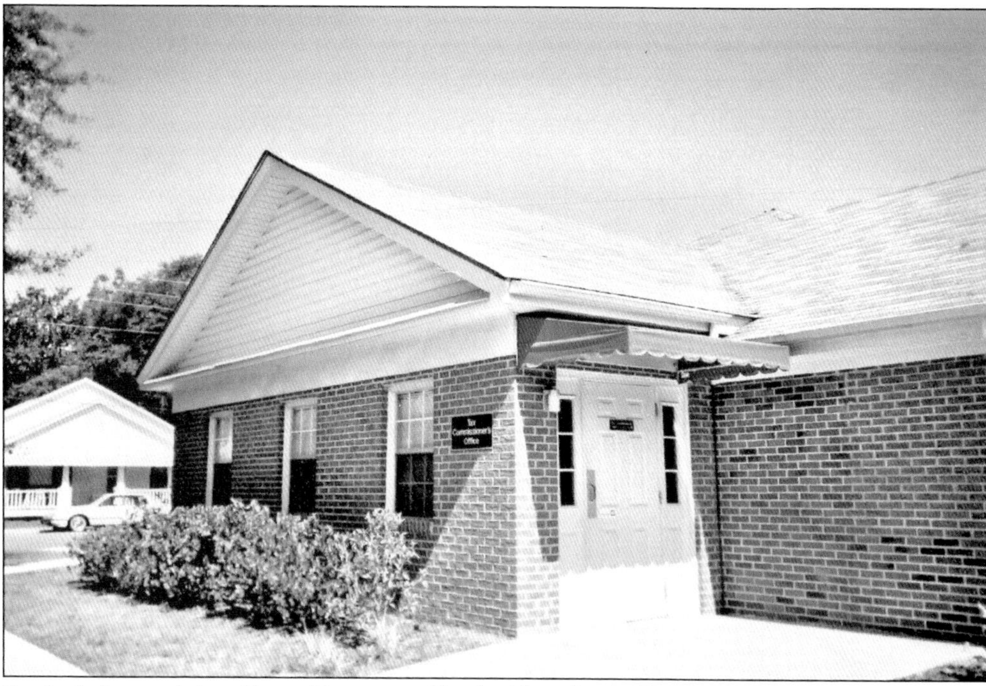

Pembroke's growth is evidenced by a new office building for the Bryan County Tax Commissioner's Office. A satellite tax commissioner's office is located in nearby Richmond Hill.

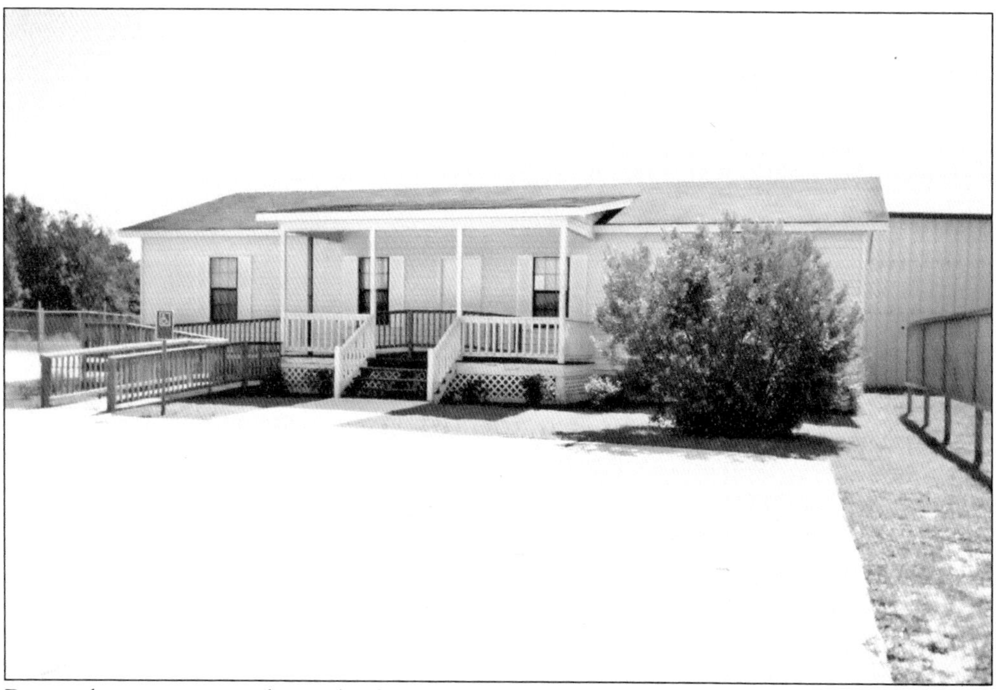

Due to the expansion and growth of Pembroke and Bryan County, there was a need to relocate the planning and zoning department to a separate office. In 2003, the office moved to its new location on Industrial Boulevard in East Pembroke.

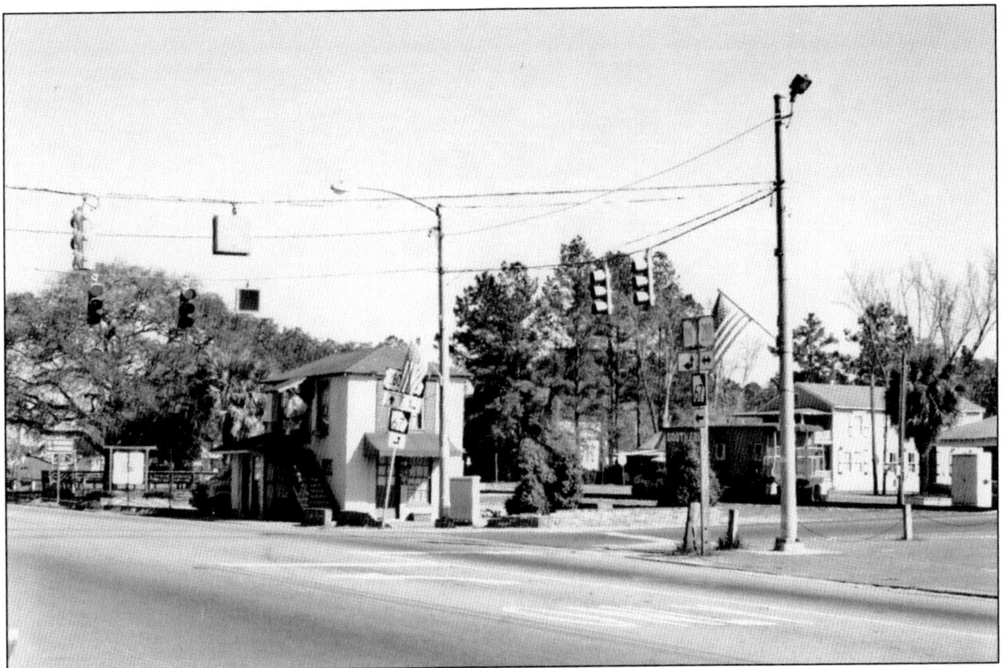

These two photographs show Pembroke's Welcome Center, located on Main Street. At one time, this building served as the Pembroke Police Station.

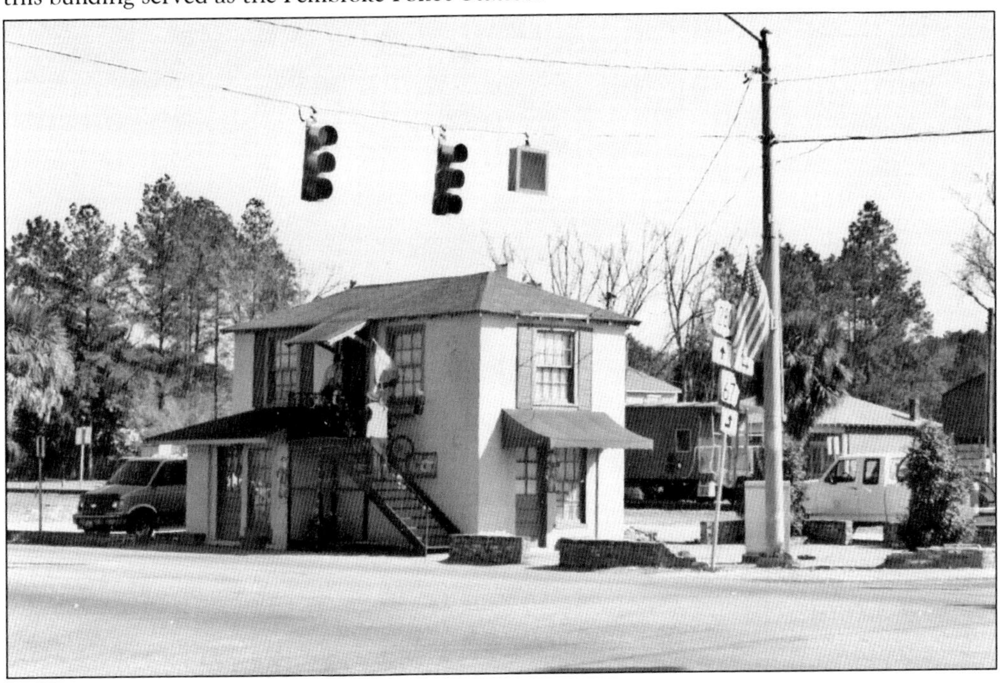

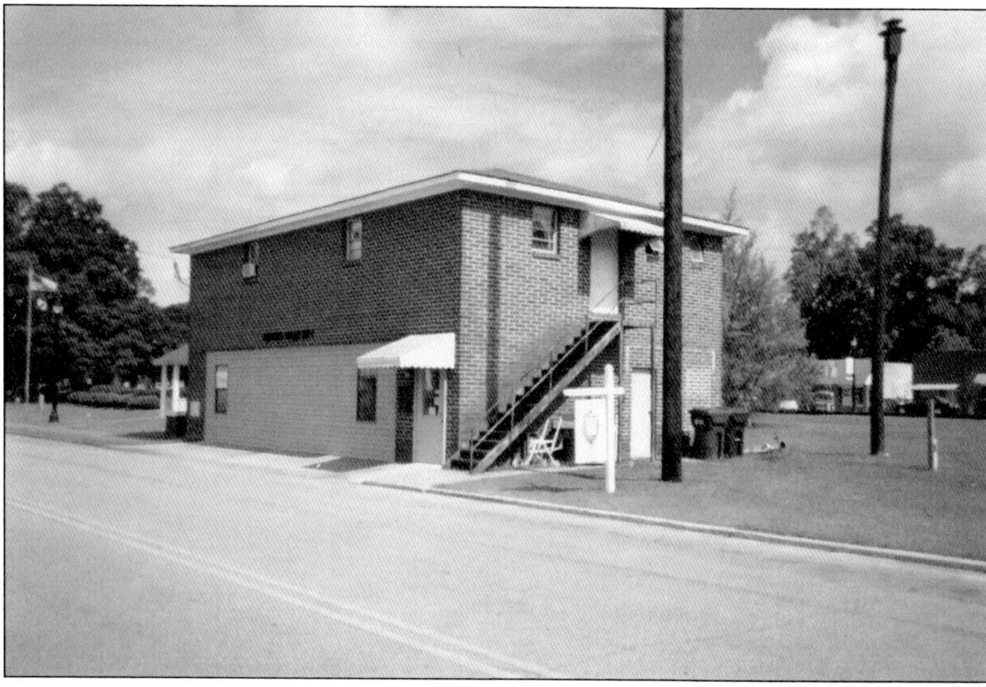

A new police station for Pembroke was built in 1998 and is located on Railroad Street.

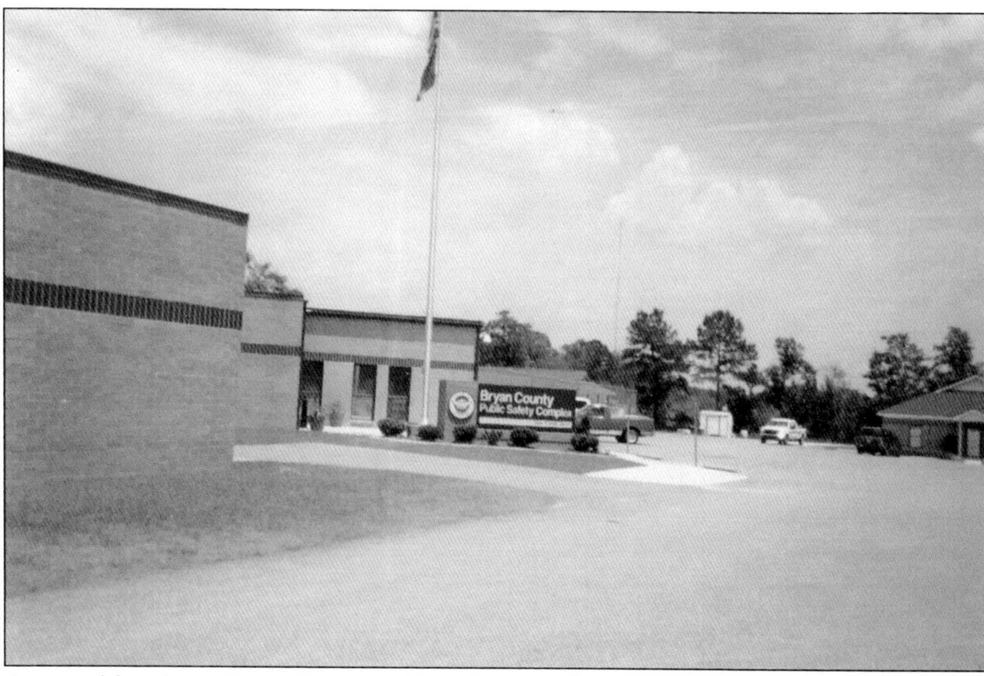

As a need for a larger Bryan County public safety complex grew, one was constructed in 1998. It houses several judicial offices and also serves as the headquarters of Meals on Wheels.

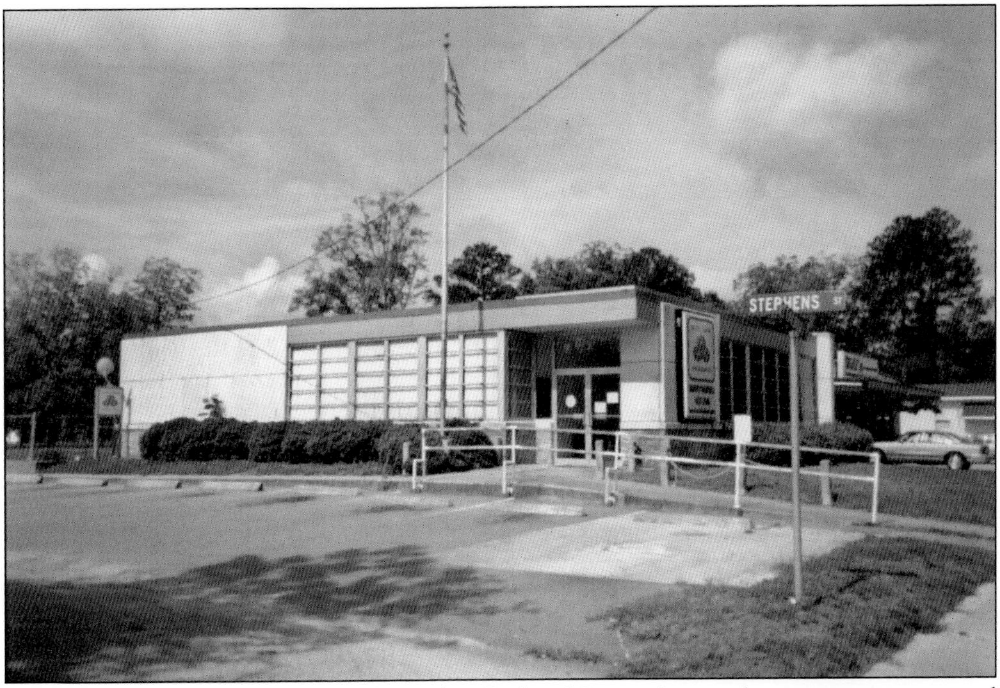

The old post office in Pembroke was located on Railroad Street. Among the many postmasters and postmistresses were Jessie Hope, Helen Graham, George Dewey Hendrix, and Earlest Pevey.

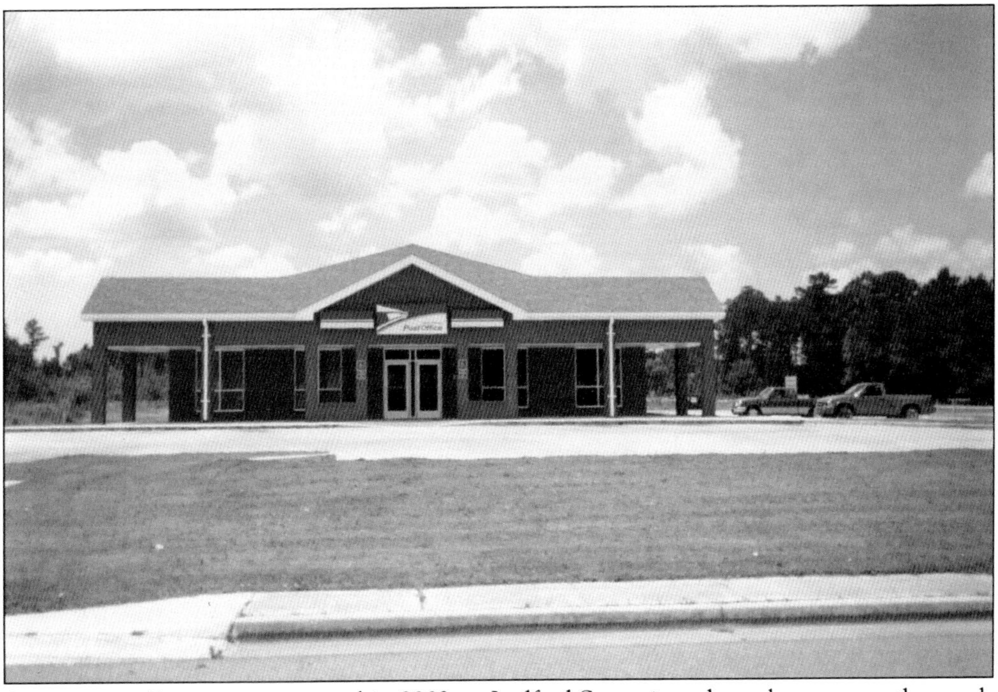

A new post office was constructed in 2003 on Ledford Street in order to better serve the needs of the community.

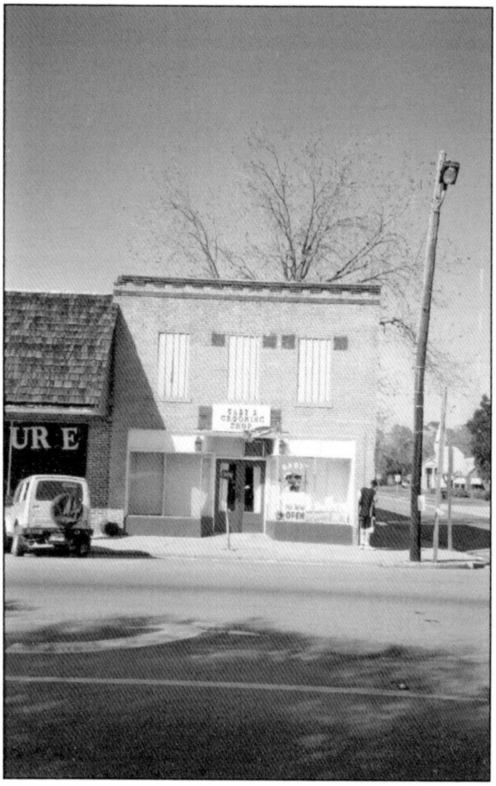

Gaby's Grooming Shop, located on Main Street in Pembroke, has bathed, groomed, and made beautiful many of Pembroke's four-legged citizens. This site at one time housed the post office.

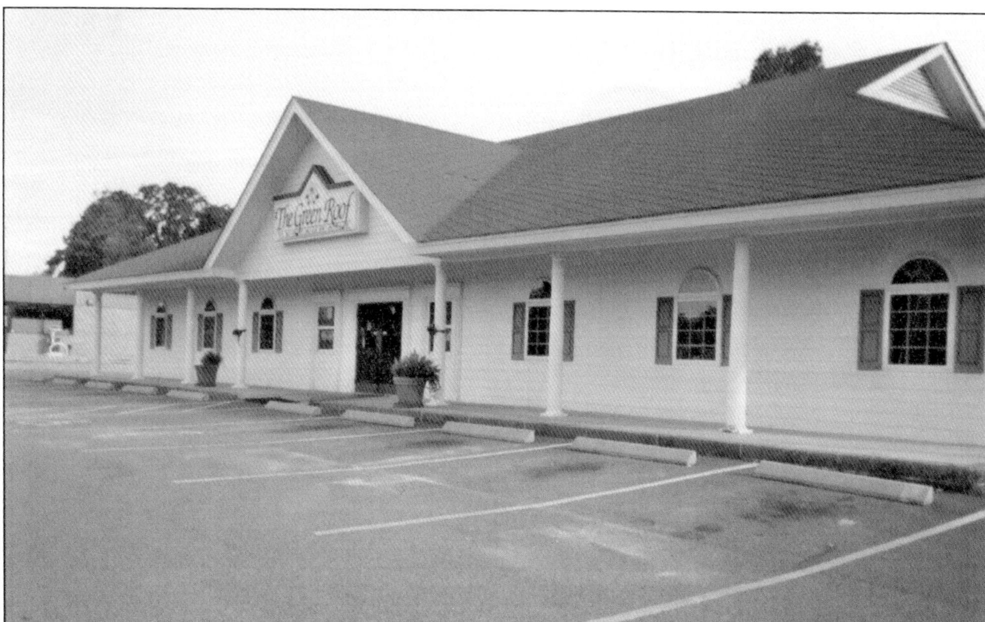

A new addition to Pembroke's restaurants was The Greenroof, established in the late 1990s and specializing in "country cooking" cuisine. The original owner was Billy Conley. Recently the restaurant was acquired by Jimmy Cowart, and its new name will carry on his family tradition in the restaurant business as Cowart's Café.

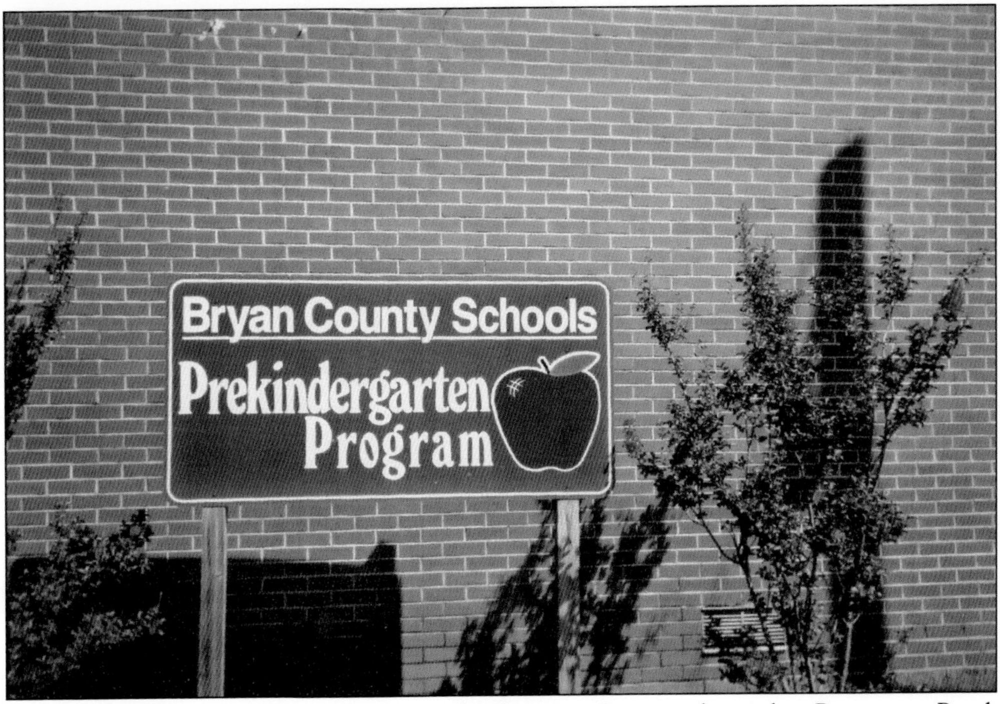

The building that houses Bryan County Prekindergarten Program, located on Bacontown Road, was originally the Pembroke High School. After the schools became integrated in 1970, the building was used as Bryan County Elementary School.

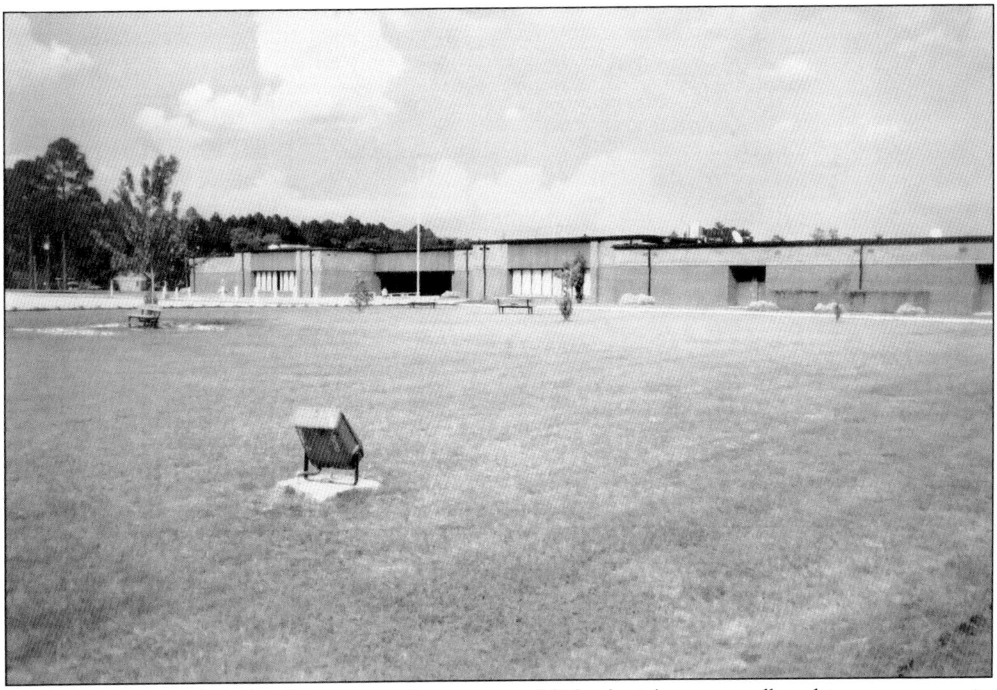

Bryan County High School, as it is today, was established with a groundbreaking ceremony in the fall of 1985.

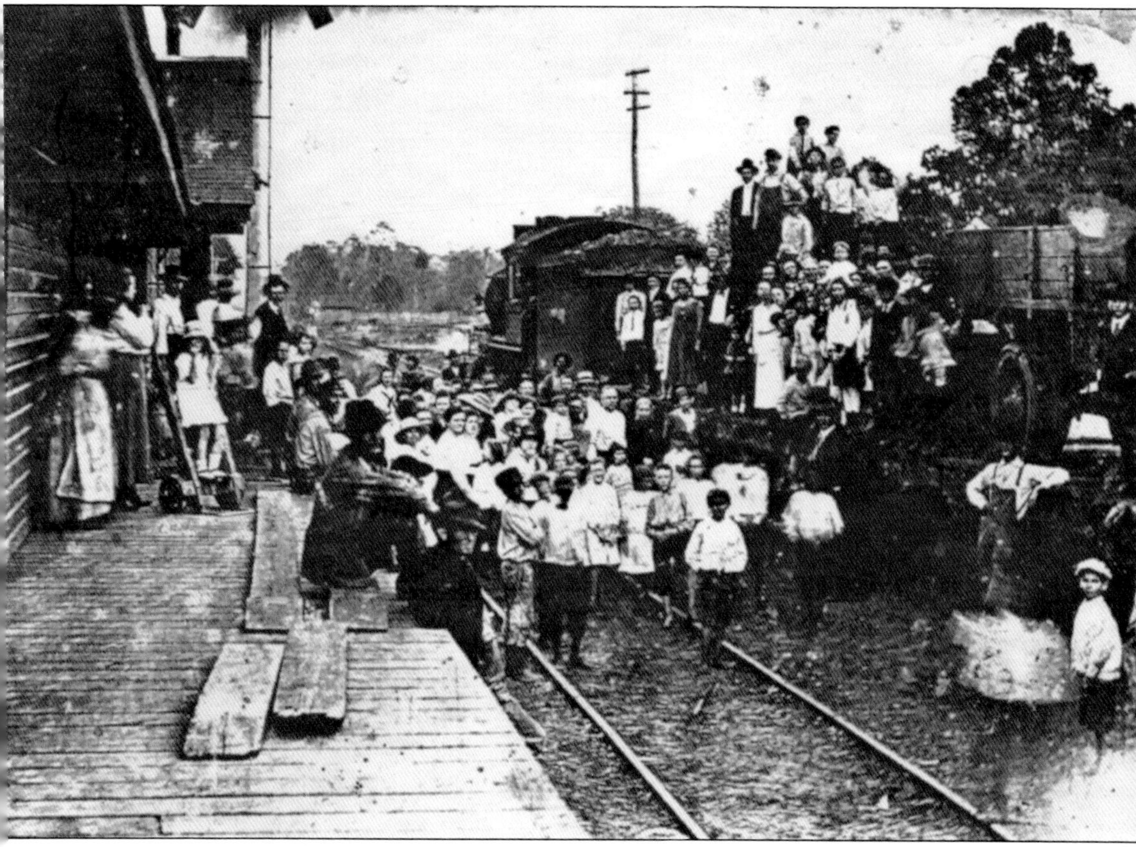

A c. 1890 image depicts "waiting on the train in Pembroke." This was a big event, and people would gather to watch the train come in and leave.

Two

PEOPLE

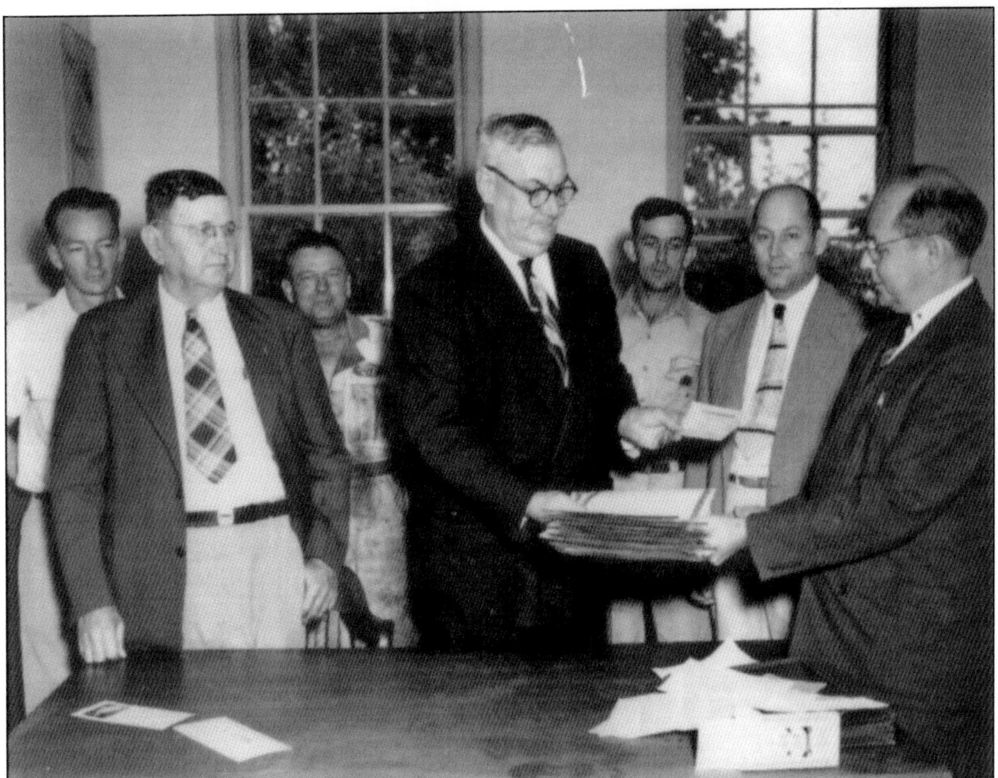

The Pembroke City Council is pictured at work in the 1950s. Pictured from left to right are Gene Mock, Albert Bacon, Joe Brewton, Mayor Frank Miller, Hawley Bozemore, Hagin Dubose, and unidentified.

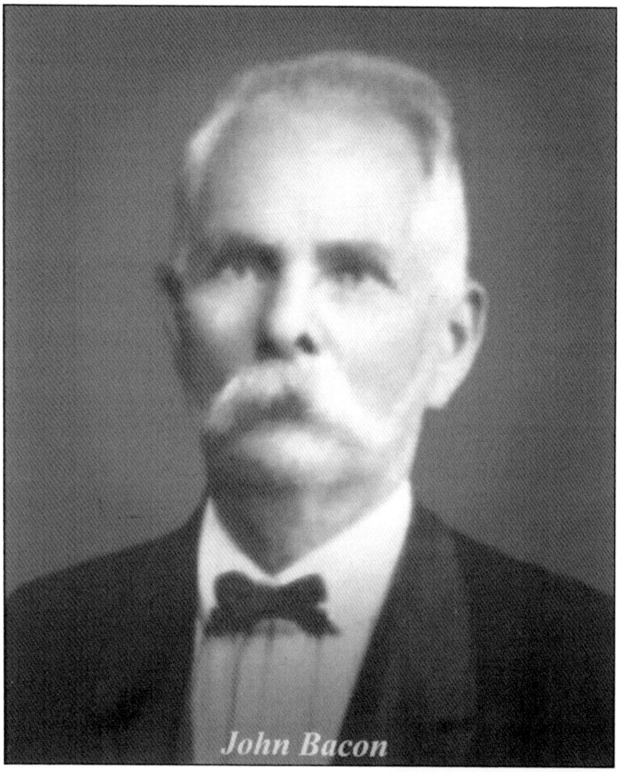

John Bacon served as a state representative. He is the great-grandfather of Pembroke's current mayor, Judy Bacon Cook. Bacon introduced the bill for Pembroke to become incorporated on August 23, 1905, by an act of the legislature.

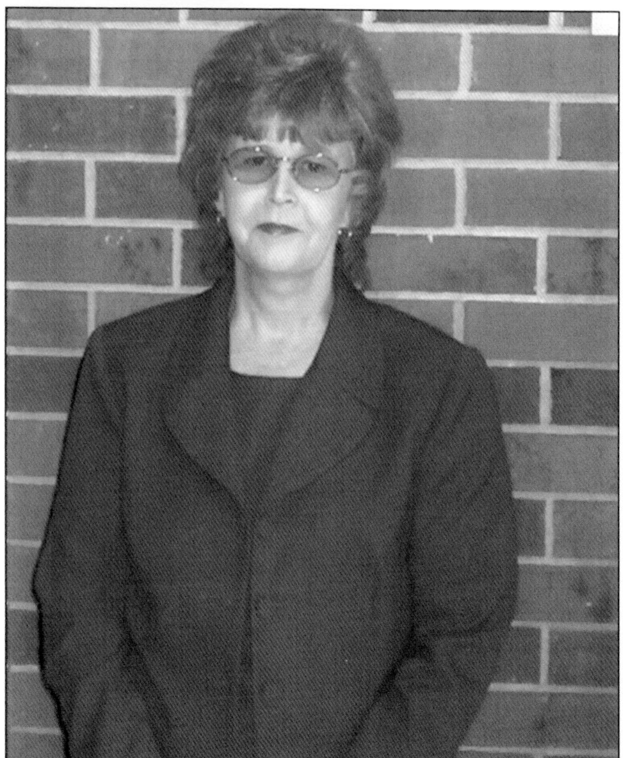

Judy Bacon Cook served as city clerk for 20 years before retiring. She is currently serving a second term as Pembroke's mayor, first being sworn in on January 11, 2000. Mrs. Cook is the first female to serve as Pembroke's mayor.

Oh, those were the days! A beautiful Pembroke belle posed in front of Cowart's Grocery in the 1940s.

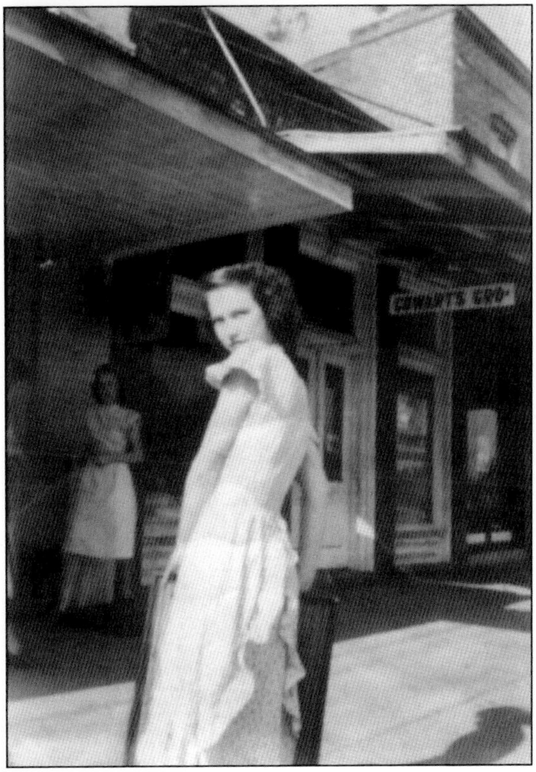

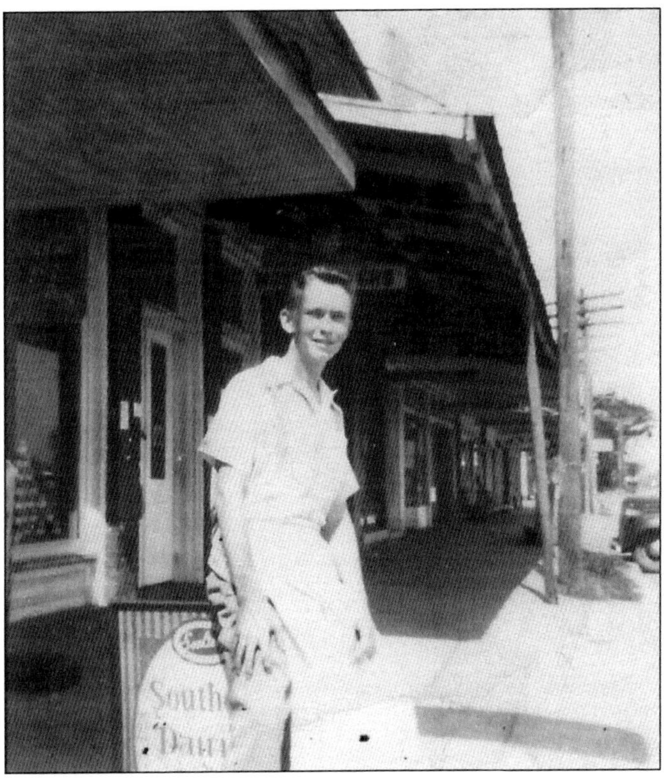

Remember when an ice cream cone cost 5¢? In the 1940s, this was a cool treat. This man is standing in front of the Pembroke drug store on Main Street.

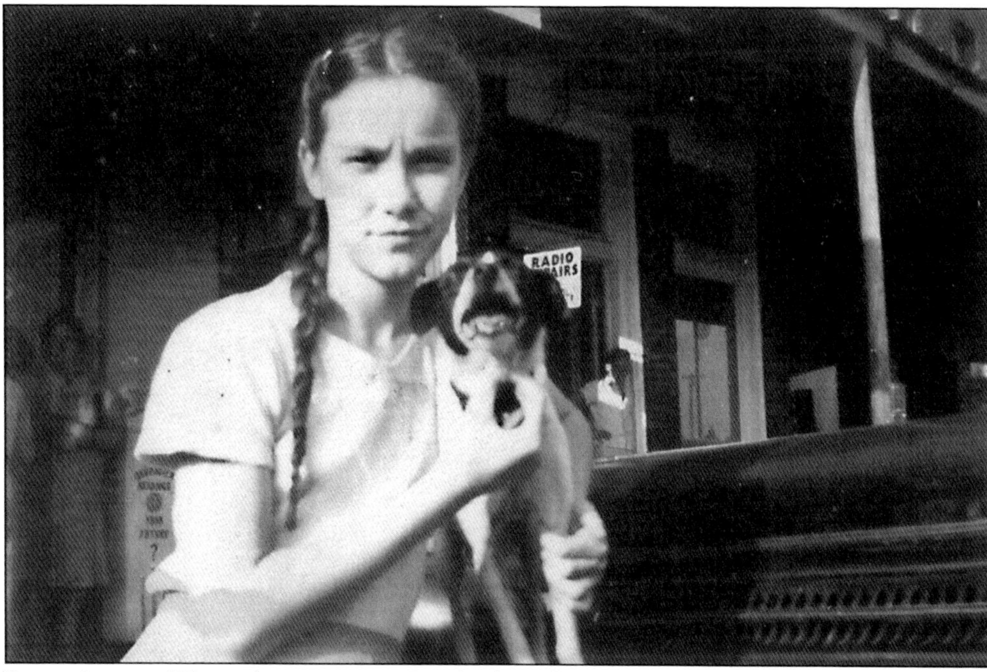

Renee Lanier (Houser) grew up in Pembroke. She is standing in front of her parents' pharmacy and ice cream parlor in the 1940s. Renee still lives in Pembroke and is active in the Veterans Administration.

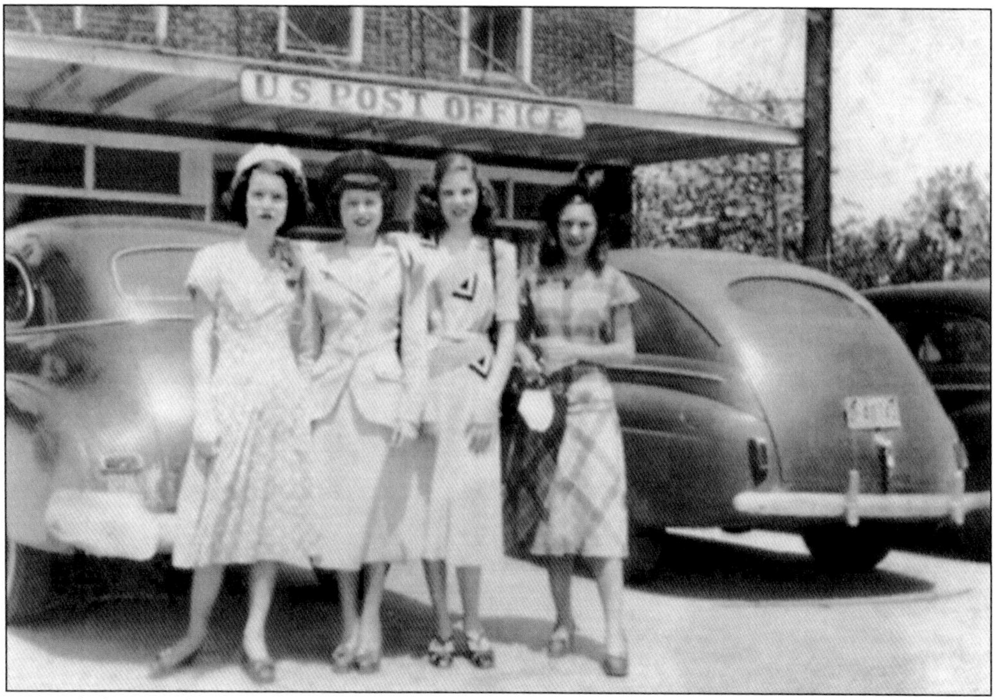

Young ladies are the same today as yesterday. Here are some of Pembroke's finest posing in front of the post office in the 1940s. From left to right are Renee Lanier Houser, Evelyn Owens, Patty Deal, and unidentified.

Mr. and Mrs. James Hobbs Lanier, owners of Lanier's Drug Store in Pembroke, were longtime residents of Bryan County. Mr. Lanier had several careers before purchasing the pharmacy in 1939; he served one term as county treasurer.

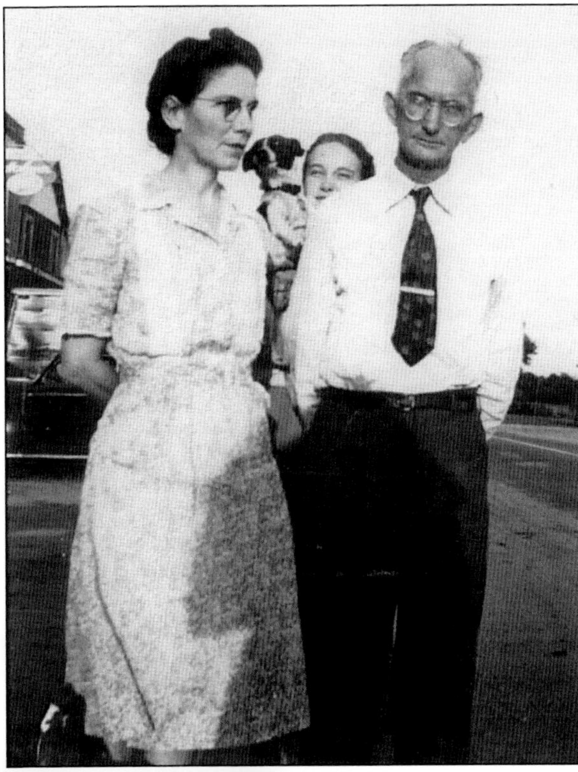

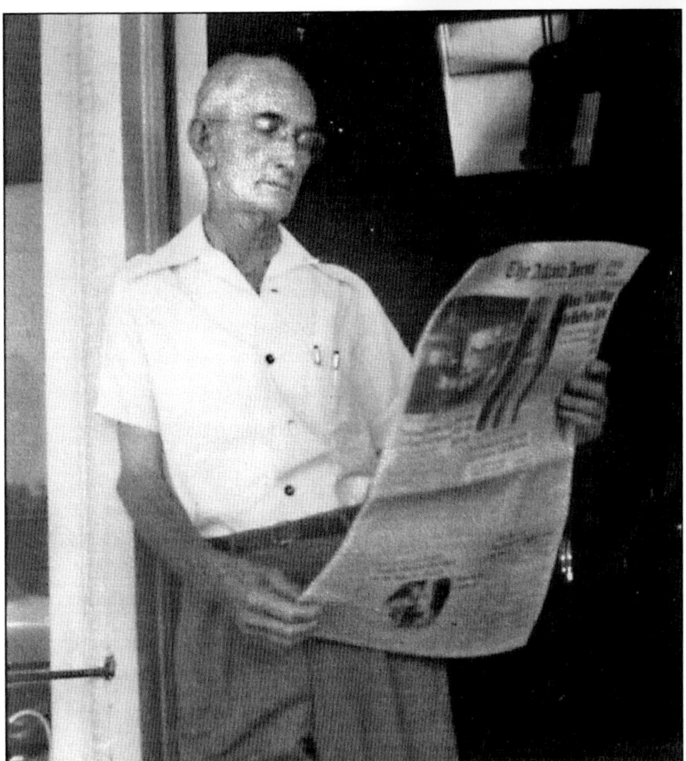

Mr. James Hobbs Lanier is pictured reading *The Atlanta Journal* in his spare time in front of his drug store. An interesting fact about Mr. Lanier was that he was born in the Tindol Hotel on October 3, 1925. His drug store remained active until his death in 1959.

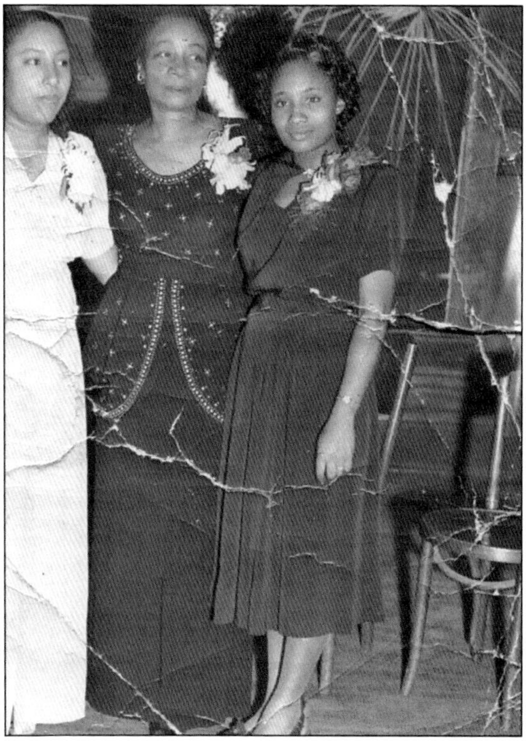

Miriam Bush (right) is pictured with C. J. Walker and her daughter, Michelle. This was Miriam's graduation from Boyce's Beauty School in 1948; she subsequently opened the first African American beauty shop in the community.

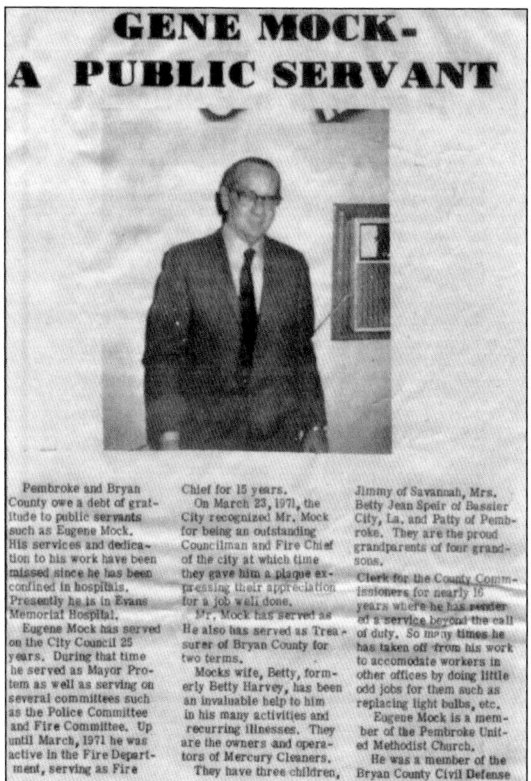

GENE MOCK-
A PUBLIC SERVANT

Pembroke and Bryan County owe a debt of gratitude to public servants such as Eugene Mock. His services and dedication to his work have been missed since he has been confined in hospitals. Presently he is in Evans Memorial Hospital.

Eugene Mock has served on the City Council 25 years. During that time he served as Mayor Protem as well as serving on several committees such as the Police Committee and Fire Committee. Up until March, 1971 he was active in the Fire Department, serving as Fire Chief for 15 years.

On March 23, 1971, the City recognized Mr. Mock for being an outstanding Councilman and Fire Chief of the city at which time they gave him a plaque expressing their appreciation for a job well done.

Mr. Mock has served as He also has served as Treasurer of Bryan County for two terms.

Mocks wife, Betty, formerly Betty Harvey, has been an invaluable help to him in his many activities and recurring illnesses. They are the owners and operators of Mercury Cleaners.

They have three children, Jimmy of Savannah, Mrs. Betty Jean Speir of Bassier City, La. and Patty of Pembroke. They are the proud grandparents of four grandsons.

Clerk for the County Commissioners for nearly 16 years where he has rendered a service beyond the call of duty. So many times he has taken off from his work to accomodate workers in other offices by doing little odd jobs for them such as replacing light bulbs, etc.

Eugene Mock is a member of the Pembroke United Methodist Church.

He was a member of the Bryan County Civil Defense Rescue team for many years.

Mr. Gene Mock was a dedicated public servant. He served the Pembroke City Council for 25 years, and he also served as fire chief for 15 years. Gene and his wife, Betty, had three children, Jimmy, Betty Jean, and Patty.

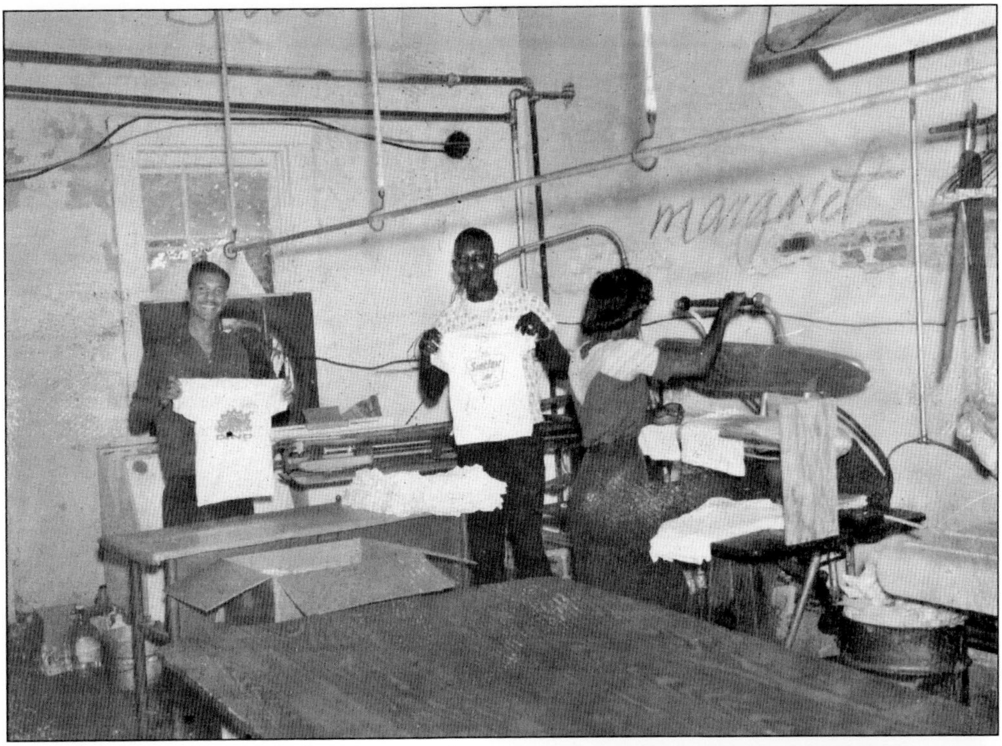

Mercury Cleaners was owned and operated for many years by Gene Mock. This photograph shows Buster Bunch and Margaret Bacon working. Mr. Mock blew the fire station siren every day at noon to alert everyone that it was lunch time; everyone in town set their watches by the blowing of the siren.

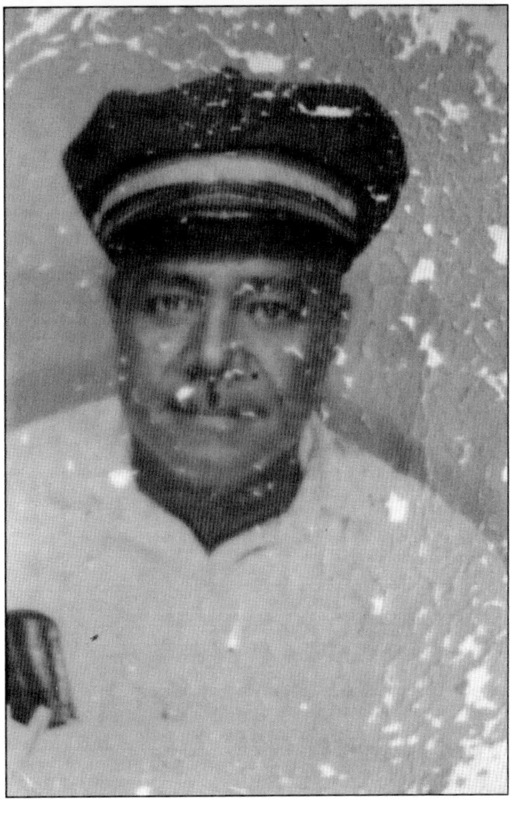

Oscar Bunch is pictured in the 1950s, when he drove a school bus for the Bryan County School System. He also worked for the city.

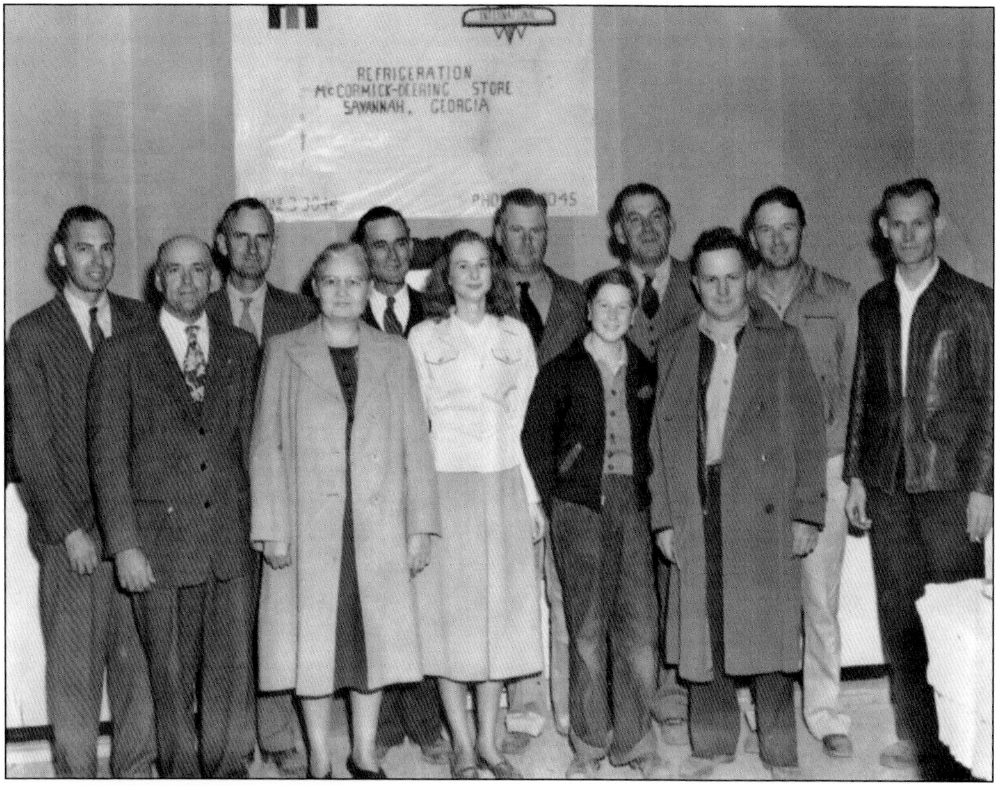

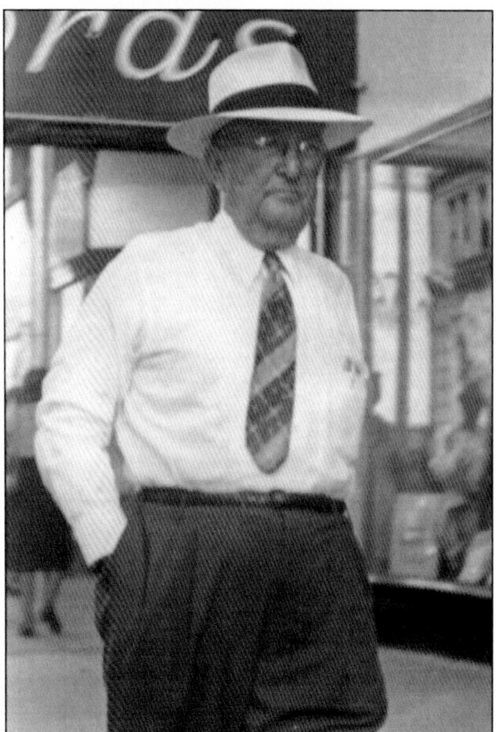

The International Harvester Presentation comes to Pembroke in the 1950s. Pictured from left to right are (first row) F. C. Drexel, Ora C. Payne, Mrs. Sikes, Herbert Smith (student), and Gerald Bacon; (second row) Alton Smith, Dewey Medders, Clyde Payne, Charles Warnell, Emory Smith, an unidentified International Harvester representative, and Mr. Sikes (the agriculture teacher at Bryan County High School).

Thomas Waters moved to Pembroke in 1929 and established and operated a lumber business. He died on July 13, 1970.

This picture of Thomas and Elloyce Waters was taken in the 1930s. They were married in 1922 in Statesboro, Georgia, and they had four children: Rex, Katherine, Thomas, and Nan.

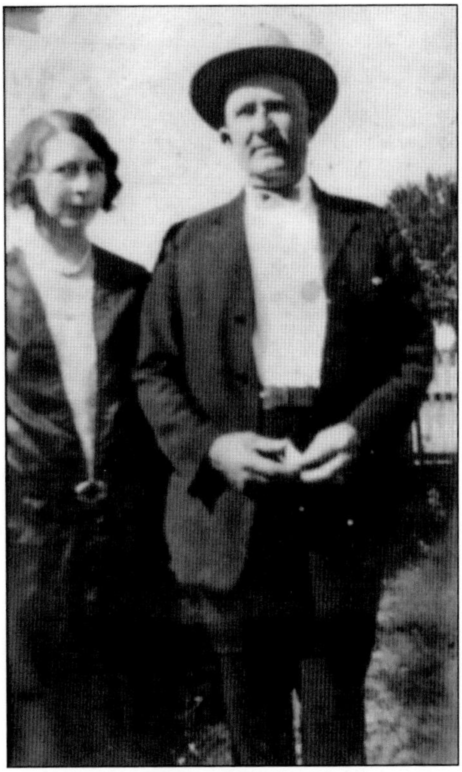

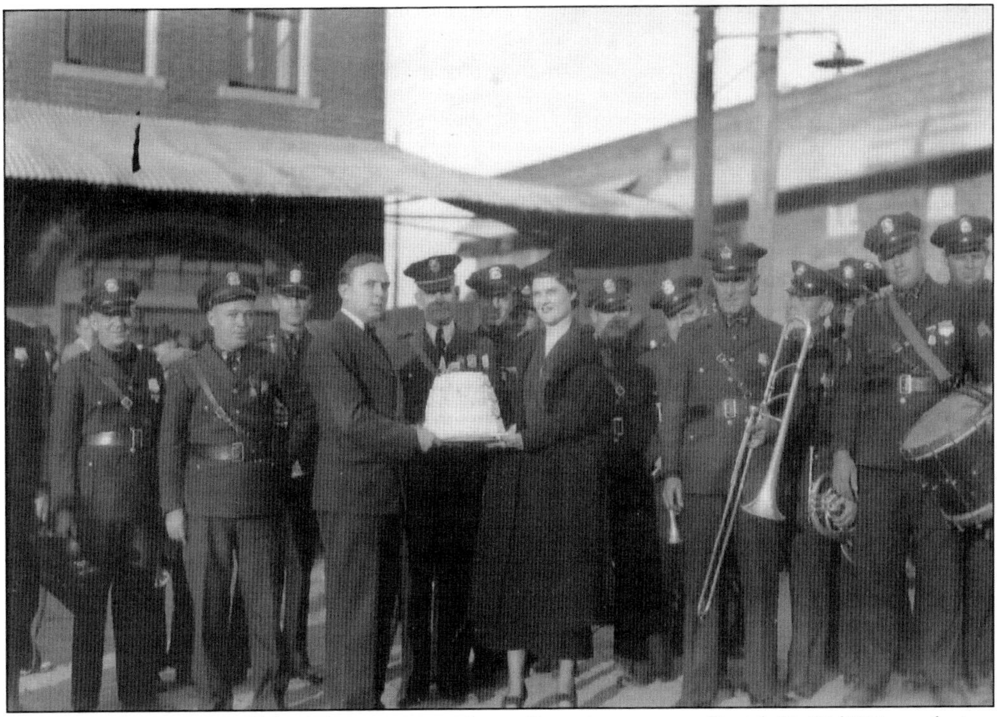

Miss Dorothy A. Warnell (right) presents a cake to Georgia governor Eurith D. "Ed" Rivers during festivities celebrating the dedication of the Bryan County Courthouse on May 19, 1938.

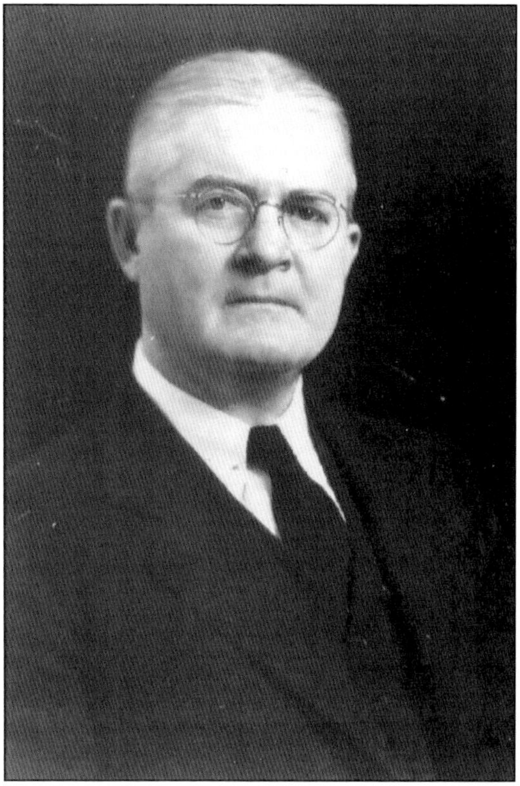

Daniel B. Warnell, state representative, introduced the bill in the Georgia legislature changing the county seat for Bryan County from Clyde to Pembroke. The bill was passed by the legislature by a vote of 137 to 0 on February 11, 1937. He continued to serve Pembroke and Bryan County when he was elected state senator in 1938.

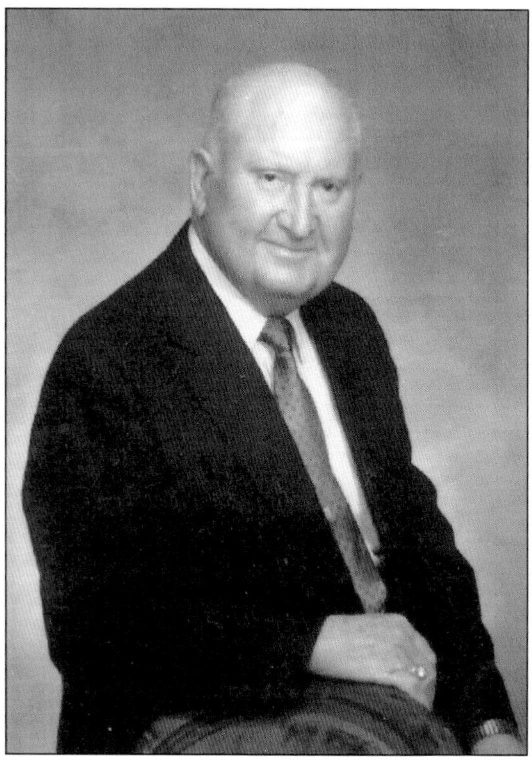

Charles F. Warnell Sr., citizen of Pembroke, was the state senator for Bryan, Liberty, and Long Counties from 1965 to 1958 and 1960 to 1962. He also served as director of the Pembroke State Bank from 1946 to 1987, as chairman from 1957 to 1987, as a member of the Bryan County Board of Education from 1951 to 1979, and as chairman from 1964 to 1979.

Mr. J. Dixie Harn Sr. was born in 1912 in Pembroke. He served as city clerk for 30 years; afterwards he also served two years as Pembroke's mayor. He served 16 years with Bryan County Board of Commissioners. Mr. Harn opened Harn's Variety Store and established many local contacts. He was a charter member of the Coastal Area Planning and Development Commission and served as the first chairman and was a member of the board of directors during his tenure as county commissioner. He was a member of Pembroke United Methodist Church for more than 50 years and was married to Elizabeth Ward of Macon.

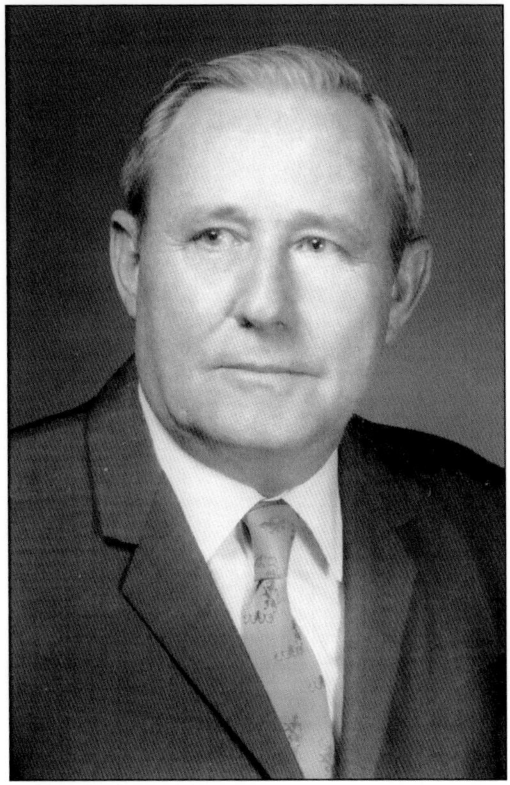

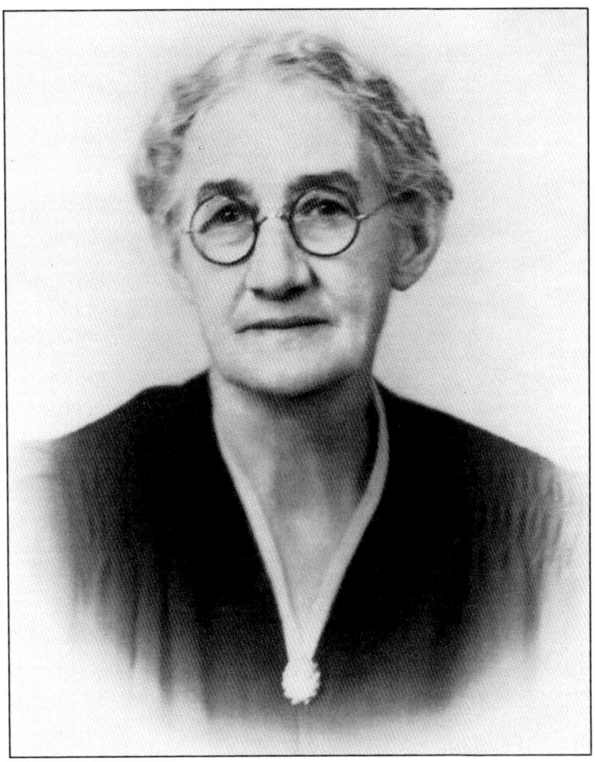

Dollie Harn married William Perry Dukes in 1913 and moved to Pembroke, where they lived in what was known as the "old hotel," which was owned by her husband. Miss Dollie moved to Savannah in 1943, living with her daughter until her death. She was born in 1877 and died in 1952.

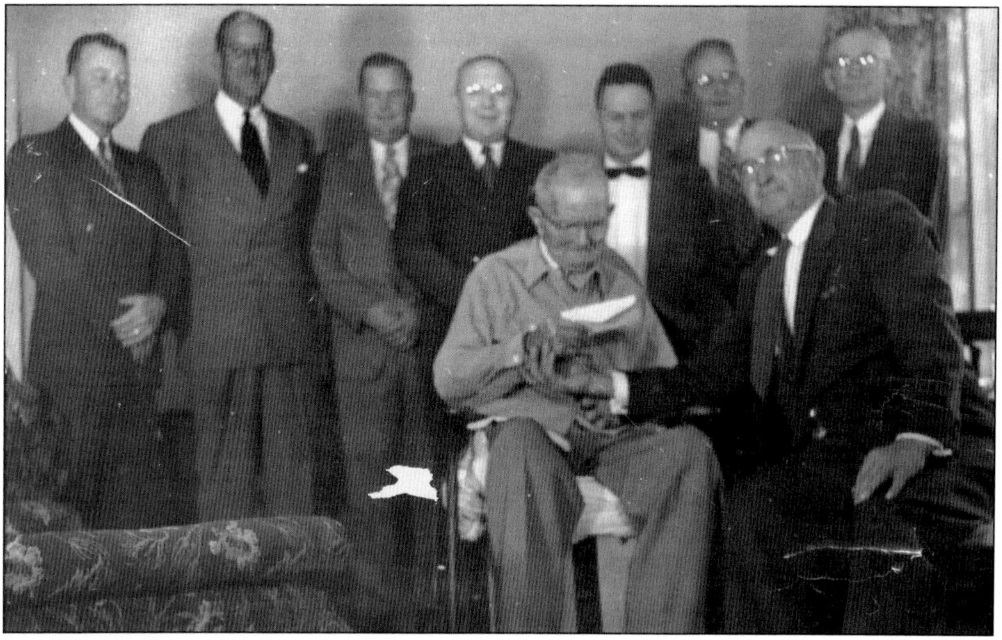

Mr. John Harn (seated on left), father of J. Dixie Harn, is shown being presented with a 50-year certificate of service with the Masons. He was a member of the Pembroke City Council when Pembroke's first city water system was installed in 1928. From left to right are (standing) unidentified, Oliver Fagnant, Harry Williamson, Herman Griner, Gerald Bacon, Johnny Mikel, and U. J. Bacon; (seated) John Harn and Herman Brewton.

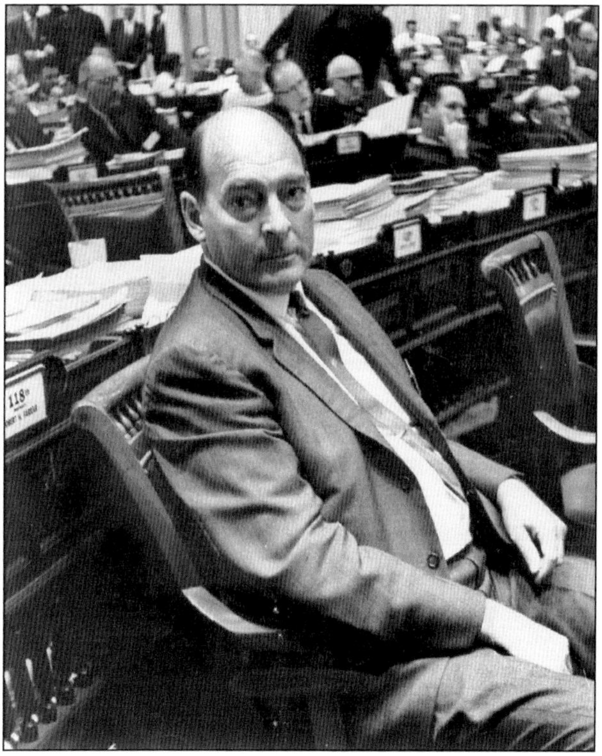

Jack W. Shuman was a native of Bryan County. He was a member of the Georgia House of Representatives from 1959 to 1968. The owner and operator of a chain of building supplies stores established in 1950, Mr. Shuman served with the U.S. Army during World War II and was injured in Germany at the Battle of the Bulge. He received an honorable discharge on December 12, 1945. An astute businessman, Jack provided employment opportunities for many Bryan County residents.

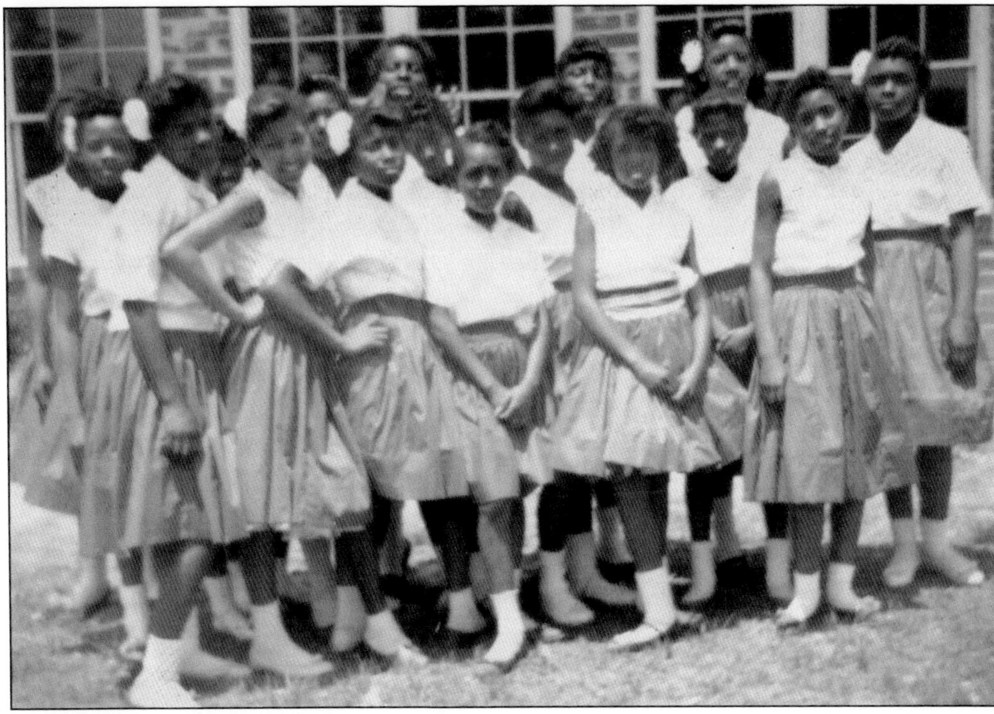

May Day is celebrated Pembroke High School in 1960. Many of the female high school students participated in the festivities.

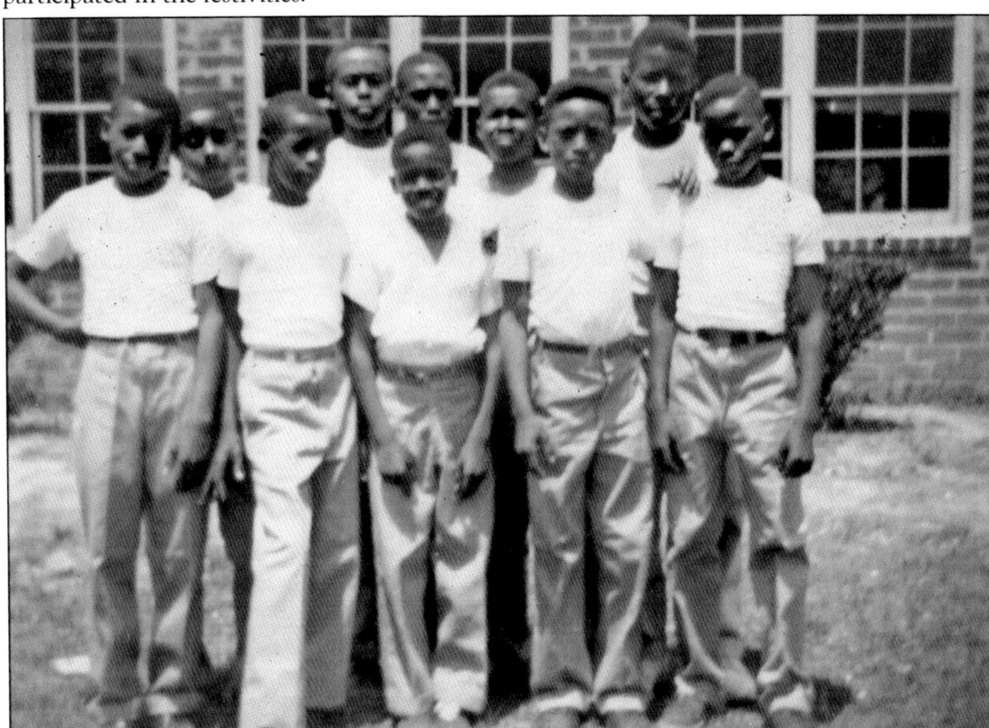

Many of the young men at Pembroke High School participated in the same festivities.

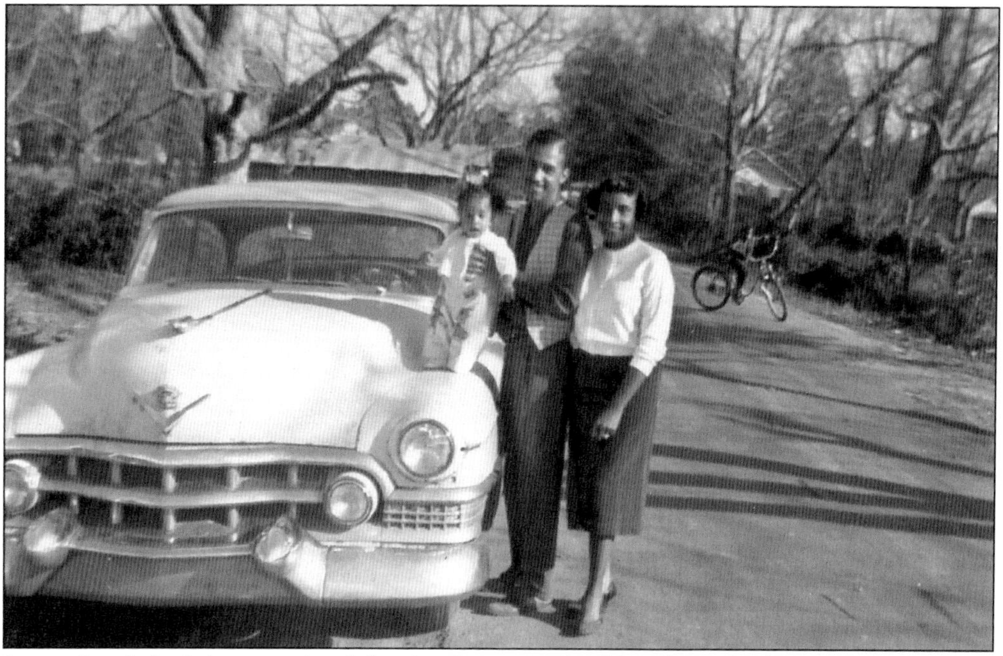

Louise Bunch (right), pictured with her family, was a school bus driver for the local school system and worked for the Bryan County Library. She was the wife of Joseph "Buster" Bunch (center) and the mother of two children, Angelo (left) and Ursula (not pictured).

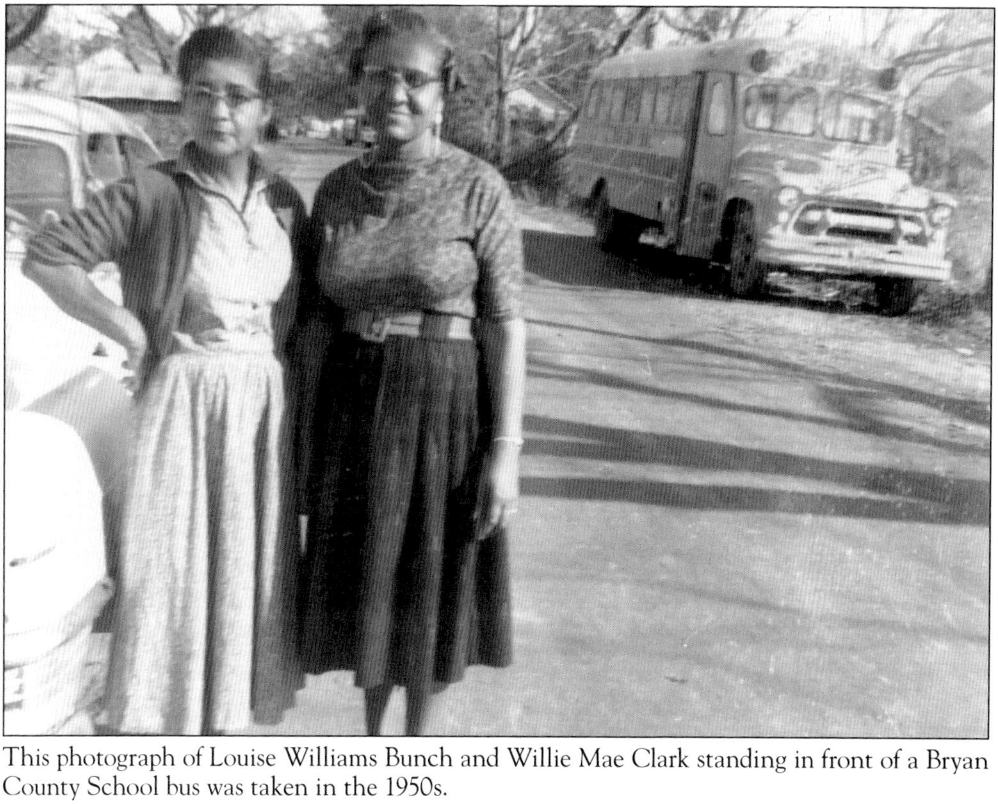

This photograph of Louise Williams Bunch and Willie Mae Clark standing in front of a Bryan County School bus was taken in the 1950s.

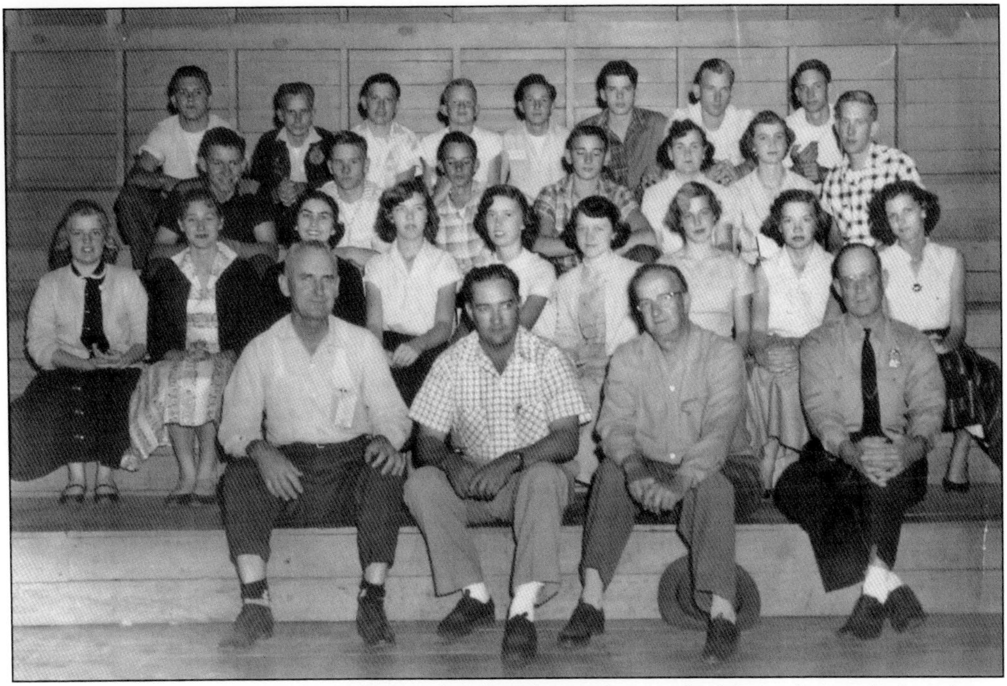

The Sky Watchers were a group of high-school students who watched for and identified airplanes for a civil defense project in the 1950s. Pictured from left to right are (first row) Dewey Medders, unidentified, Dr. Durden, and chief of police Malcolm Starling; (second row) Elizabeth Anderson, Lavone Hodges, Eva Williams, Carlene Lane, Elouise Merritt, Lou Quattlebaum, Faye Lane, Anne Lane, and Carolyn Calloway; (third row) Sonny Owens, Buddy Owens, Jimmy Hendrix, Gene Bazemore, Betty Murphy, Miriam Humphries, and Kyle Smith Jr.; (fourth row) Everett Bazemore, Sydney Bradley, Calvin Smith, Danny Warnell, Larry Foxworth, Trey Curl, Noel Osteen, and Jimmy Strickland.

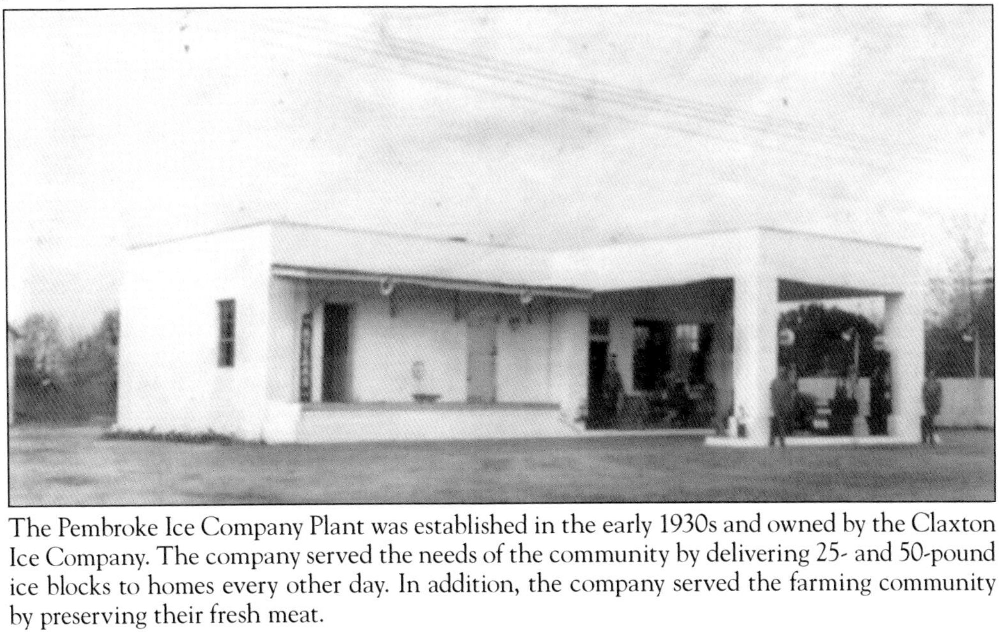

The Pembroke Ice Company Plant was established in the early 1930s and owned by the Claxton Ice Company. The company served the needs of the community by delivering 25- and 50-pound ice blocks to homes every other day. In addition, the company served the farming community by preserving their fresh meat.

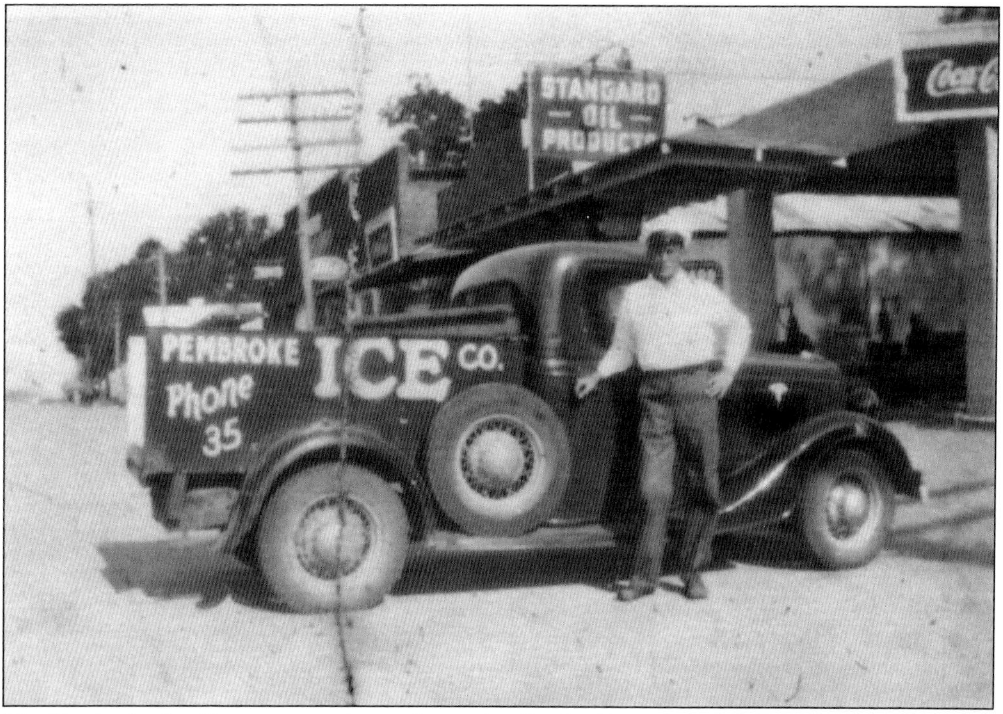

The Pembroke Ice Company truck was driven by Hawley Bazemore. Mr. Bazemore started work with the company in 1934 and retired in 1972, after 38 years.

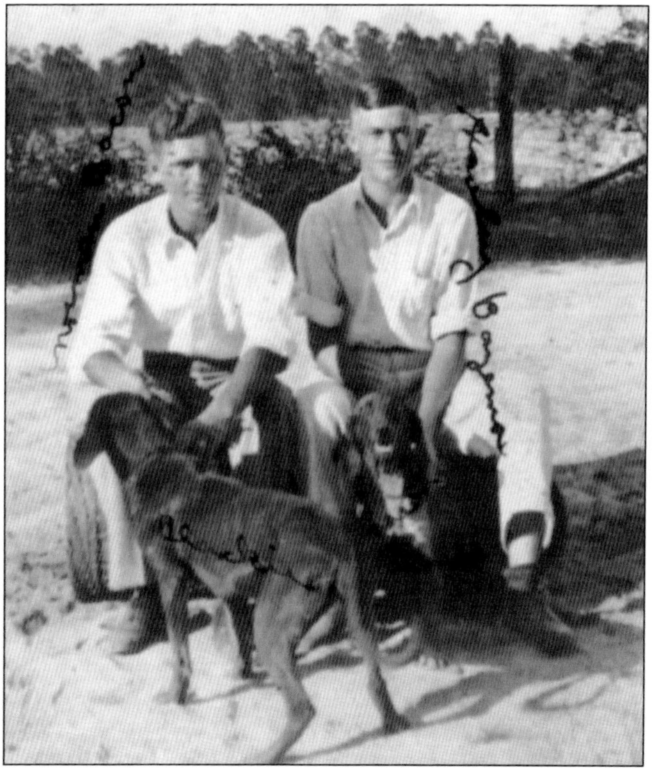

Buddies Norman Bacon (left) and Hawley Bazemore are shown with their retriever Blackie. They were both avid bird hunters. Mr. Bacon was a rural letter carrier and operated the Purina Feed Store.

James Madison Smith moved to Pembroke following the death of his first wife to furnish building materials for the Savannah and Western Railway. He later married Ida Williams Duggar of Pembroke. He served as a one-term mayor of Pembroke and was the father of Dr. W. K. Smith. He was Pembroke's first postmaster.

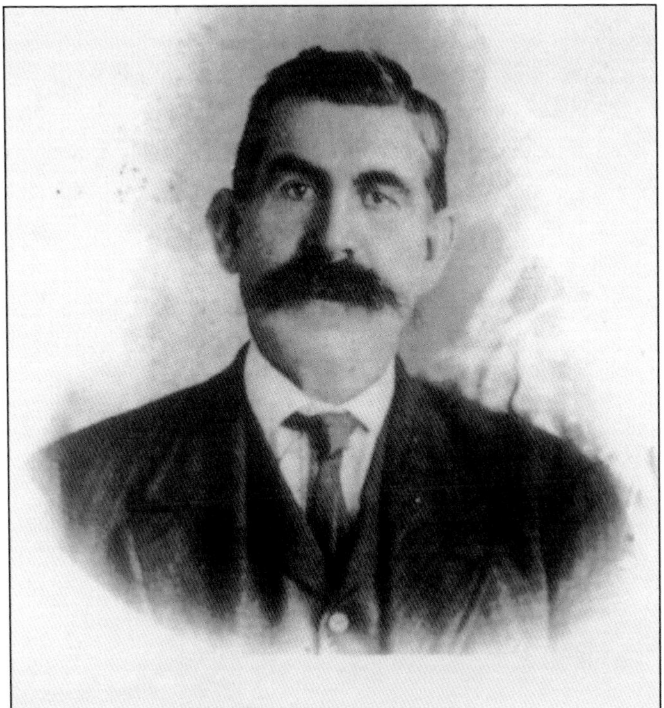

JAMES MADISON SMITH

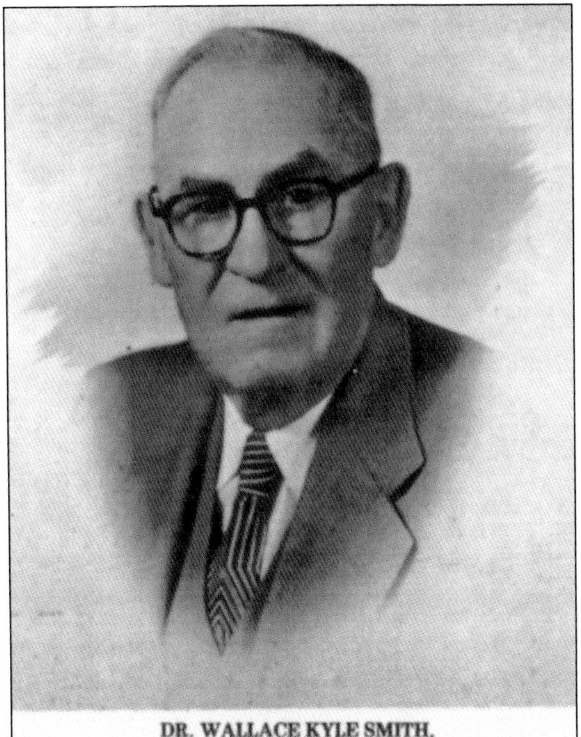

DR. WALLACE KYLE SMITH, M.D.

Dr. W. K. Smith secured the necessary funds to provide a new water system for Pembroke in order to fight typhoid fever. He started his first medical practice in Pembroke and served the community for over 50 years. He also served as state representative from Bryan County for 16 years.

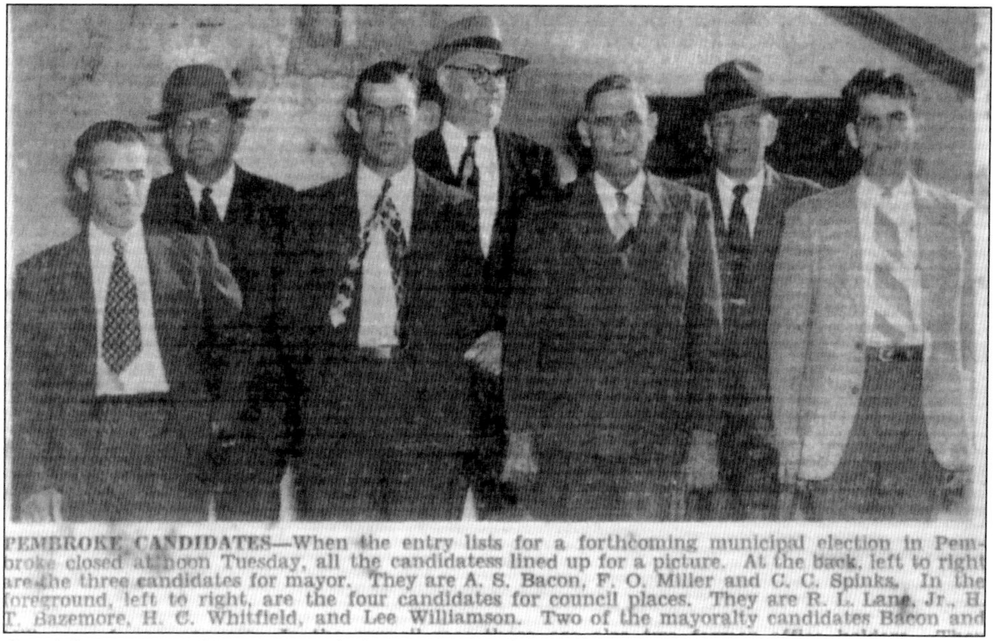
PEMBROKE CANDIDATES—When the entry lists for a forthcoming municipal election in Pembroke closed at noon Tuesday, all the candidatess lined up for a picture. At the back, left to right are the three candidates for mayor. They are A. S. Bacon, F. O. Miller and C. C. Spinks. In the foreground, left to right, are the four candidates for council places. They are R. L. Lane, Jr., H. T. Bazemore, H. C. Whitfield, and Lee Williamson. Two of the mayoralty candidates Bacon and

Candidates in a 1950s municipal election in Pembroke were, from left to right, (first row) R. L. Lane Jr., H. T. Bazemore, H. C. Whitfield, and Lee Williamson; (second row) mayoral candidates A. S. Bacon, F. O. Miller, and C. C. Spinks. Two of the mayoral candidates, Bacon and Miller, were former mayors.

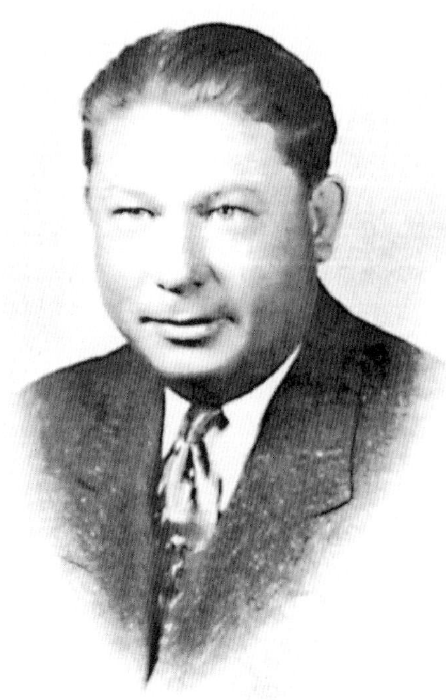
DR. WILLIAM EUGENE SMITH, M.D.

Dr. W. E. Smith followed in the footsteps of his father and practiced medicine until his death in the 1990s.

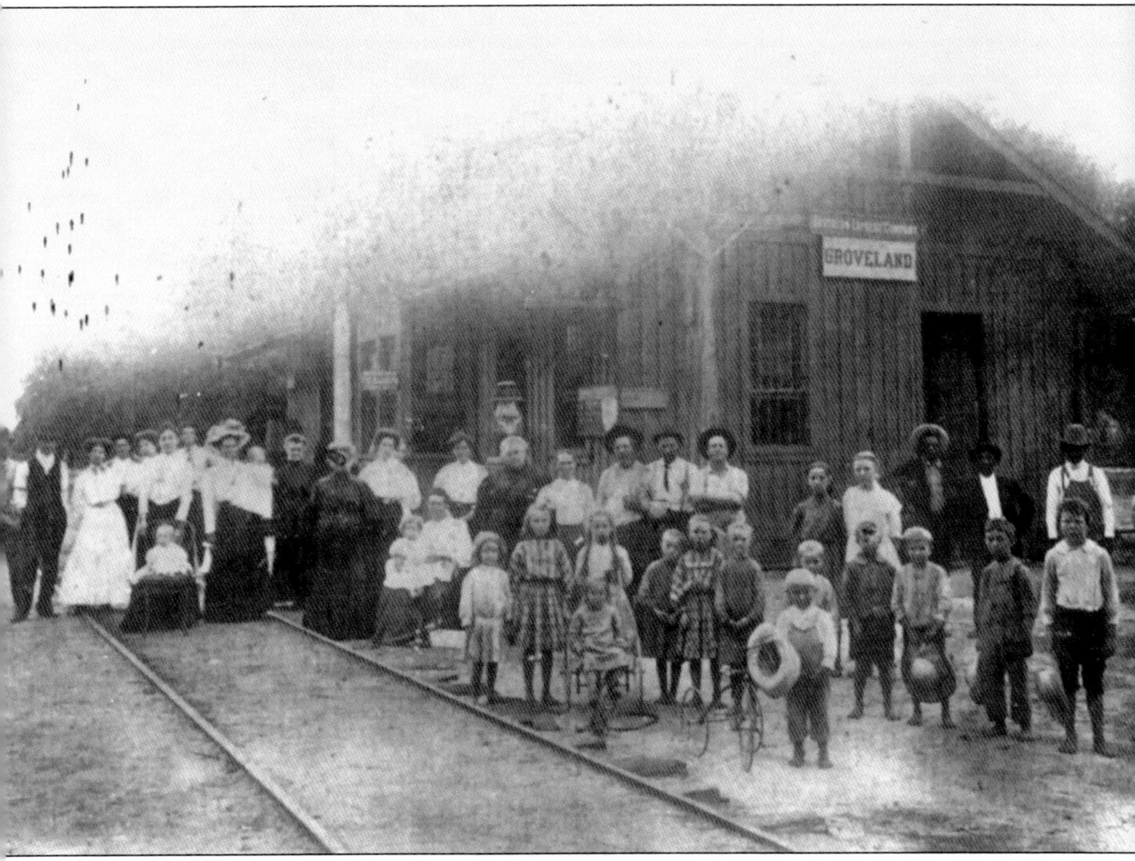

The woman seated holding the baby is Mrs. Elizabeth Green, mother of Elizabeth Lane and grandmother of Ann Lane Sanders. This picture was taken in 1909 at the Groveland Depot.

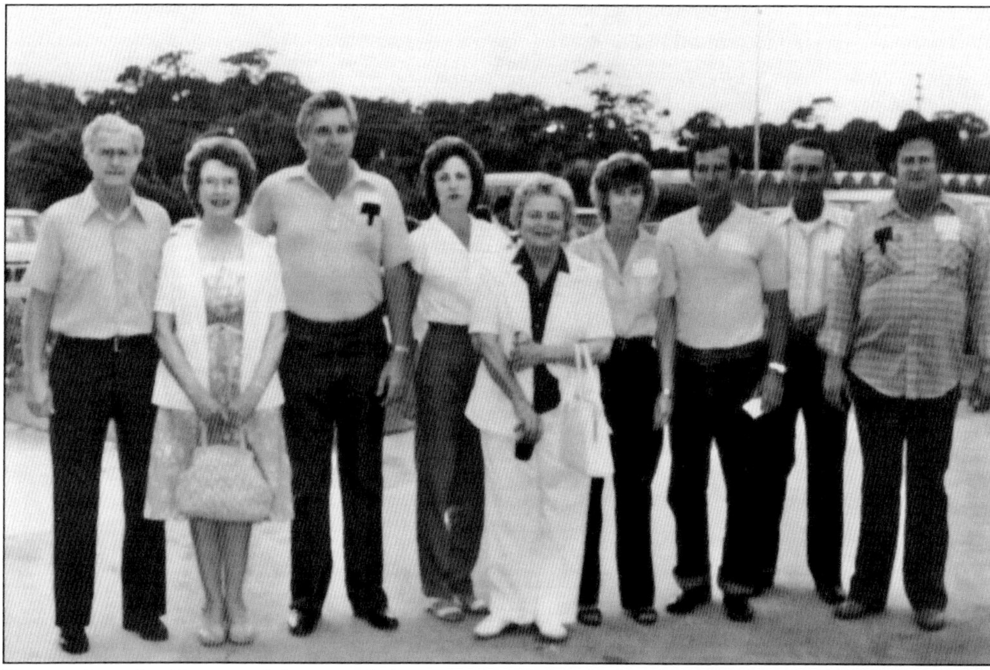

Pictured at the Georgia Municipal Association Convention in 1983 are the following, from left to right: Purvis Brannen, Louise Bacon Brannen, city councilman Gene Cowart, Montene Smith Cowart, Dorothy May Bacon Pickett, Judy Bacon Cook, city councilman Jimmy Cook, city councilman Ed Jordan, and city councilman Harvey Carruthers. Mayor Woodrow W. Pickett is missing from this picture.

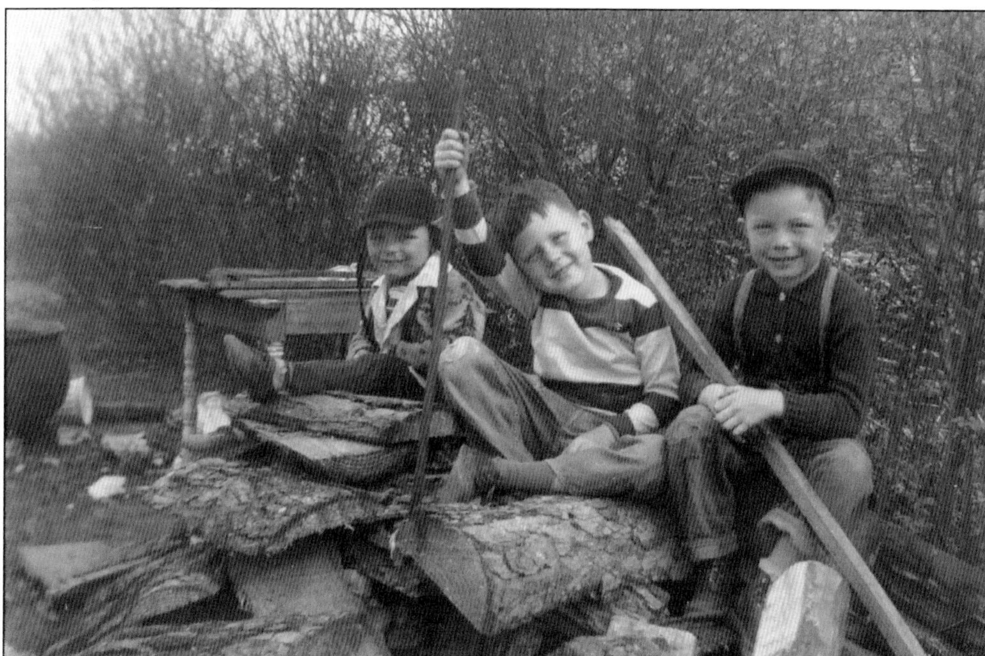

Pals on the wood pile, George Huff (left), Jim Harn (center), and Richard Owens (right) are pictured here.

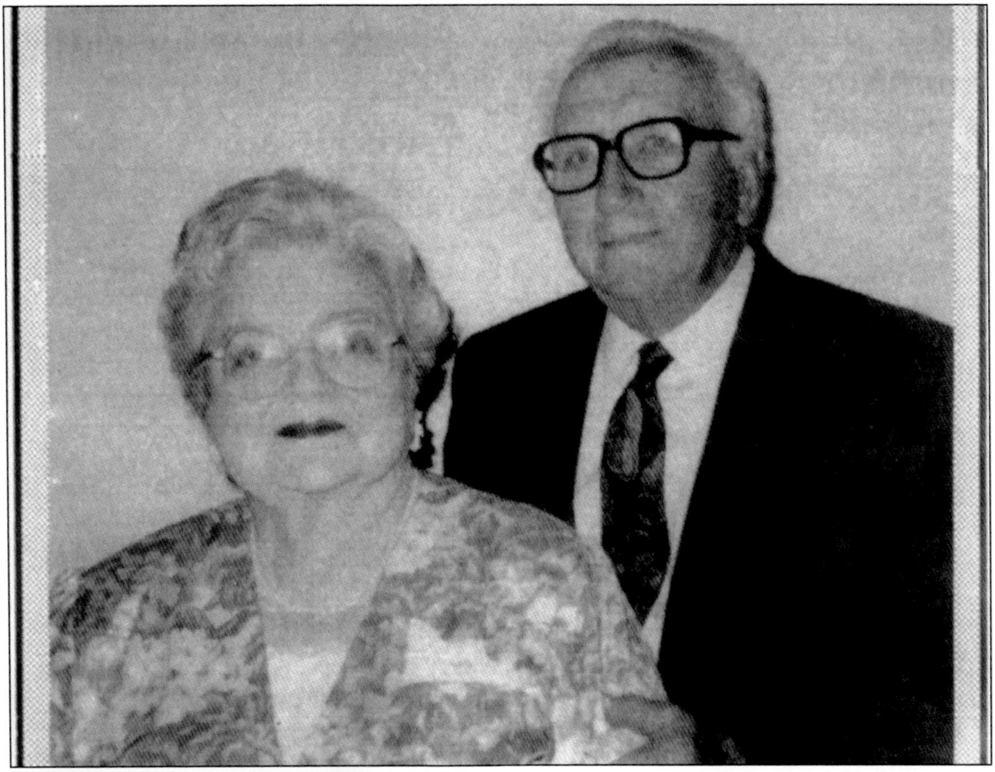

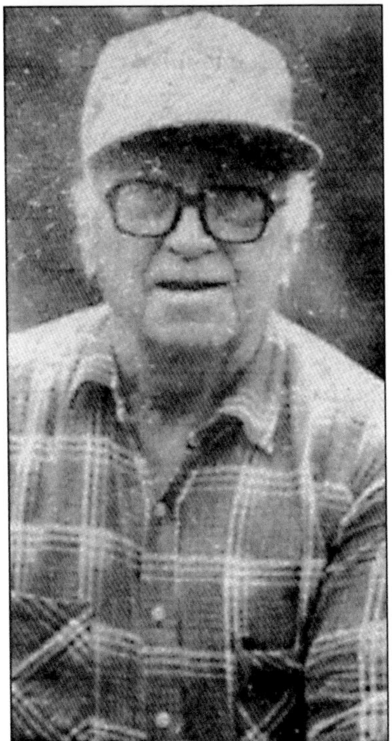

Woodrow Pickett

Mr. and Mrs. Woodrow W. Pickett observed their golden wedding anniversary in June 1992. Dorothy Mae and Woodrow Pickett, beloved members of the Pembroke community, were married in the First Baptist Church of Pembroke in 1942. Woodrow was employed by the U.S. Army for 26 years, and Dorothy Mae was a school teacher for 31 years.

Mr. Woodrow Pickett was mayor of Pembroke for six terms. A "one-term" mayor lasted for six terms! During Mayor Pickett's first term, the City of Pembroke received four grants for paving streets, sidewalks, and gutters. He gives credit for all of the good changes to the people who served under him. One of his hobbies after retirement was raising hogs for market.

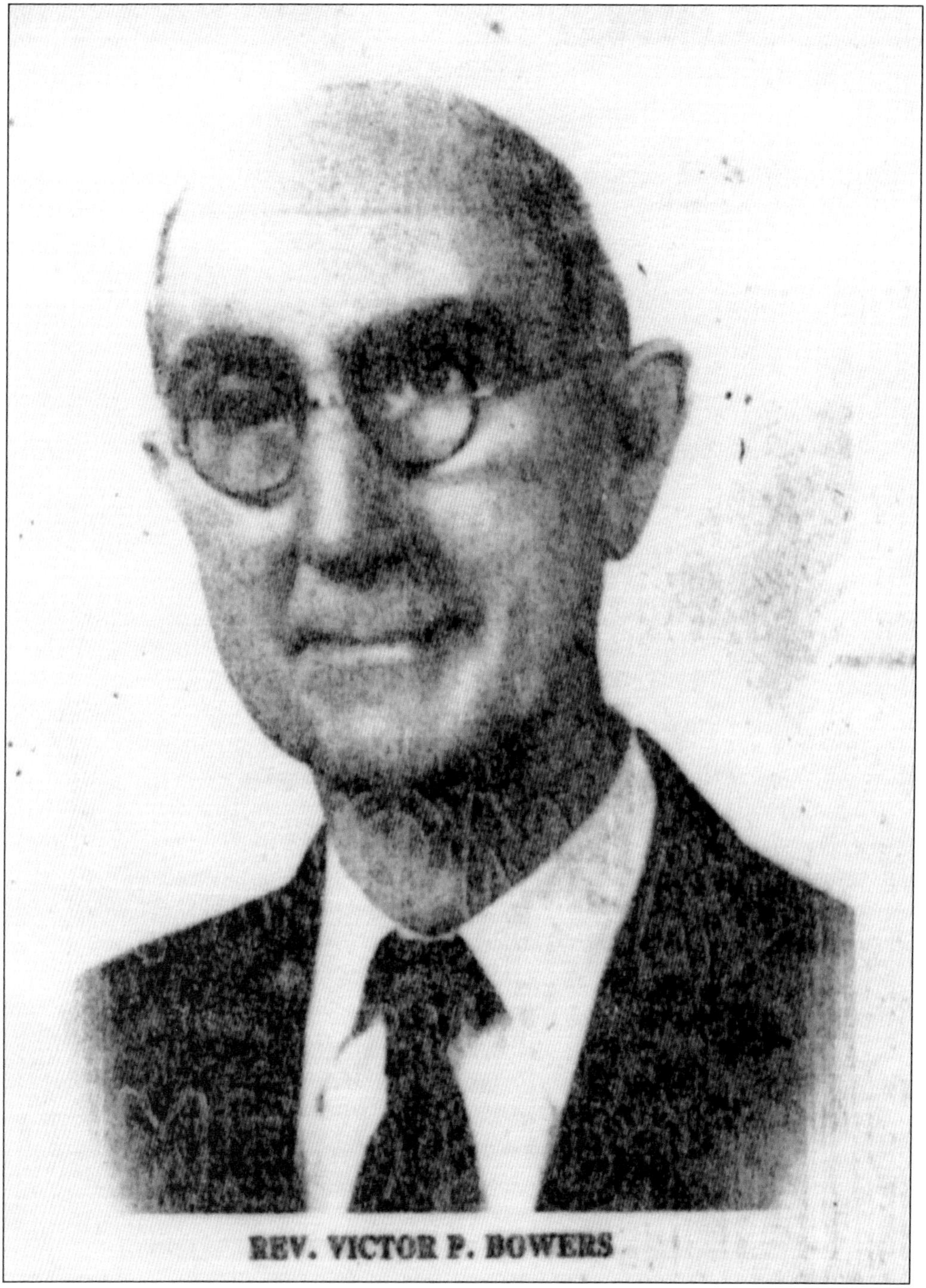

Rev. Victor P. Bowers came to this area in 1901 and organized the Pembroke Christian Church. After serving for 55 years in the ministry, he retired in 1956. In addition, he served as a director of the Pembroke State Bank and was chairman of the Bryan County Board of Education at one time.

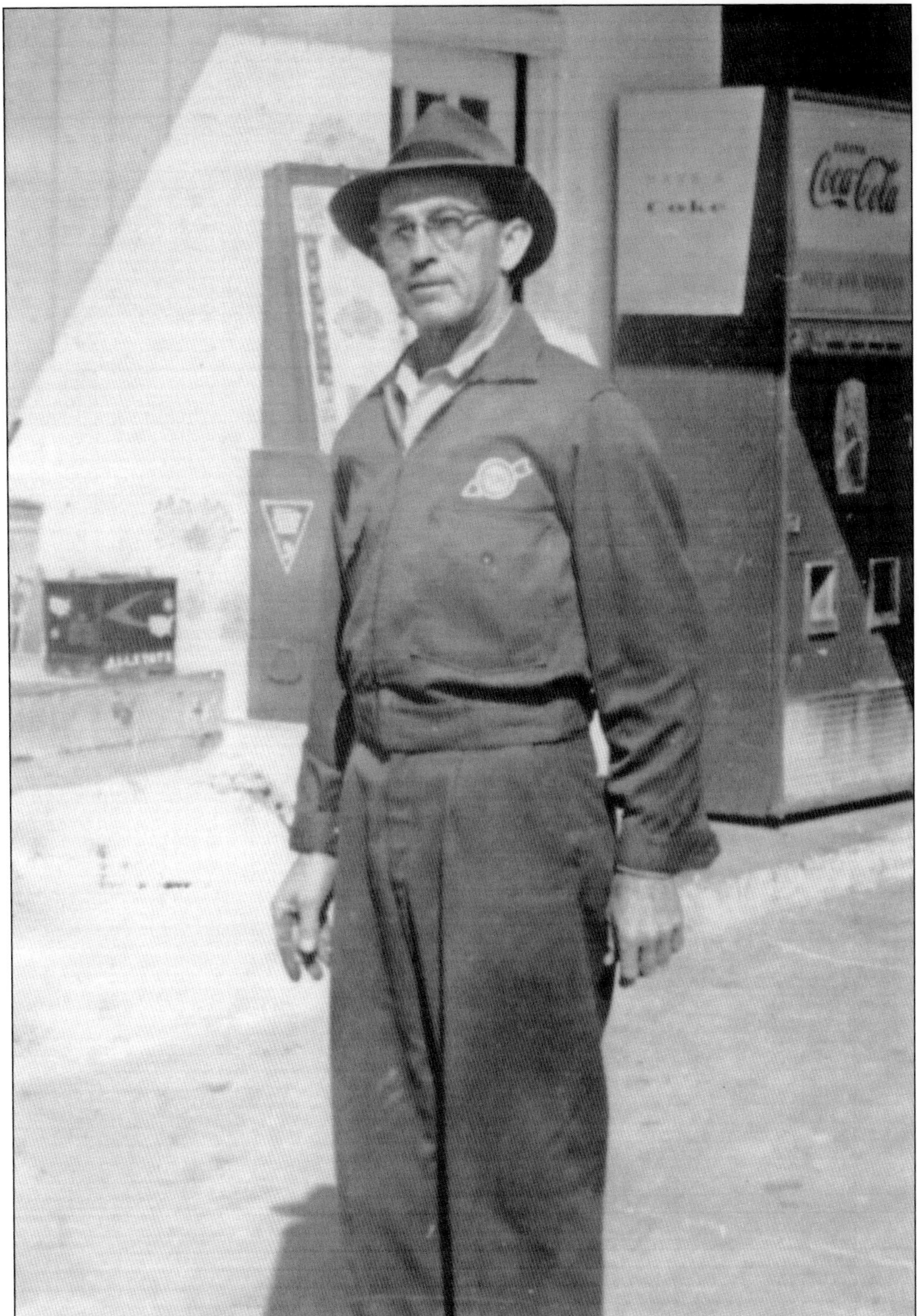

Hawley Bazemore was longtime employee of Pembroke Ice Company. He served as county commissioner for 12 years and on the City Council of Pembroke for 13 years. Hawley was married to the former Bessie Elizabeth Clanton, whom he met at a cane grinding.

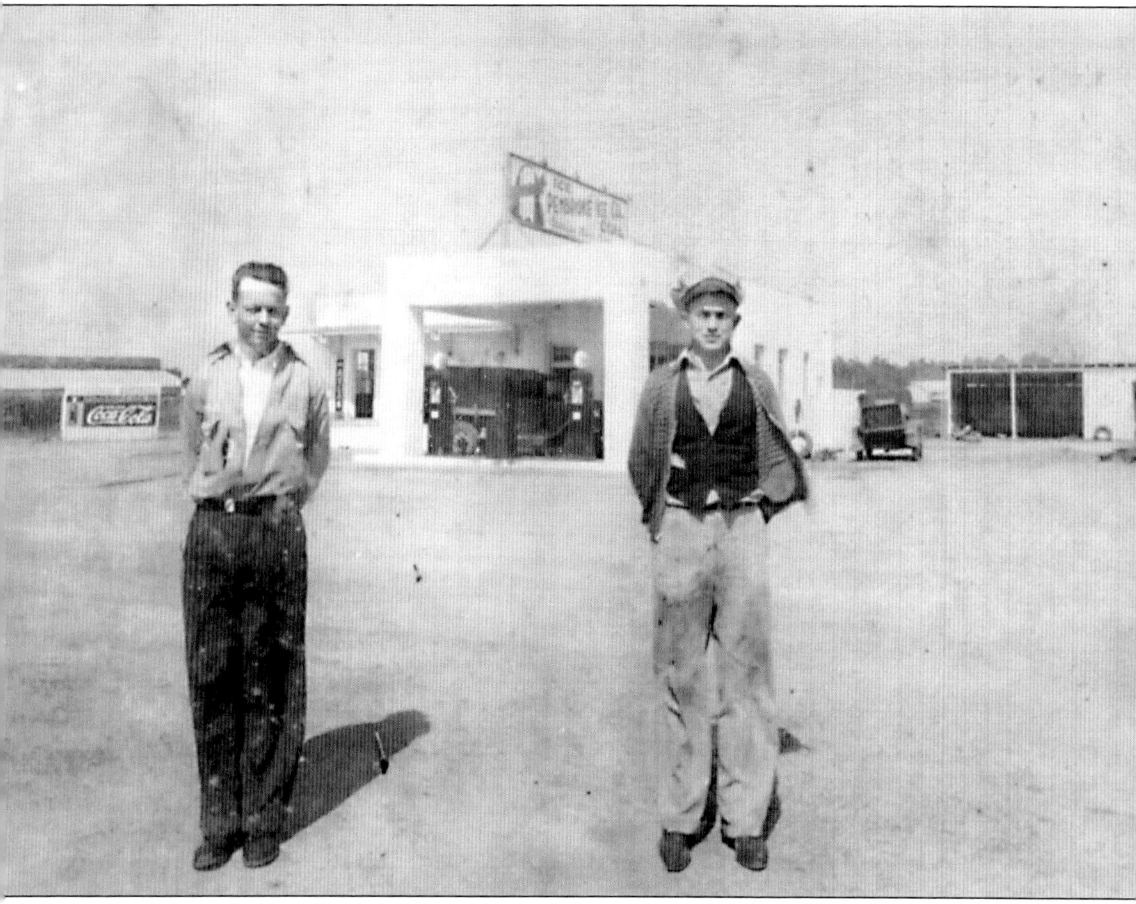

Buck Lane (left) and Hawley Bazemore (right) are pictured in front of Pembroke Ice Company in 1939. Buck was manager of the company, and Hawley delivered the blocks of ice.

Margie Bacon Nolan, a native of Pembroke, is seen standing in front of a school bus in the early 1930s.

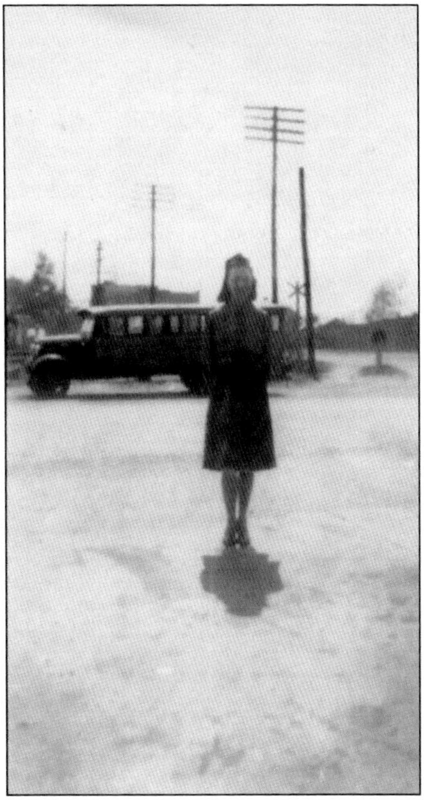

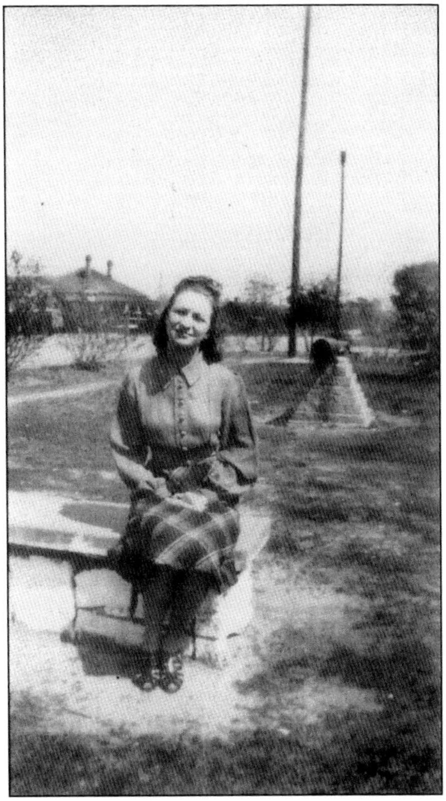

Here, Margie Bacon Nolan is seated in front of the Civil War cannon that was located in downtown Pembroke. The Jones Hotel, in the background, was one of the first hotels in Pembroke. The owner, Mrs. Jones, made a trip every Friday to Savannah to purchase groceries for the boarders for the coming week. Since Mrs. Jones could not drive, Geneva Futch, a first-grade teacher at Pembroke, drove for her, and all the other boarding teachers went along for the ride.

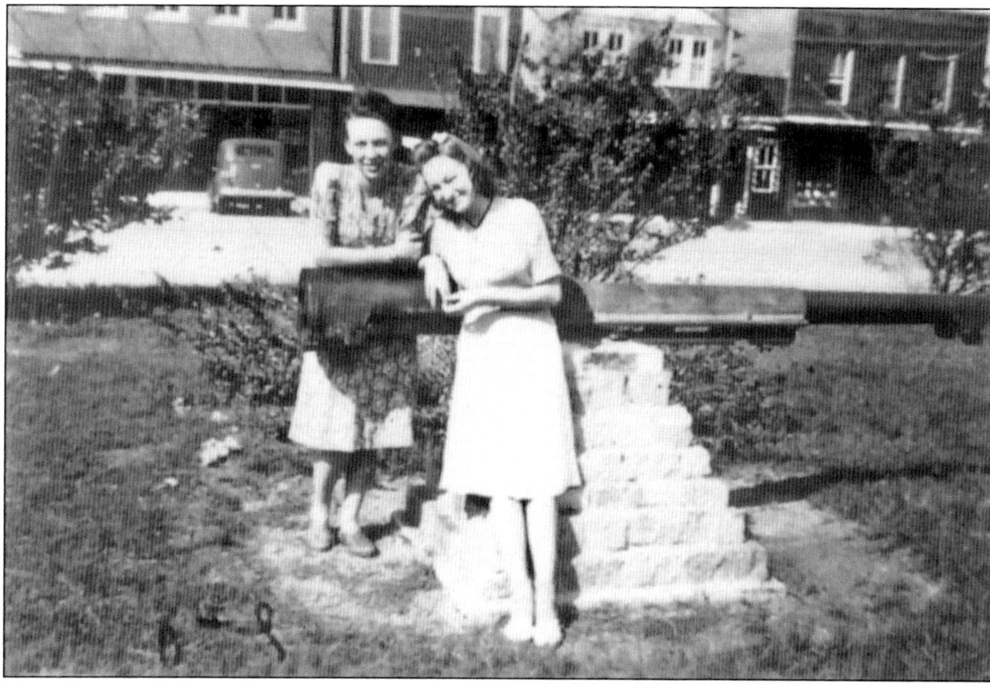

Mary Sims and Margie Bacon are pictured with Pembroke's Civil War cannon. The cannon was removed during World War II for scrap metal.

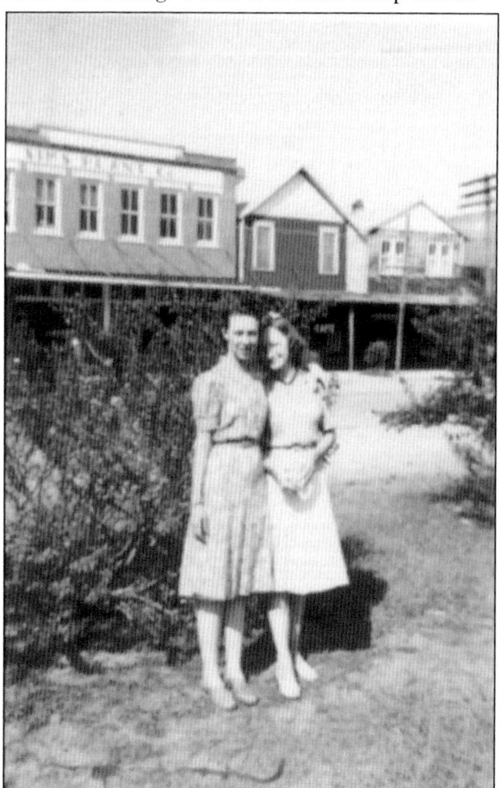

Mary Sims and Margie Bacon are pictured standing in front of the Sims Plant Company in the 1940s. Mary Sims was the daughter of the owner of Sims Plant Company. They grew and packaged tomato plants that were shipped all over the country.

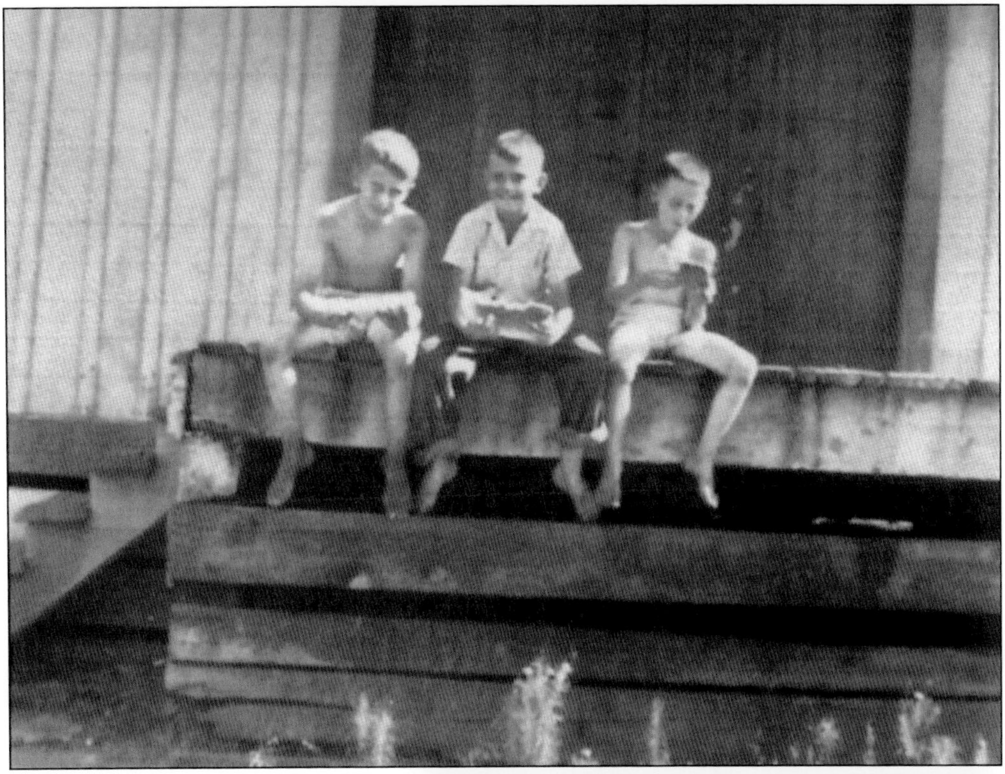

Albert Bacon (center) and his buddies are photographed sitting on the old railroad depot.

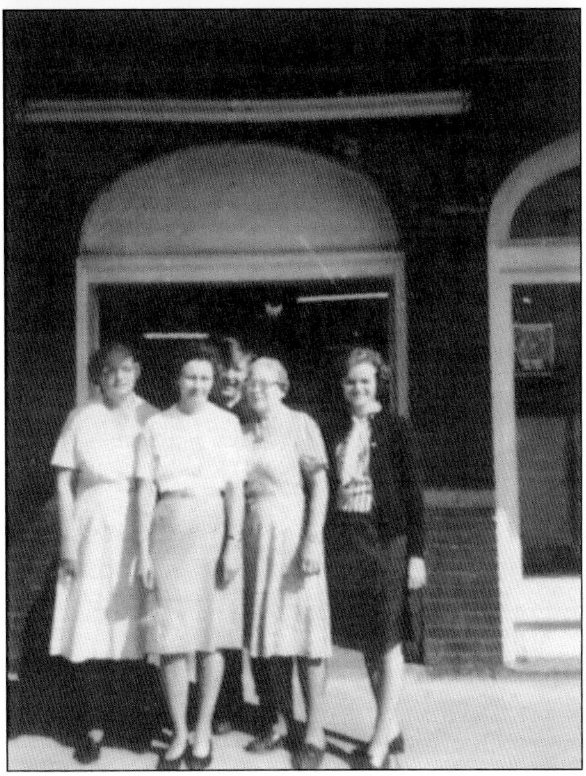

Employees of the Star Department Store served the needs of many people in Bryan County. Pictured from left to right are Loraine Warren, Needa Bragg, Wayne Bragg, Mrs. R. L. Jackson, and Brenda Futch, in the 1960s.

PEMBROKE'S NEW GRASS CUTTING TRACTOR BEING DELIVERED

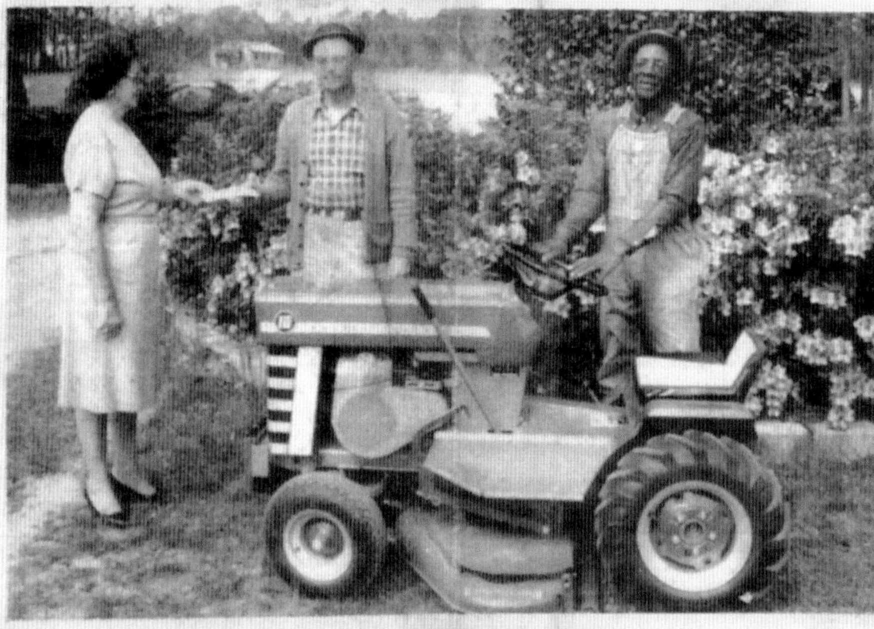

Shown above is H. G. Shuman, of the Shuman Implement Company of Hagan, delivering the handsome Massey Ferguson Tractor to Mrs. L. M. Anderson, who has charge of the Northside Cemetery Grounds, and the public squares in the city. Mrs. Anderson is handing Mr. Shuman a City of Pembroke check in full payment for this fine tractor. Looking on with a broad smile is Harley Surrency, who will operate and have charge of the tractor, which will be used only in the cemetery, the parks and squares downtown, and the Community House Grounds.

It is a small Tractor made by Massey Ferguson, recognized as being one of the largest and leading builders of farm tractors in the United States and sold in this section by:

Pembroke's new grass-cutting tractor was delivered by H. G. Shuman of the Shuman Implement Company in Hagan, Georgia, to Mrs. L. M. Anderson, who was in charge of the Northside Cemetery grounds and public squares in the city. Here, she is handing Mr. Shuman a City of Pembroke check for full payment of this fine tractor. Looking on is Harley Surrency, who would operate and have charge of the Massey Ferguson tractor.

Capt. F. C. Drexel's term as Pembroke City Court Judge was interrupted by World War II. He was granted a leave of absence from the judgeship by a special act of the General Assembly, conditional upon the fact that he would reassume these duties within the four-year term.

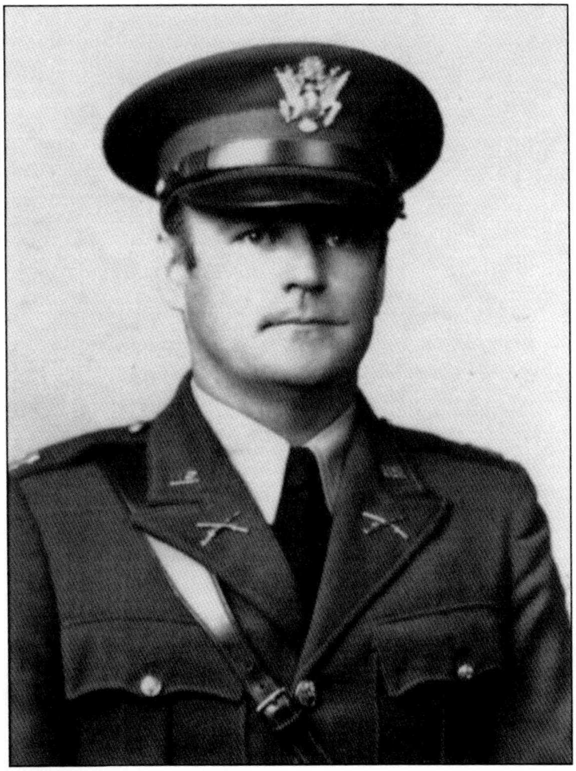

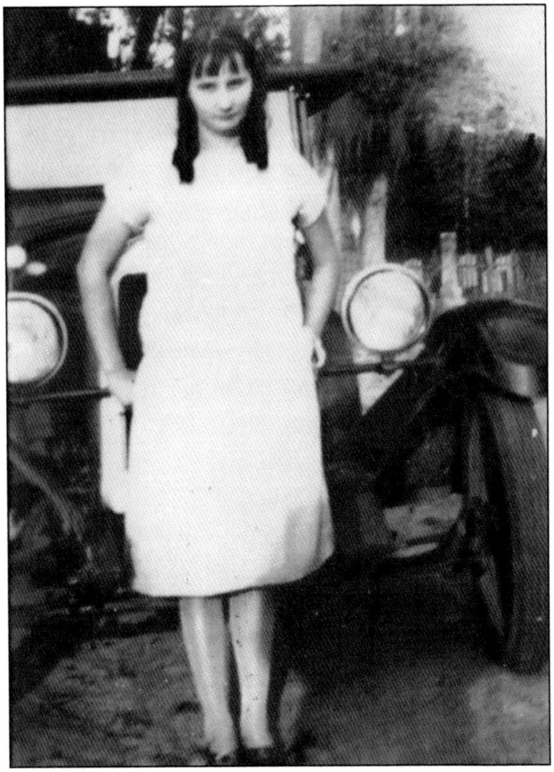

Geneva Futch Drexel, wife of F. C. Drexel, is shown standing in front of a 1925 vintage automobile. Mrs. Drexel served eight years as first-grade teacher at Pembroke School and taught a total of 37 years.

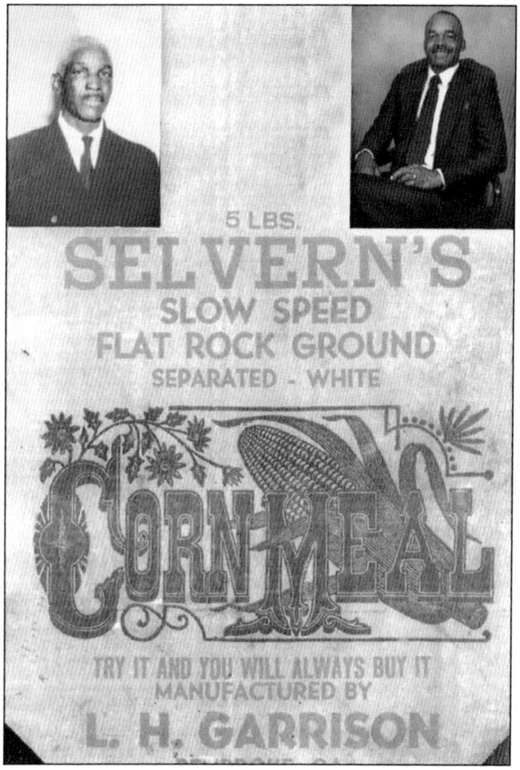

Lucius and James Garrison were owners and operators of L. H. Garrison Corn Meal Mill for 14 years, from 1948 to 1962. This mill was a slow speed, flat rock, ground corn meal mill. The corn meal was ground the old-fashioned way with no preservatives in order to produce the freshest baked goods. Meal could be bagged in five-pound bags for customers.

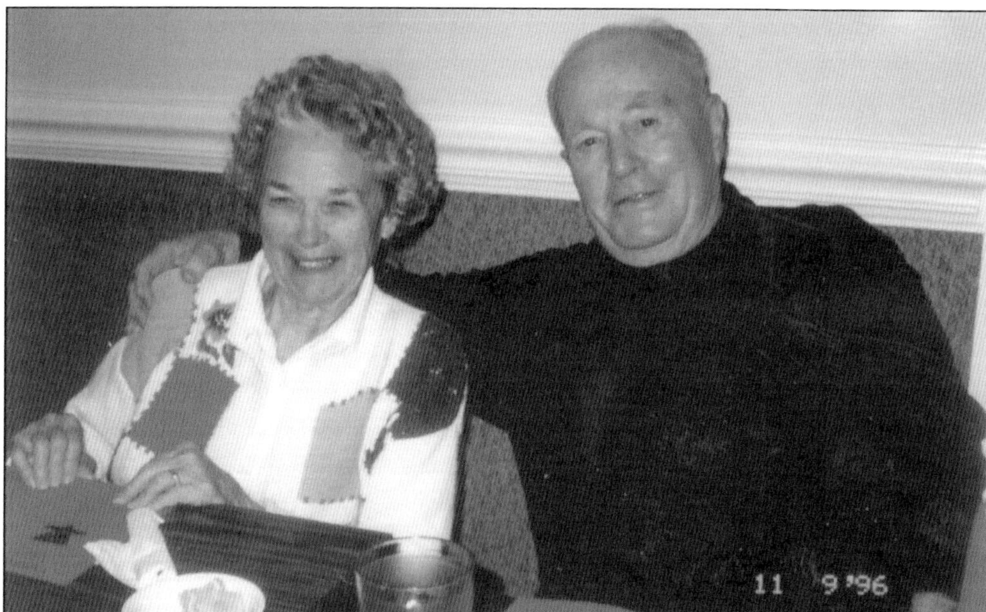

Robert Bowers served as teacher, coach, and principal of Bryan County High School from 1950 to 1974. From 1974 until retirement in 1981, he served as an administrative assistant in charge of transportation for the Bryan County Board of Education. Mary Jane Clark Bowers came to Pembroke as the home-economics teacher in 1950, after her marriage to Mr. Bowers; she taught until 1953, when she opened Pembroke Floral Shop.

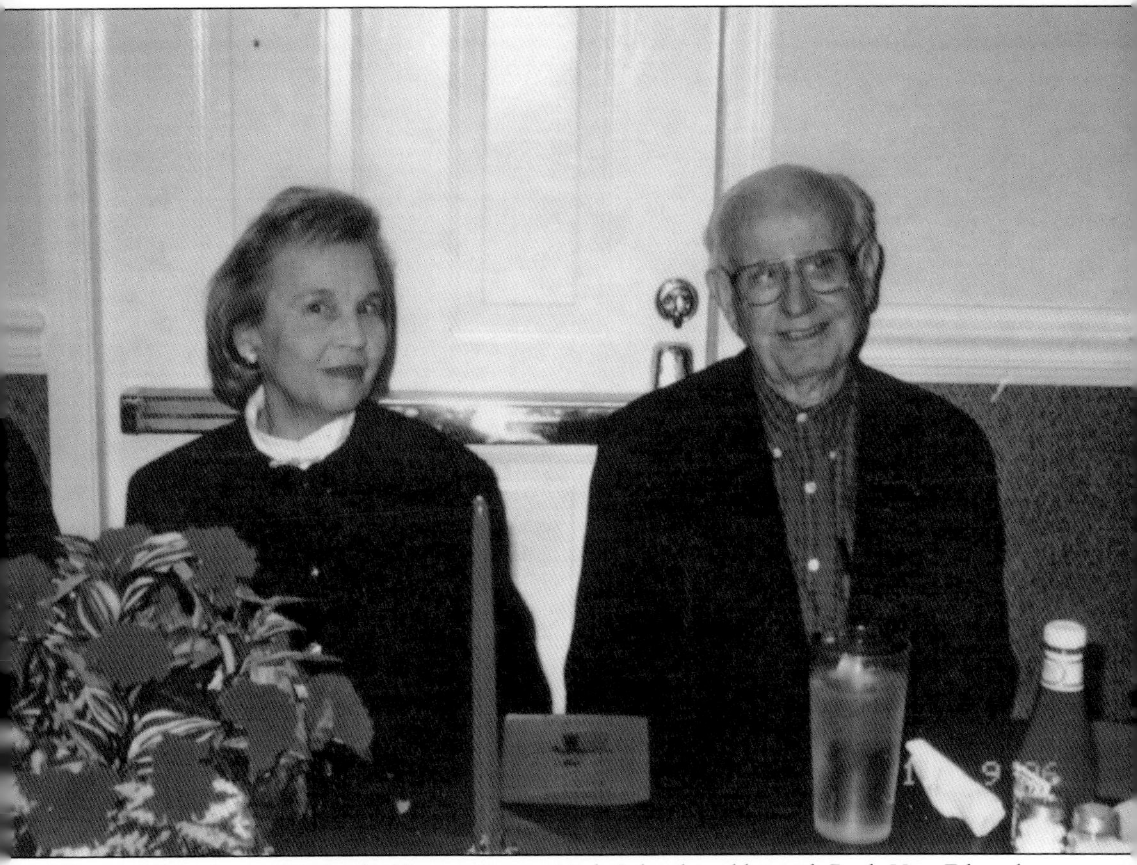

Thomas Edwards was principal of Bryan County High School, and his wife Ruth Hart Edwards was an elementary-school teacher. Thomas was a native of Pembroke, the son of Mr. and Mrs. Tom Edwards. Ruth was a native of Statesboro, Georgia.

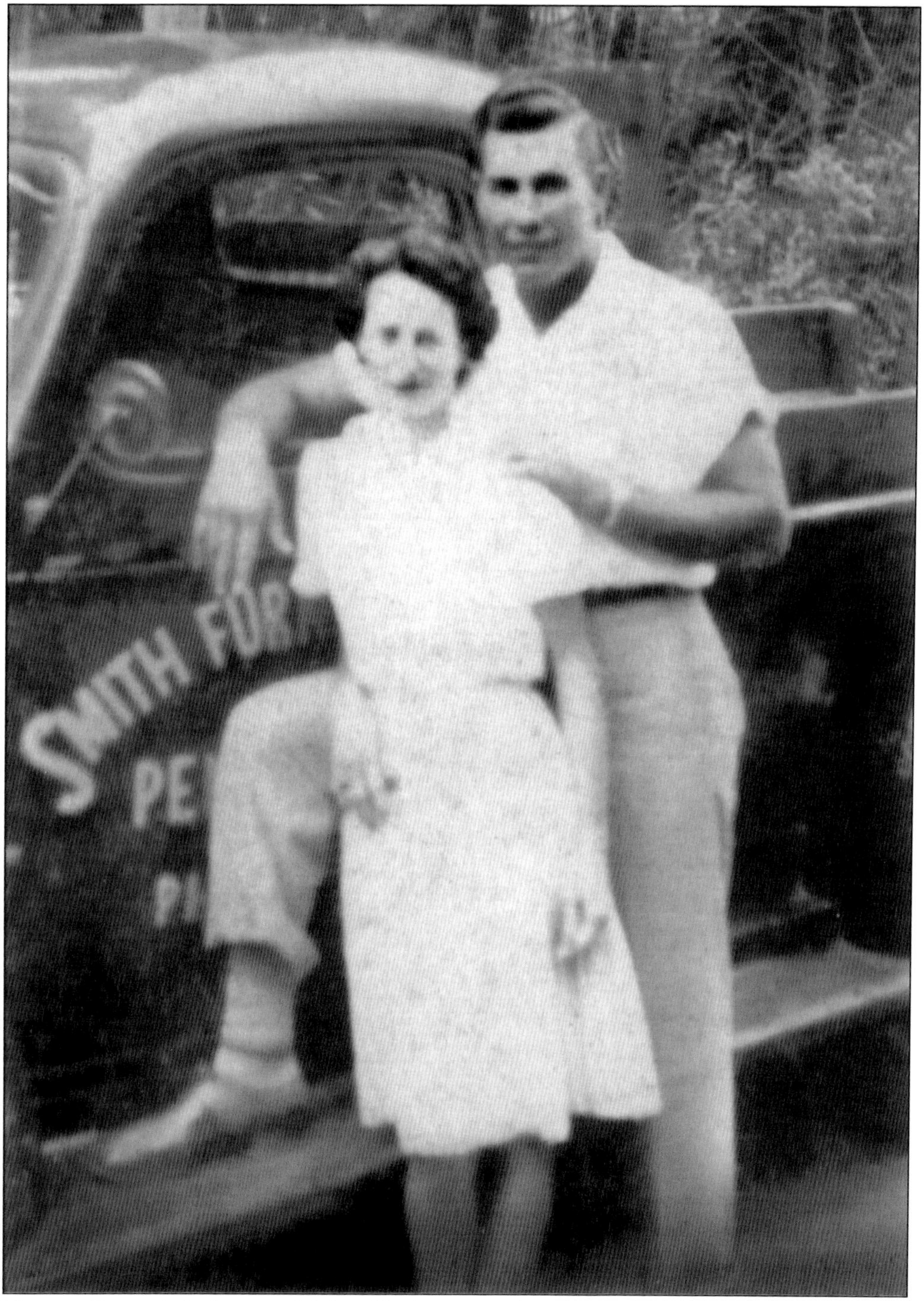

Virginia (Lanier) Buckner and Julian Buckner were longtime residents of Pembroke. He was an employee with Smith Furniture Company and also worked for Shuman Supply Company. Virginia retired from Pembroke Telephone Company and was a wonderful cook and homemaker for her family.

Pictured here are members of the Civilian Conservation Corps (CCC). This was one of Pres. Franklin D. Roosevelt's New Deal programs (1933–1942) to enhance the economy of the United States.

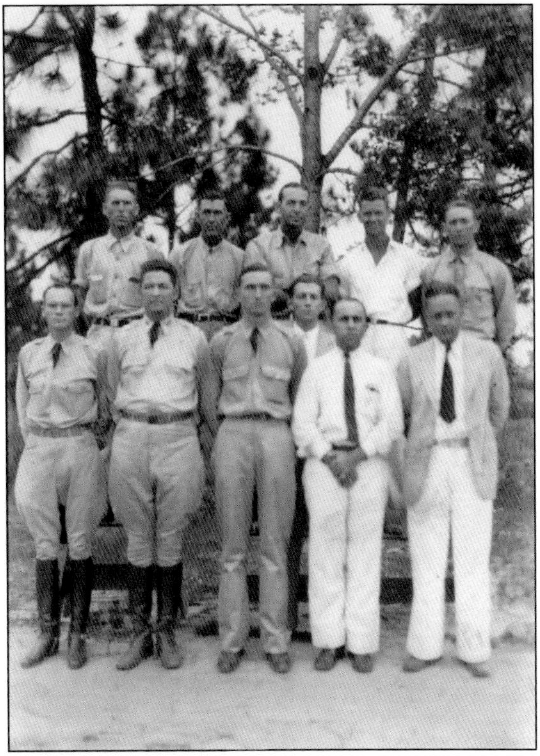

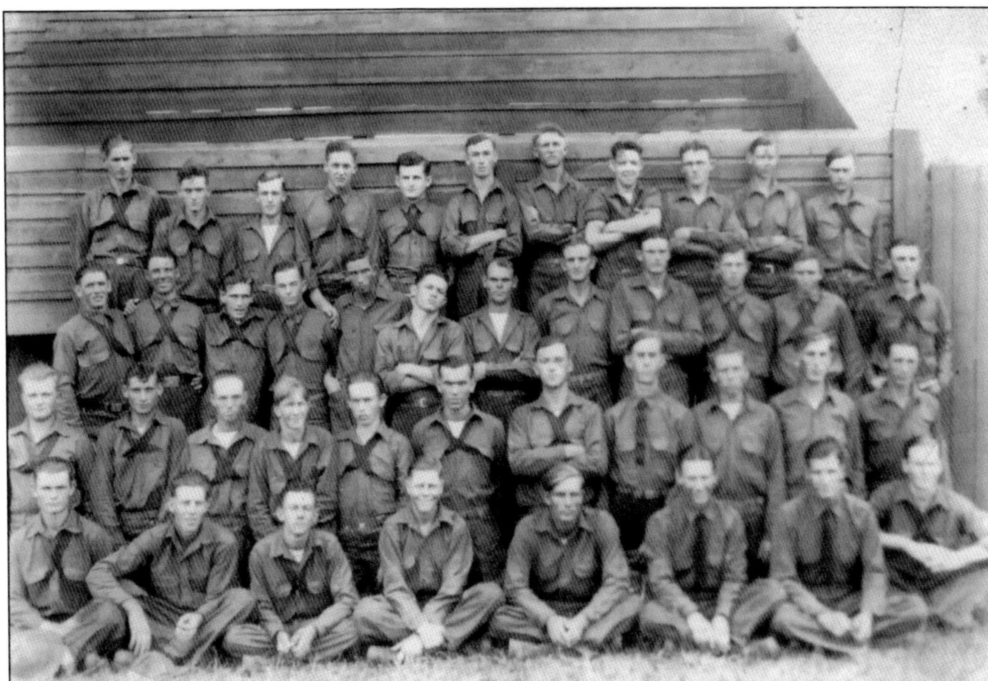

This photograph is representative of the Work Progress Administration (WPA) in 1939–1943. The WPA was another one of President Roosevelt's New Deal programs, providing work for millions of people during the Great Depression.

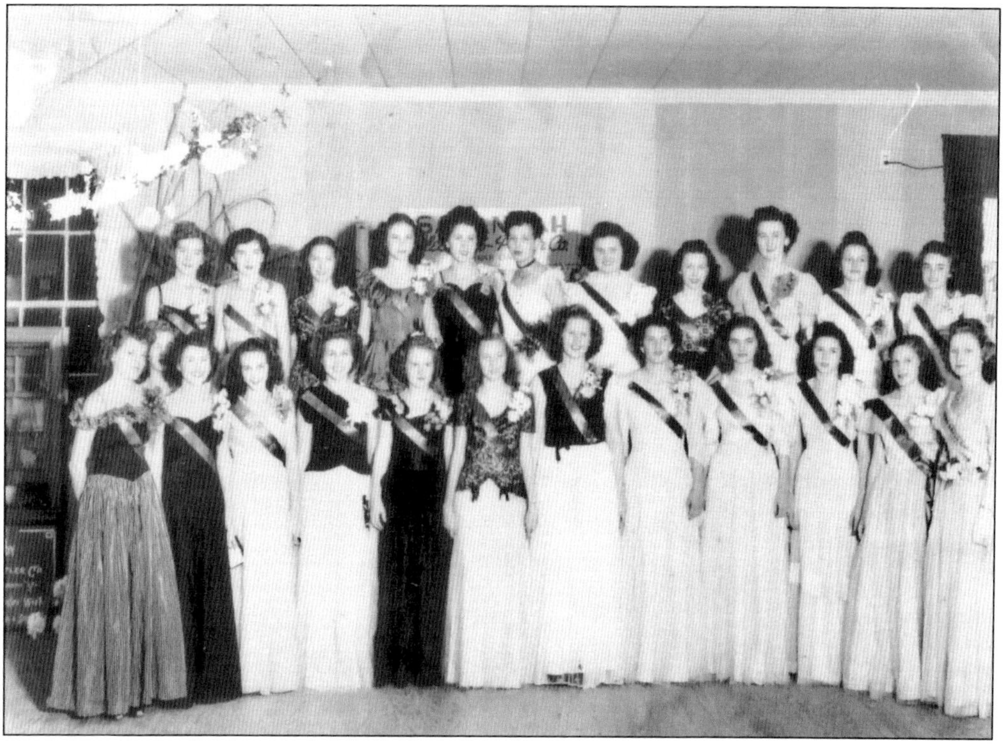

A 1940s sample of Pembroke's beauties includes, from left to right, (first row) Ruth Miller, Freida Speir, Shirley Owens, Gayle Croom, Jean Williamson, Delores Kennedy, Doris Shuman, Ruth Hutchinson, Mary Ann Spinks, Jetta Ellis, Jewel Cowart, Barbara Smith, and Evelyn Sims; (second row) Kitty Bacon, ? Strickland, Virginia Shuman, Patty Deal, Nellie Page, Virgie Sutton, Willa Fay Starling, Faye Owens, Doris Owens, Eva Mae Clark, and unidentified.

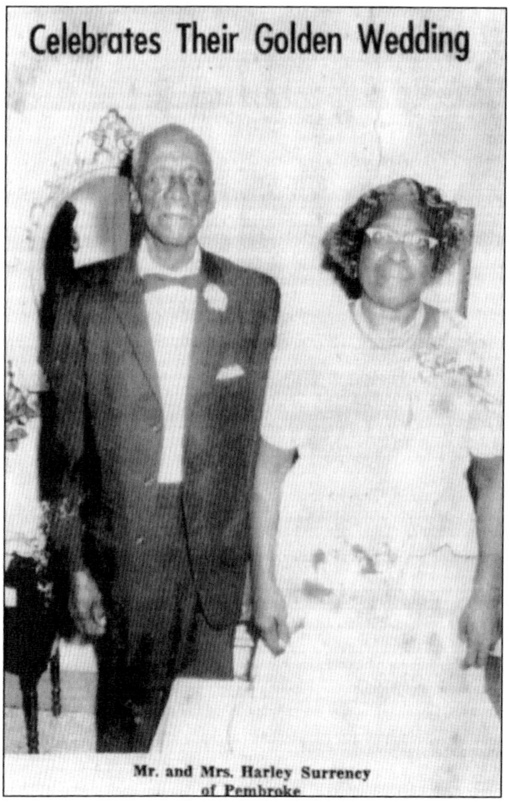
Celebrates Their Golden Wedding

Mr. and Mrs. Harley Surrency
of Pembroke

Mr. and Mrs. Harley Surrency celebrated their golden wedding anniversary. Mr. Surrency served as a deacon at Mount Moriah Baptist Church. He was known by many Pembroke citizens for his famous barbeque.

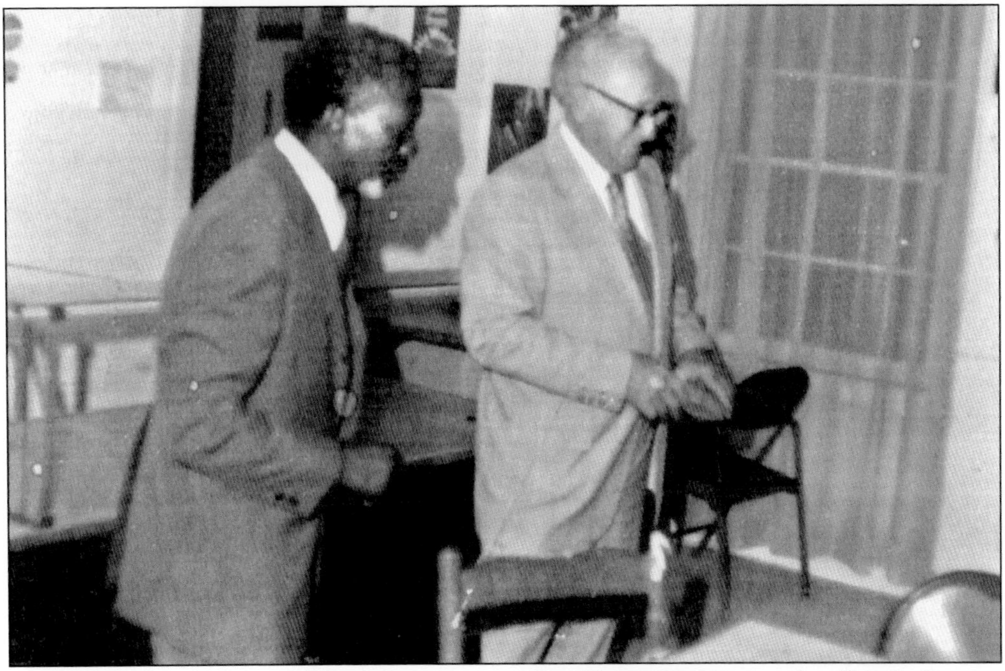

Mayor Woodrow Pickett and Fred George are pictured here representing the Client's Citizens Council in 1980. A client's council is a strong, unified group of individuals whose purpose is to act as a voice for poor people in their local community and throughout Georgia.

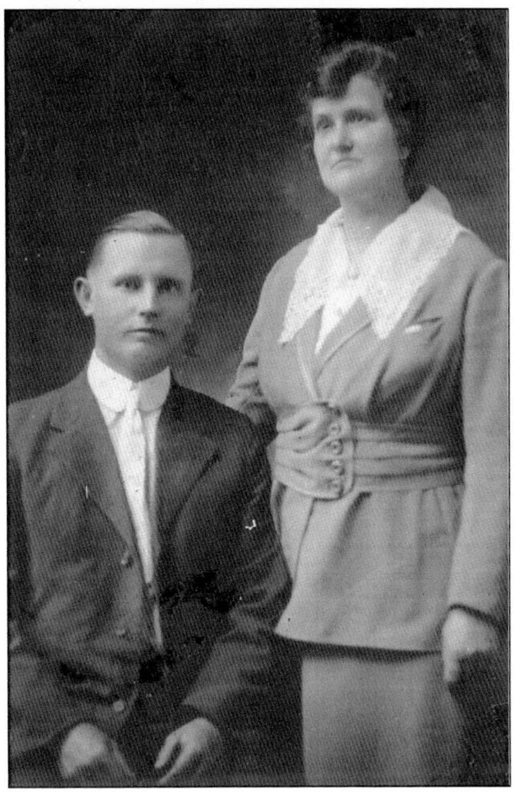

Dana and Beulah Brown Garrett were early residents of the Pembroke community. This photograph was donated by the Rad Johnson family.

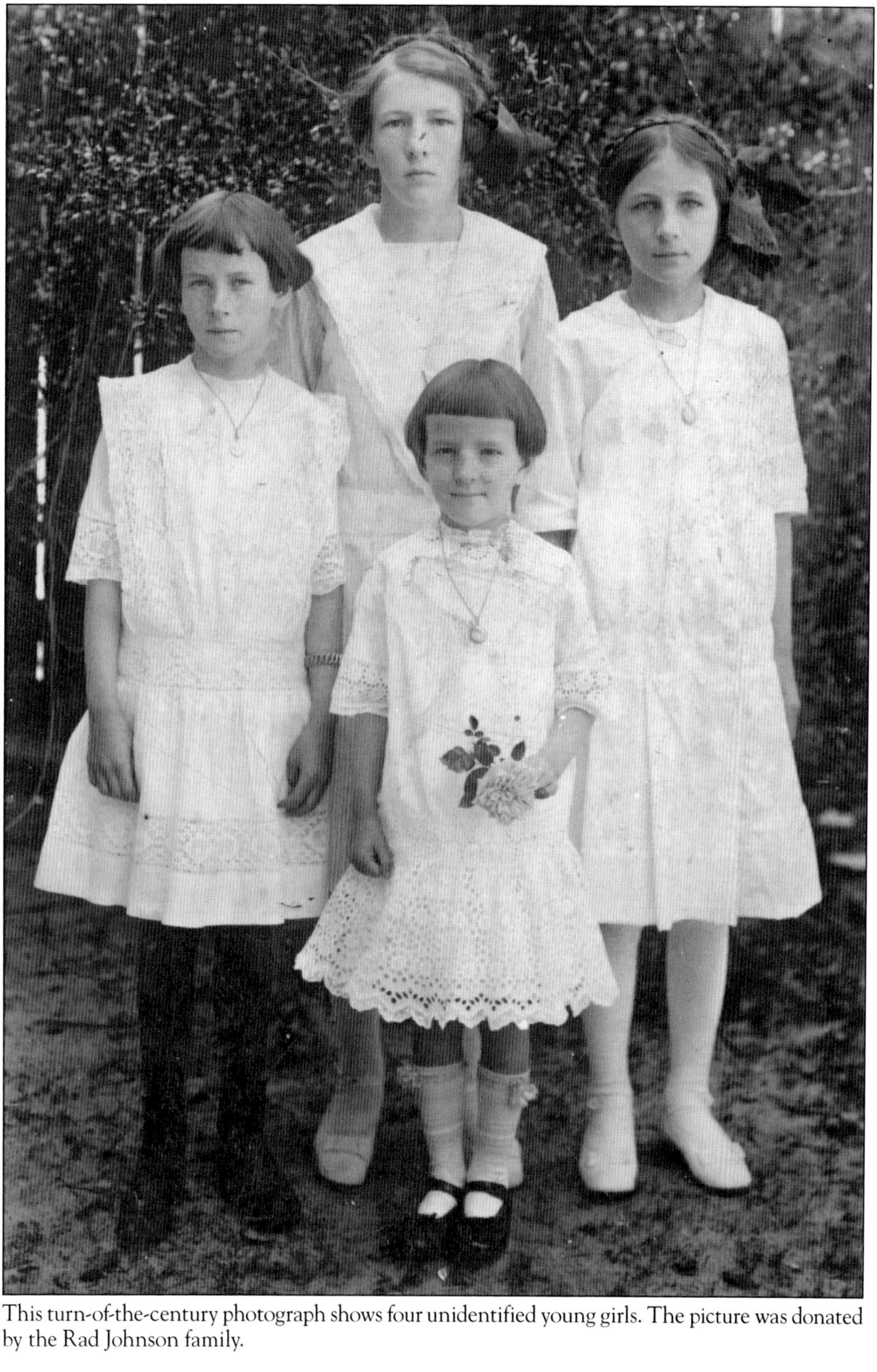

This turn-of-the-century photograph shows four unidentified young girls. The picture was donated by the Rad Johnson family.

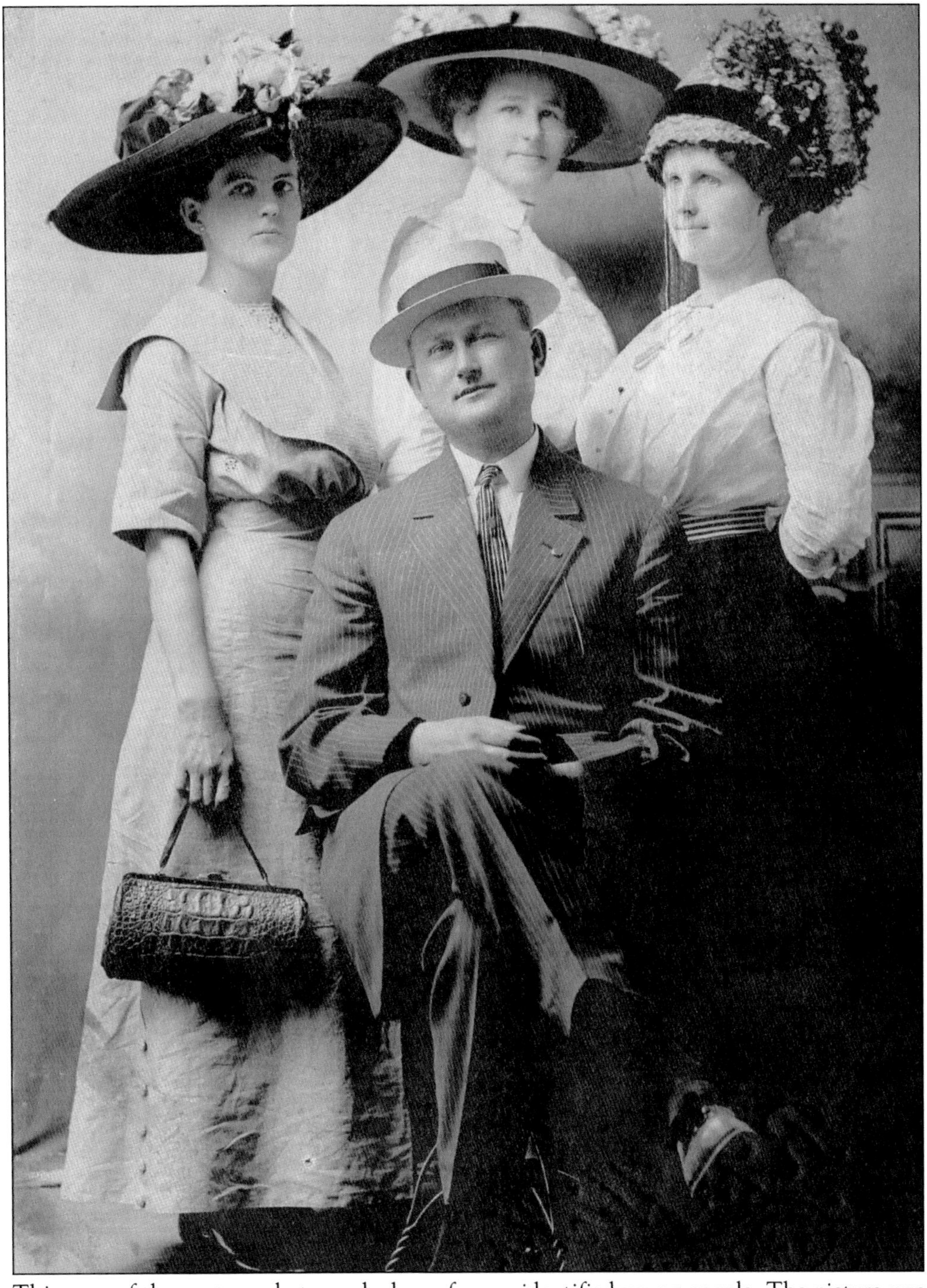

This turn-of-the-century photograph shows four unidentified young people. The picture was donated by the Rad Johnson family. Rad Johnson was a large landowner in the region in the early 20th century. By the mid-20th century, much of his land had been sold off.

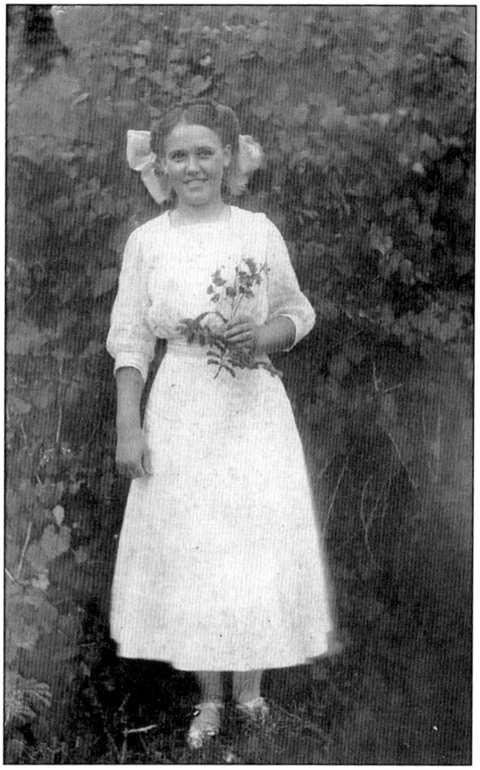

This period photograph shows an unidentified but happy young girl. The picture was donated by the Rad Johnson family. Rad Johnson's descendants, the Daniel Johnson family, are natives and life-long residents of Pembroke.

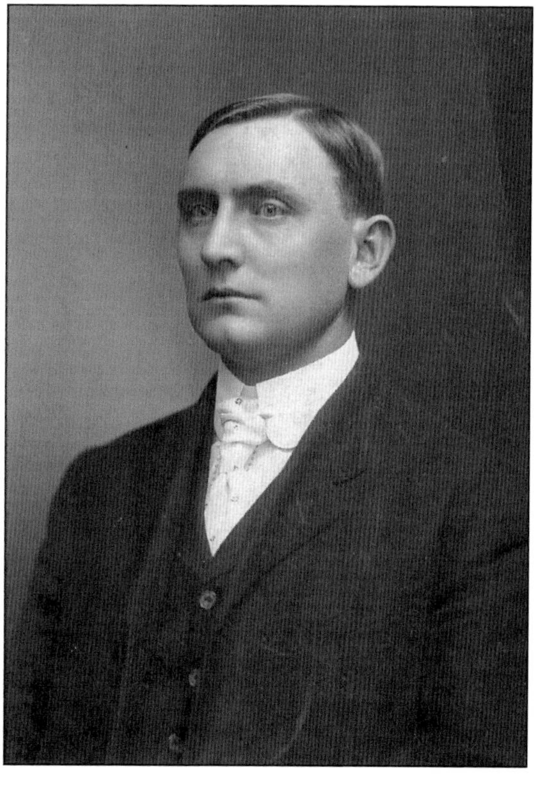

This period photograph, donated by the Rad Johnson family, shows an unidentified but dour-looking man. The Johnson family produced turpentine in the pine forests around Pembroke.

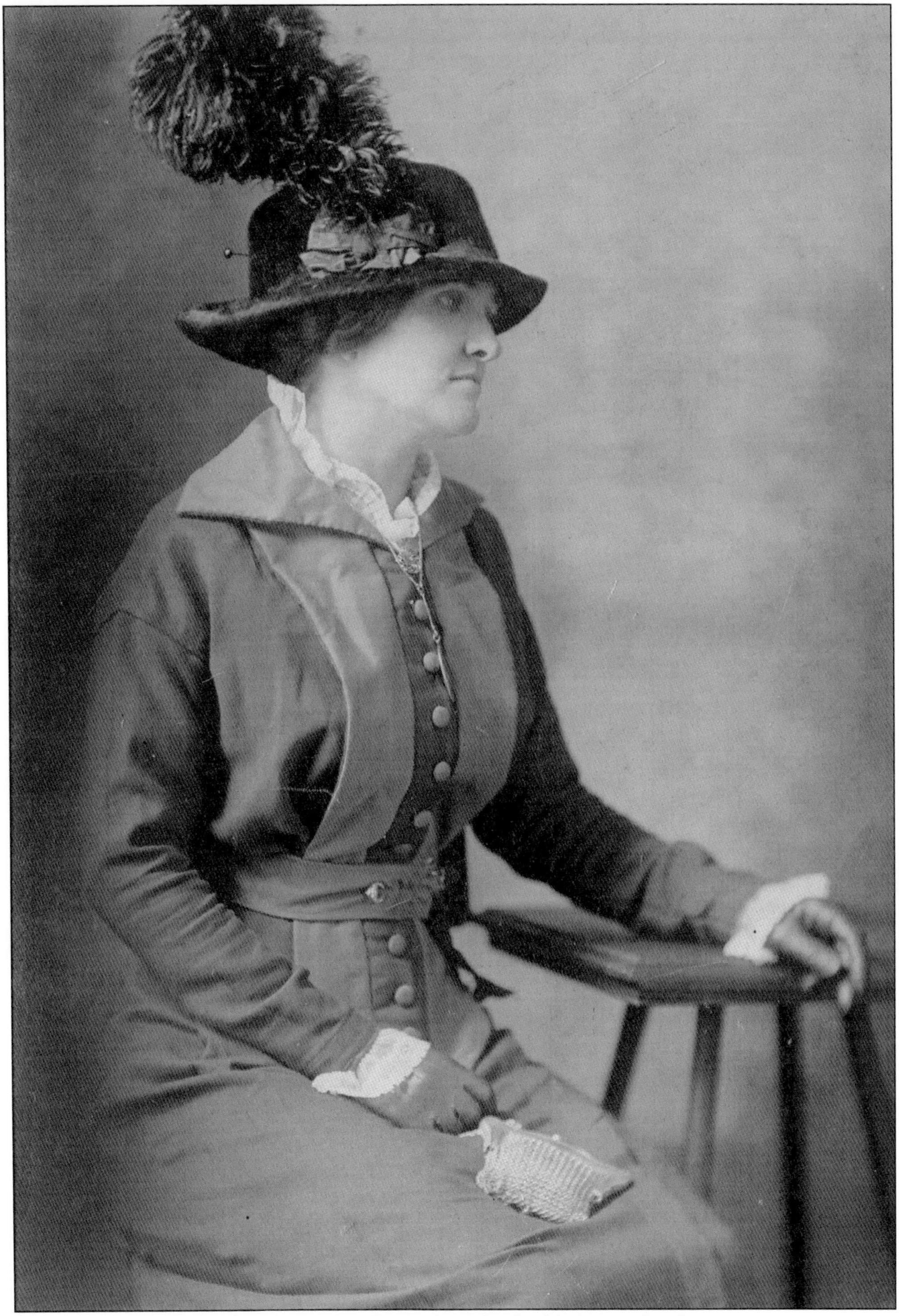

This picture of Mary Julia Rogers was donated by the Rad Johnson family.

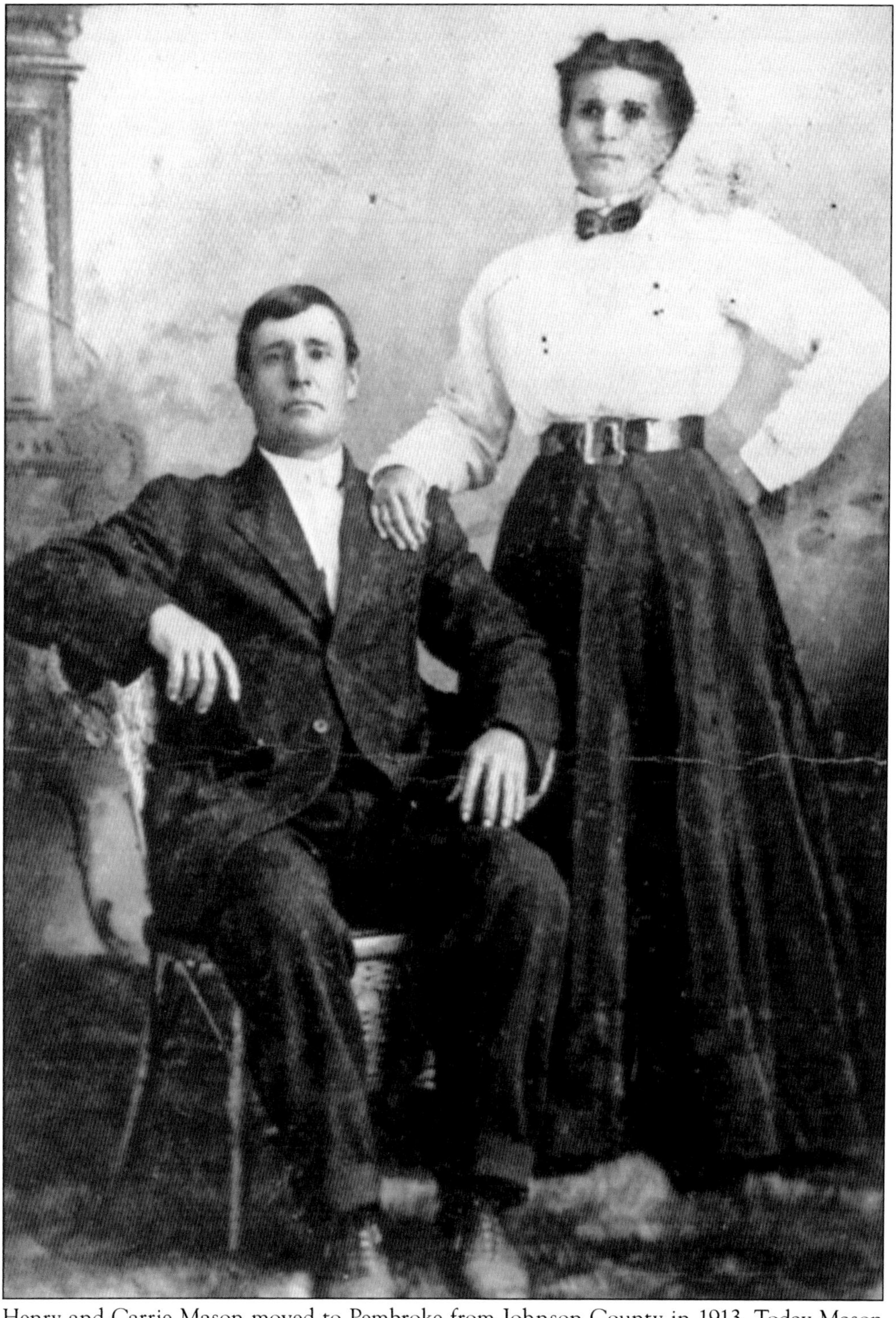

Henry and Carrie Mason moved to Pembroke from Johnson County in 1913. Today Mason Road, connecting Highway 67 and Lawrence Baptist Church Road, is named for them and their descendants.

Three

EDUCATION

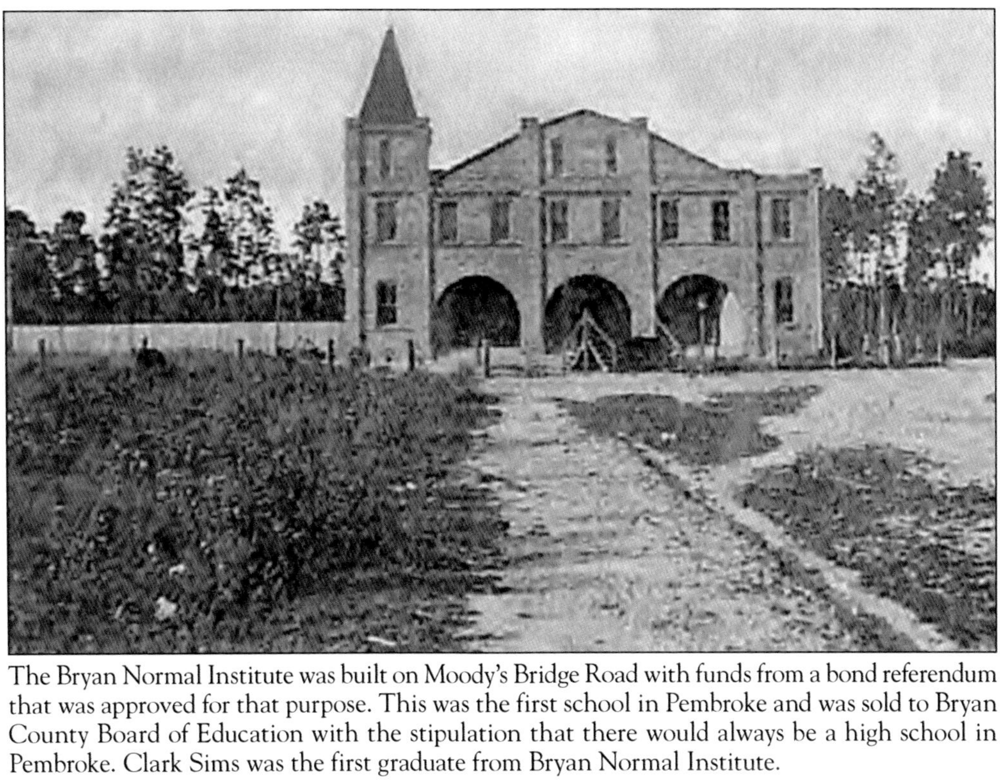

The Bryan Normal Institute was built on Moody's Bridge Road with funds from a bond referendum that was approved for that purpose. This was the first school in Pembroke and was sold to Bryan County Board of Education with the stipulation that there would always be a high school in Pembroke. Clark Sims was the first graduate from Bryan Normal Institute.

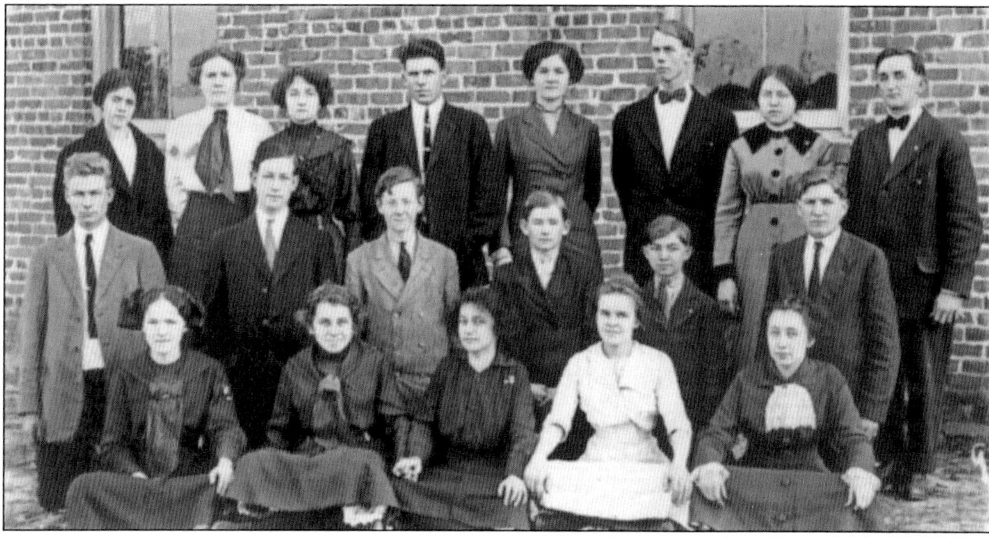

Pictured here are the proud graduates of the class of 1911 at Bryan Normal Institute in Pembroke.

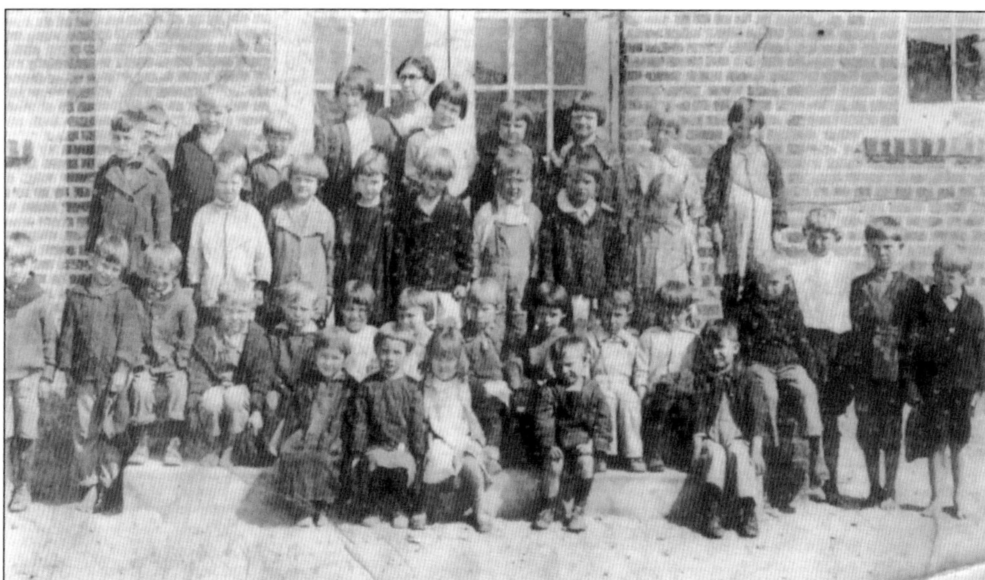

This photograph shows one of the early-20th century classes at Bryan Normal Institute.

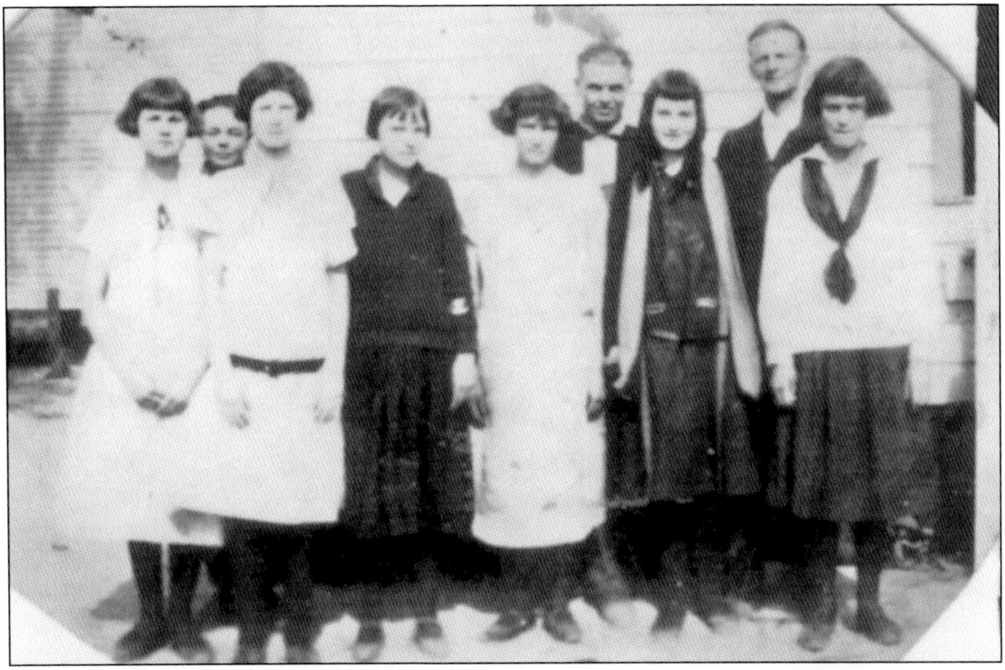

Pictured here is a 1920s class of Bryan Normal Institute.

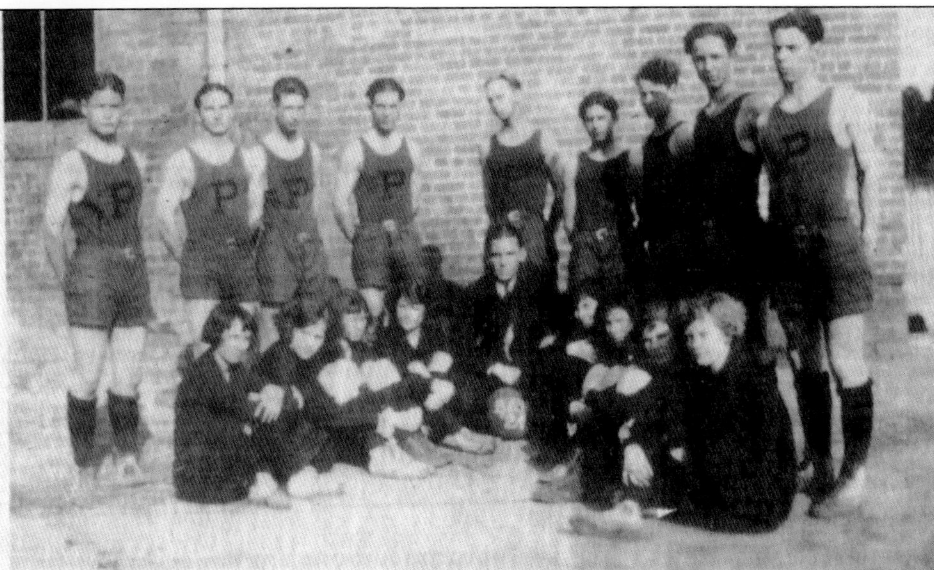

Shown L to R. are: Oren Bacon, Leffler Smith, Lamar Adams, Thomas Adams, William Roberts, Sego Morgan, Harry Roberts, Oscar Purcell and Alton Clanton; Girls are L to R. Lena Purcell, Jimmie Lee Parrish, Annie Laurie Hayman, Theo Mae Bacon, Coach: Emmet Smith, Ruby Lee Purcell, Velma Hughes, Rieta McCelvan, and Louise Stephens.

With our boys attempting to reach the basketball title this year, the above picture was brought to our attention by Mr. Leffler Smith and Mr. U. J. Bacon.

This is the Bryan County High School Basketball team of 1924. During that year they played Bellville in the region tournament in Savannah at the YMCA. The tournament consisted of schools from the 16 counties in the first Congressional District. The game between Bellville and BCHS went into overtime and there's a little bit of a question as to who won that year but Mr. Alton Clanton believes Bellville won and BCHS took second. Then in 1925 BCHS came in 3rd and in 1926 came in first but was defeated in a state playoff by Dalton. The team shown above is much of the team that took 1st in 1926.

Bryan County High School's basketball team is pictured in 1924. Can you identify anyone?

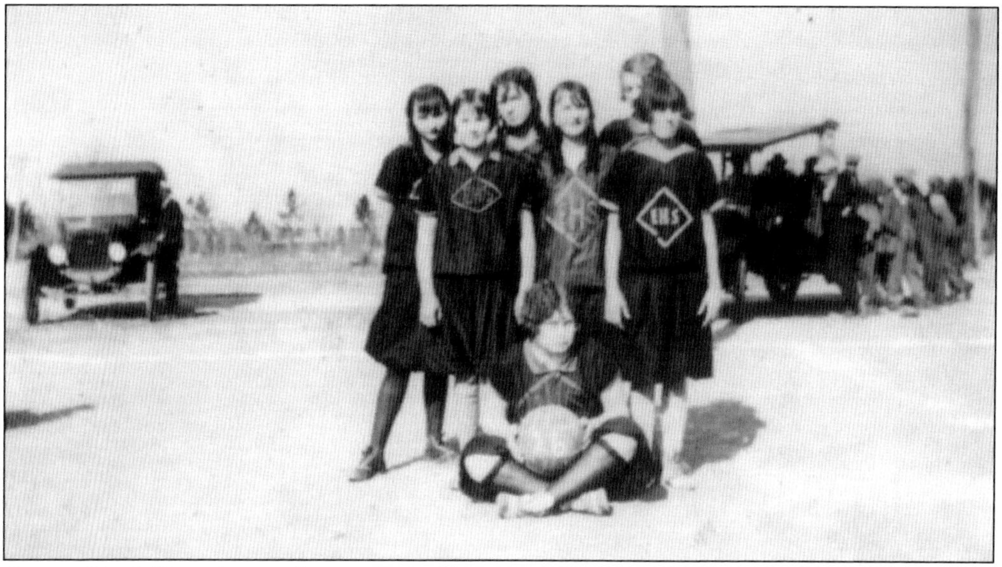

Geneva Futch Drexel was a first-grade teacher in Pembroke in the 1950s. She was a member of the Ellabell High School basketball team of 1926. Ms. Drexel is the girl with the long black hair in the center of the back row. The other girls in the picture are unidentified.

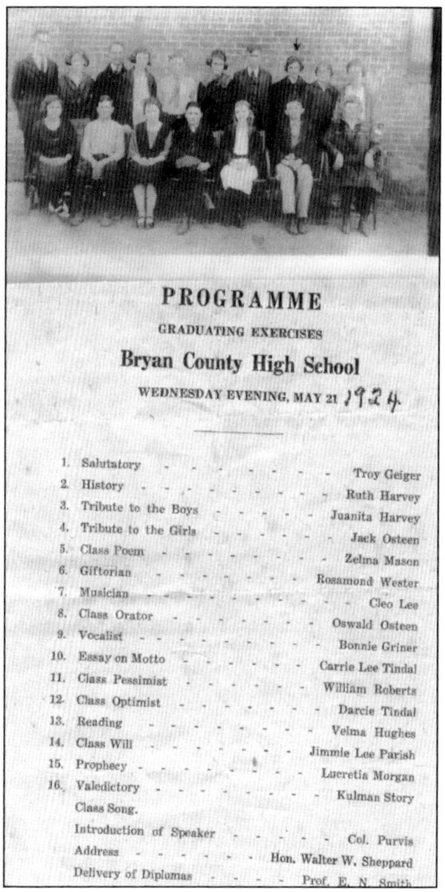

PROGRAMME

GRADUATING EXERCISES

Bryan County High School

WEDNESDAY EVENING, MAY 21 1924

1. Salutatory - - - - - - - - Troy Geiger
2. History - - - - - - - - - - Ruth Harvey
3. Tribute to the Boys - - - - - Juanita Harvey
4. Tribute to the Girls - - - - - - Jack Osteen
5. Class Poem - - - - - - - - - Zelma Mason
6. Giftorian - - - - - - - - Rosamond Wester
7. Musician - - - - - - - - - - - Cleo Lee
8. Class Orator - - - - - - - - Oswald Osteen
9. Vocalist - - - - - - - - - Bonnie Griner
10. Essay on Motto - - - - - - Carrie Lee Tindal
11. Class Pessimist - - - - - - William Roberts
12. Class Optimist - - - - - - - - Darcie Tindal
13. Reading - - - - - - - - - - Velma Hughes
14. Class Will - - - - - - - Jimmie Lee Parish
15. Prophecy - - - - - - - - Lucretia Morgan
16. Valedictory - - - - - - - - Kulman Story

Class Song.

Introduction of Speaker - - - - - Col. Purvis

Address - - - - - - - Hon. Walter W. Sheppard

Delivery of Diplomas - - - - - Prof. E. N. Smith

These proud graduates were a part of the Bryan County High School Class of 1924.

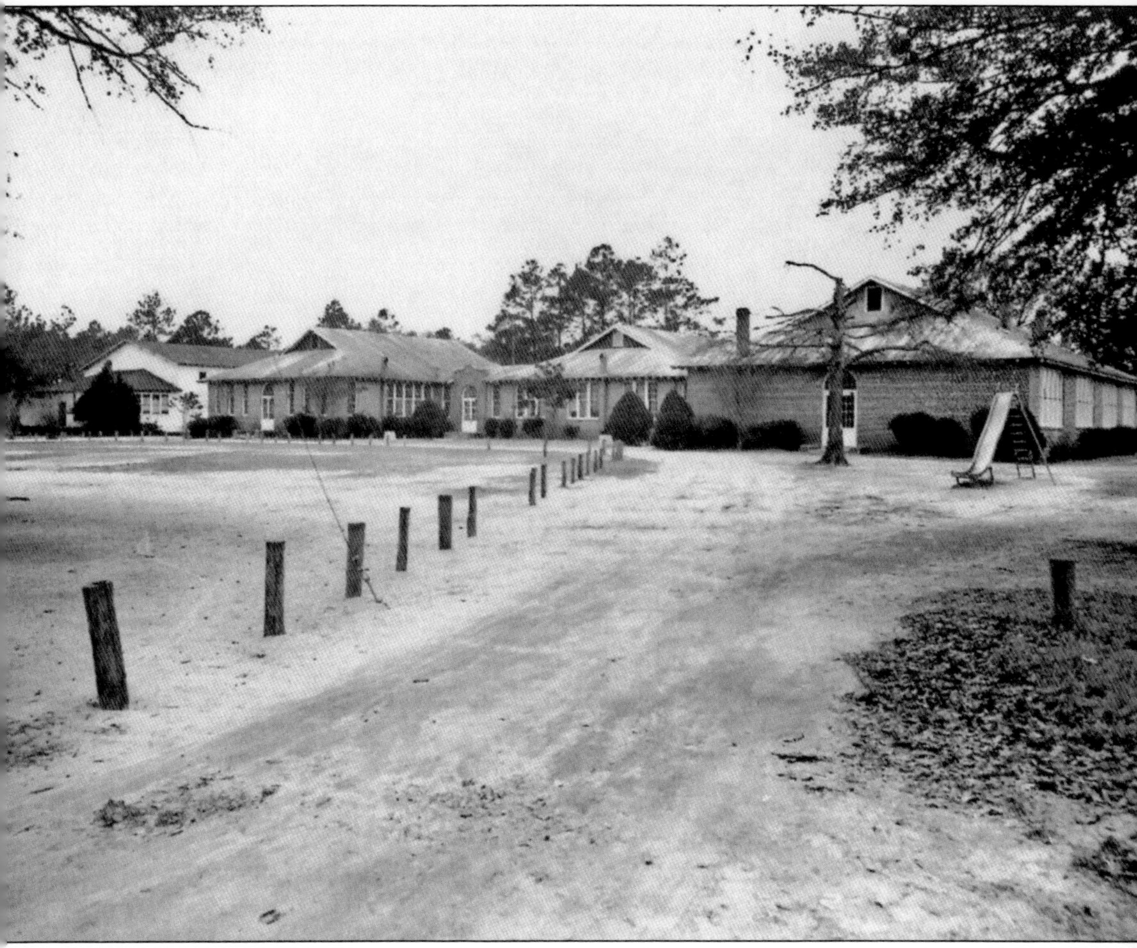

The Bryan County School System is the only one in the United States totally dissected by a military reservation. With the establishment of the Fort Stewart Reservation in 1940, the government took 105,000 acres of land from Bryan County. This completely separated the people in the northern and southern ends of the county

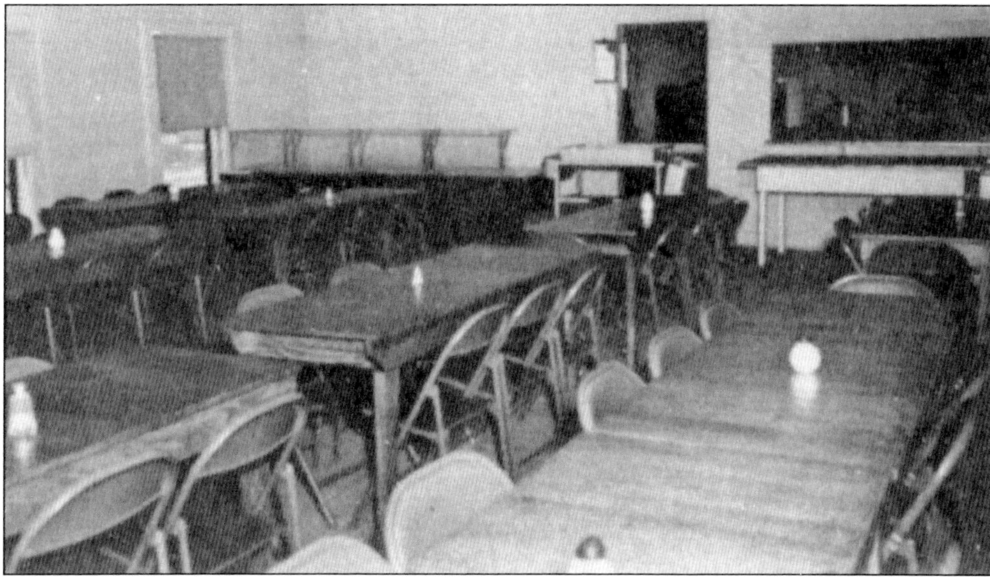

The Bryan County High School lunchroom in the early days provided hot, healthy lunches to all students for 5¢ a day. It was started as a WPA project and served as a model for schools throughout the state.

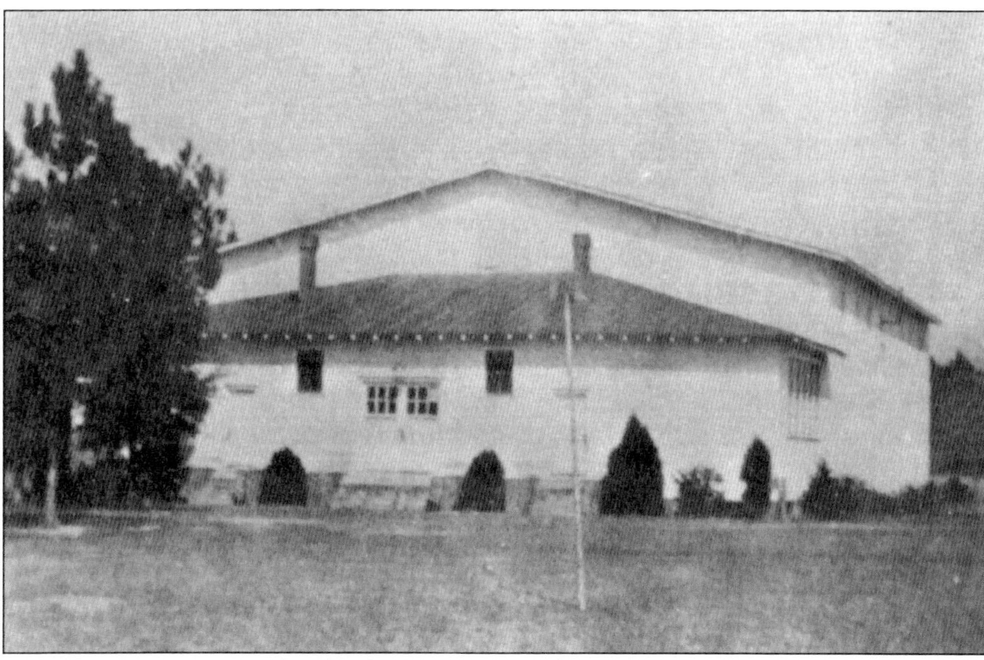

The old Bryan County High School gymnasium was the site of many exciting basketball games. Assemblies and, at one time, skating activities were also enjoyed by the community. It also served as first-grade classrooms

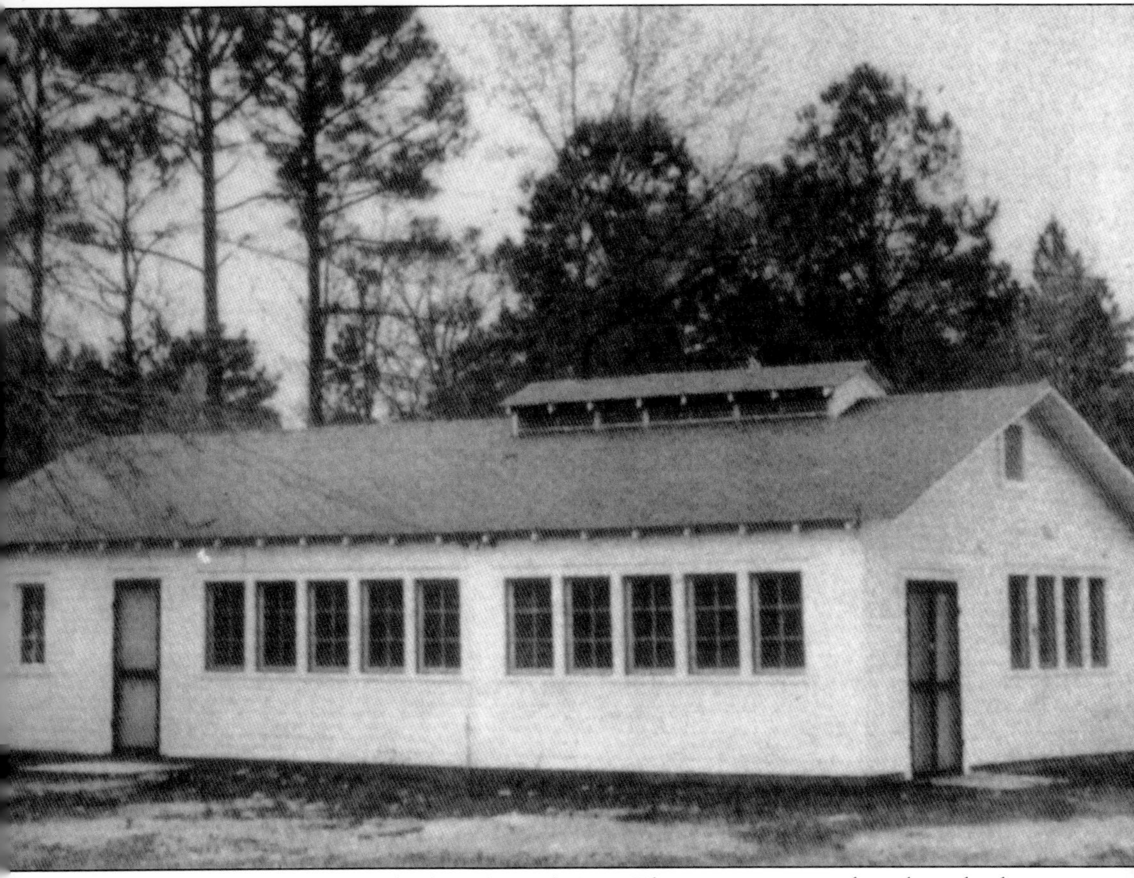

The Bryan County Cannery was built in the mid-1940s. The community residents brought their vegetables here to be canned for home use.

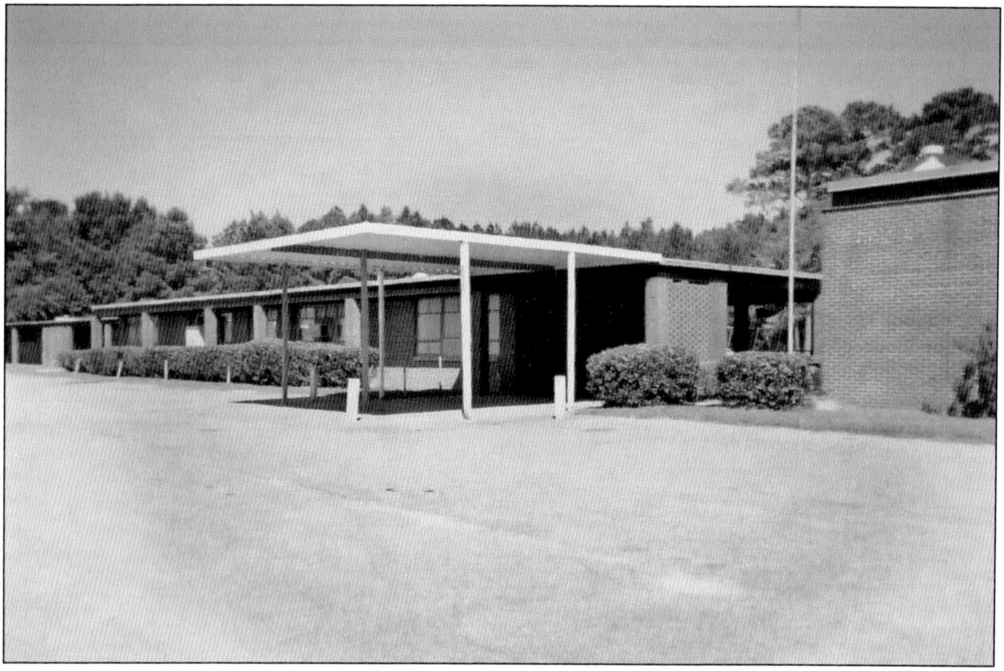

Bryan County Pre-K School at Pembroke is pictured as it appears today. This building was the former Pembroke High School.

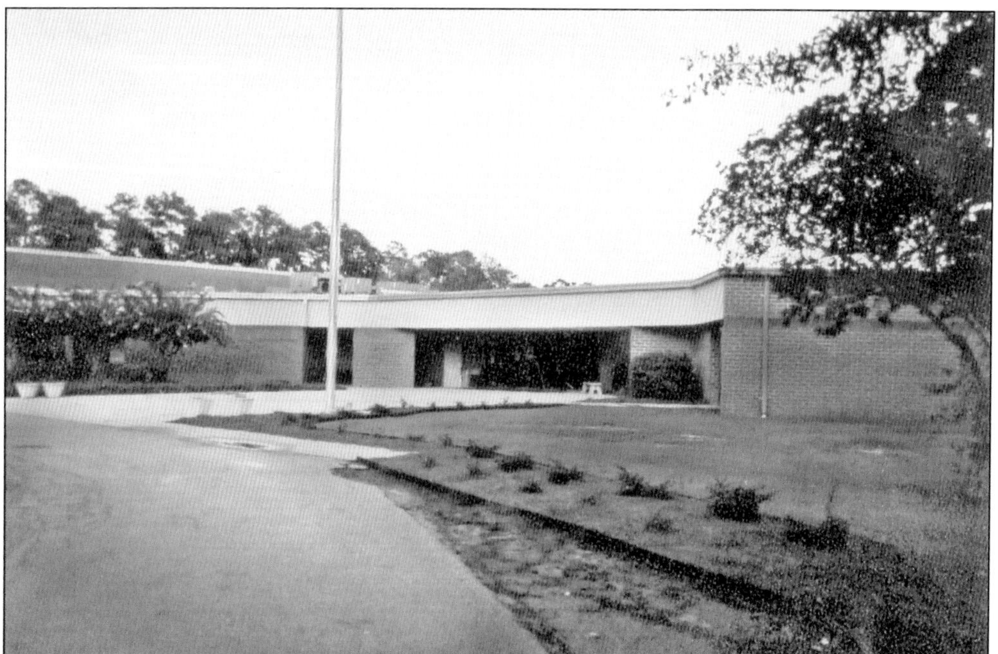

The Lanier Primary School groundbreaking occurred in 1980 under the auspices of Bryan County School superintendent June Baylor. The school was opened for classes in 1981. It houses prekindergarten through second grade. Pattie Newman serves as the principal.

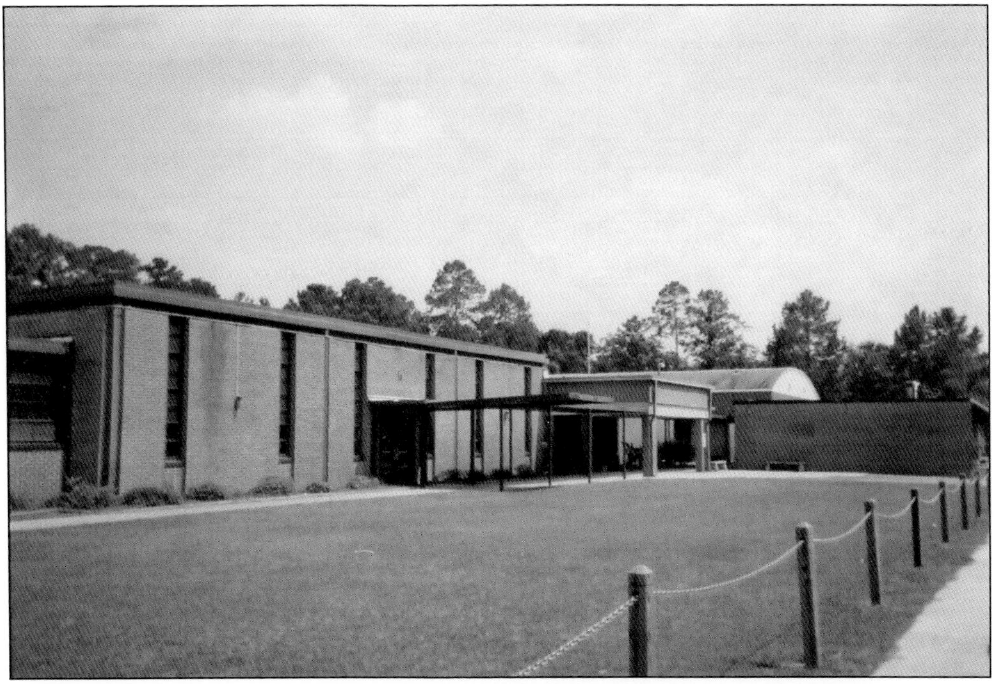

Bryan County Elementary School serves grades three through five. The principal is Mrs. Debbie Laing.

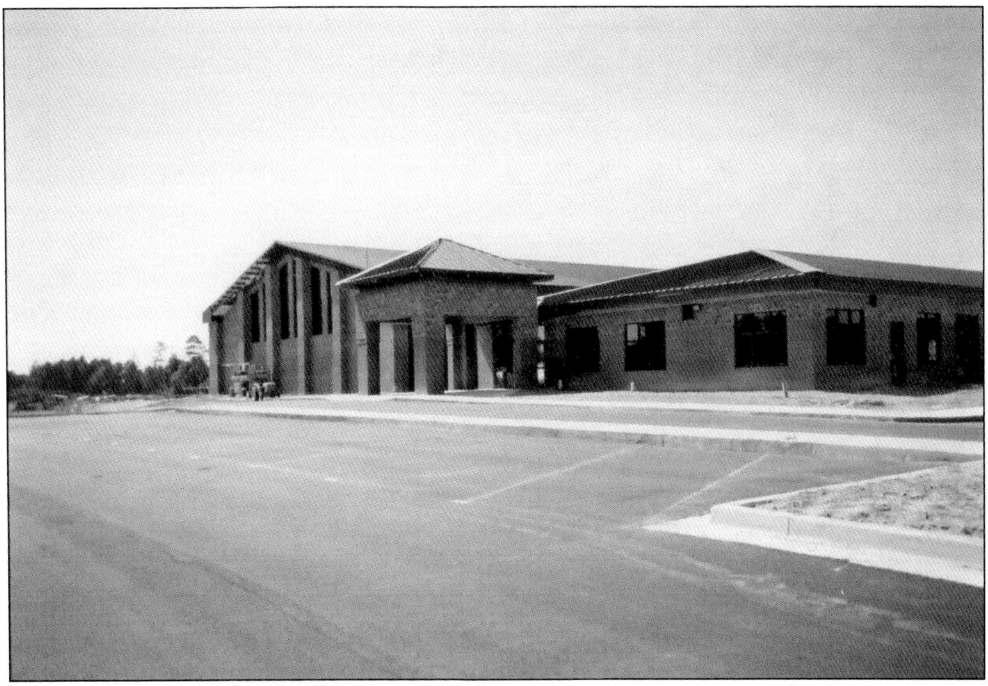

Bryan County Middle School is shown under construction. It was completed in 2005. The school is located on Payne Drive, and Debbie Ham serves as principal. It houses grades six through eight.

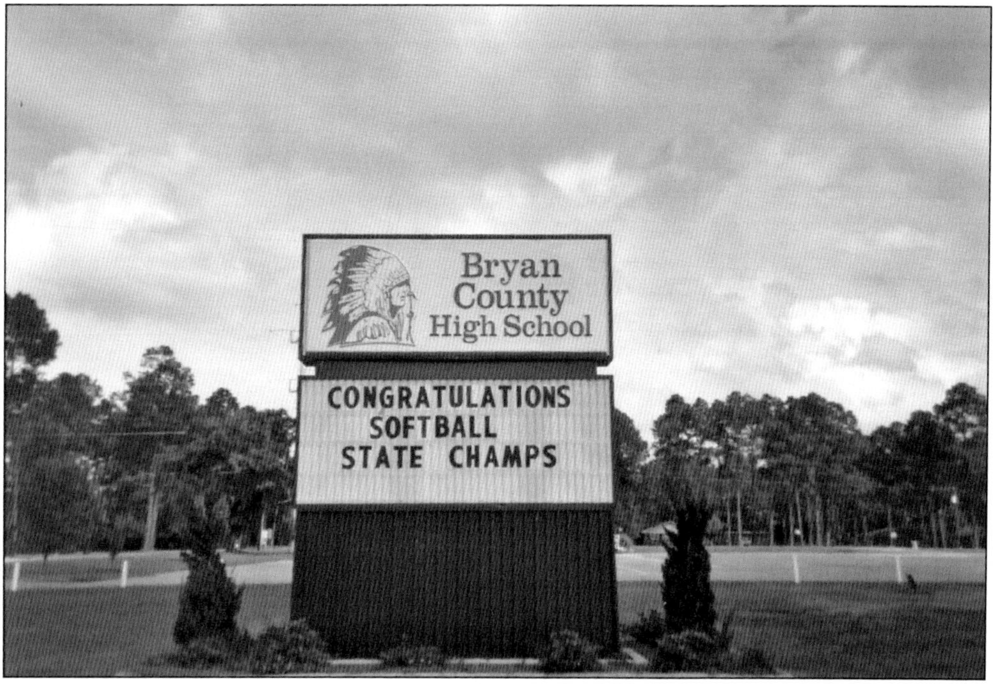

The Bryan County High School marquee is used to announce the activities of the school.

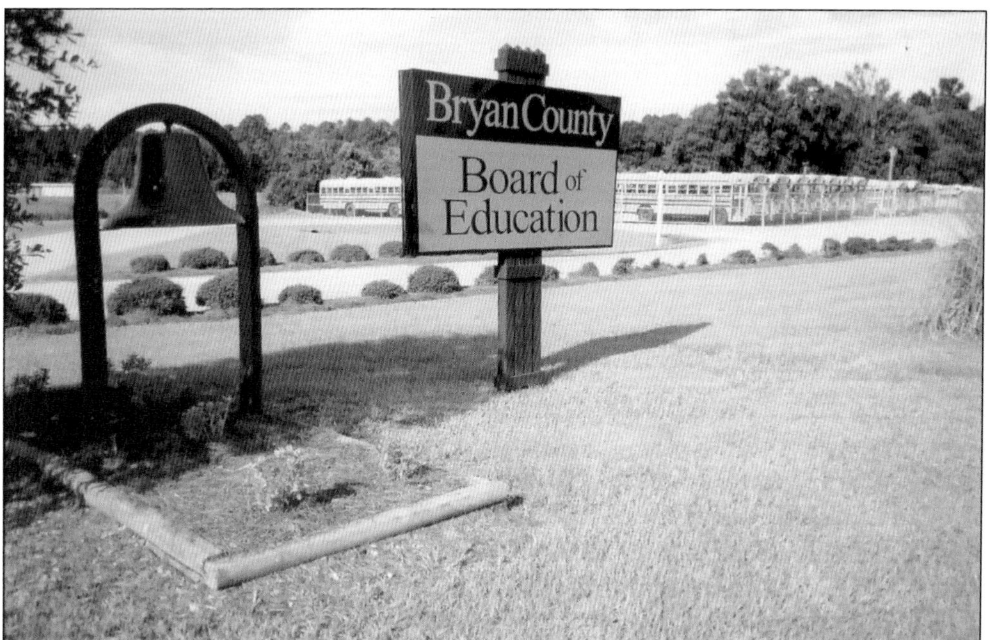

The marquee for the Bryan County Board of Education is located in the J. Dixie Harn Industrial Park in Pembroke.

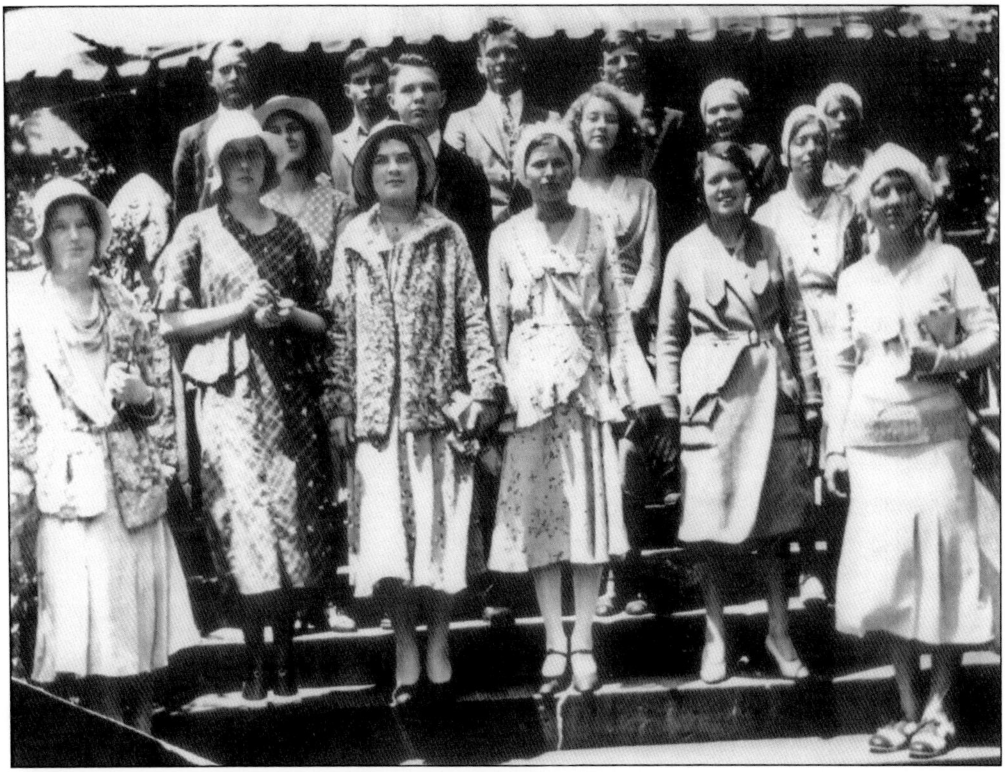

Pictured here is the 1931 class of Bryan Normal Institute.

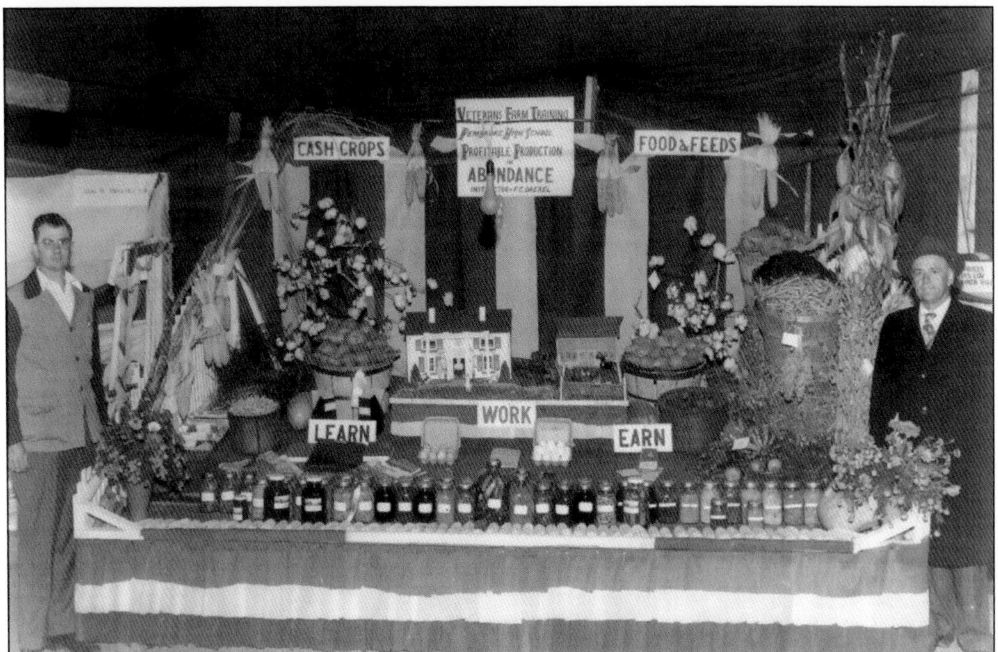

In this 1940s photograph, a display of Veterans Farm Training at the local fair includes instructor F. C. Drexel (on right). This picture was taken at the Pembroke Fair.

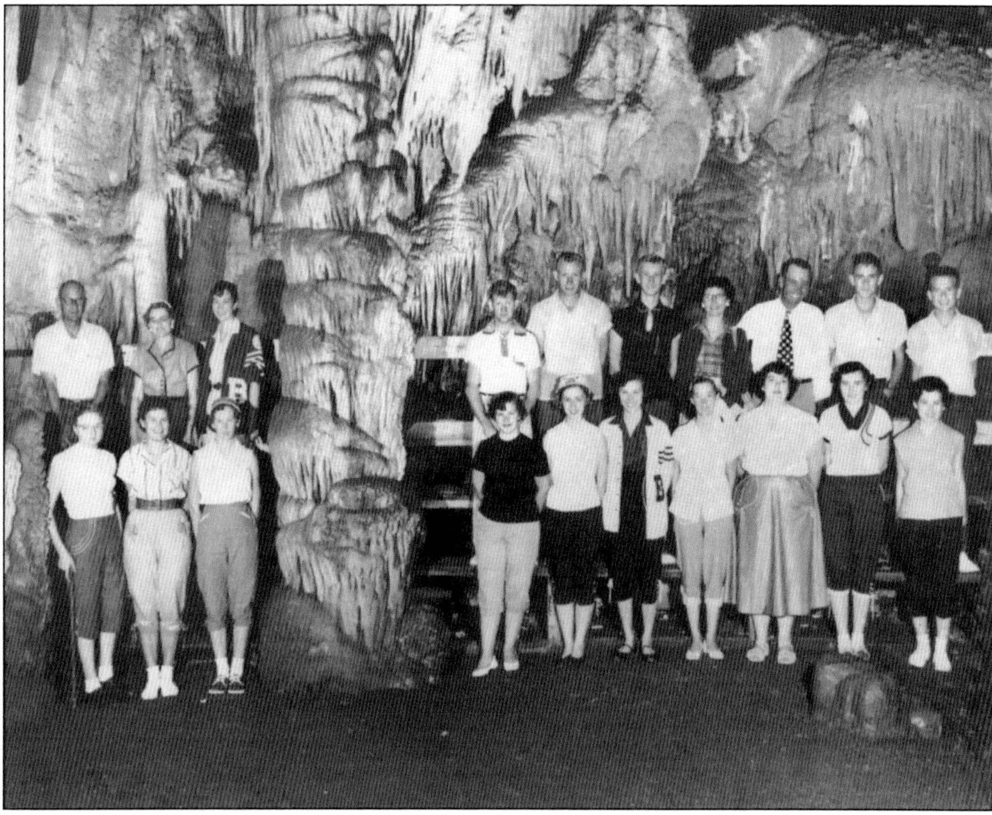

The Bryan County High School Class of 1954 made a trip to Luray Caverns in Virginia.

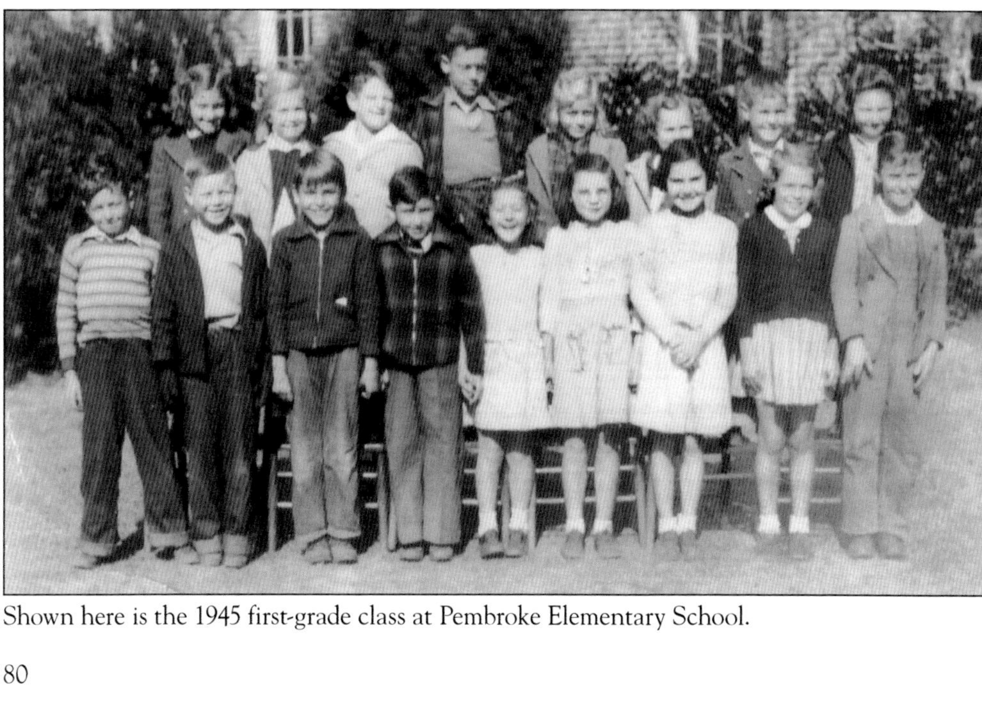

Shown here is the 1945 first-grade class at Pembroke Elementary School.

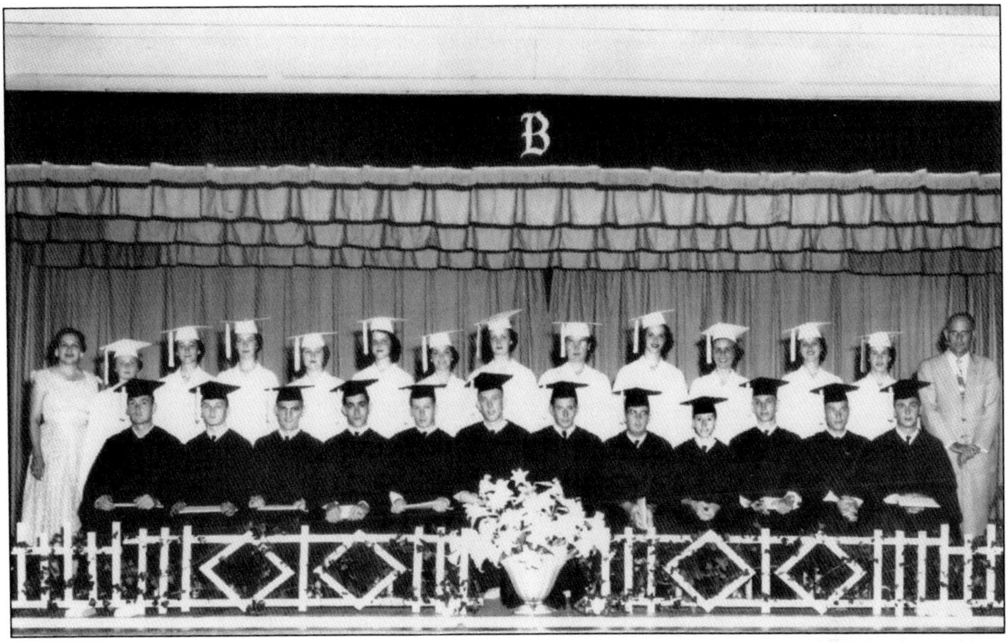

The Bryan County High School graduating class of 1957 is posed here on stage. At far right is principal J. M. Monte. Mrs. Sophie Smith, at far left, was senior class sponsor.

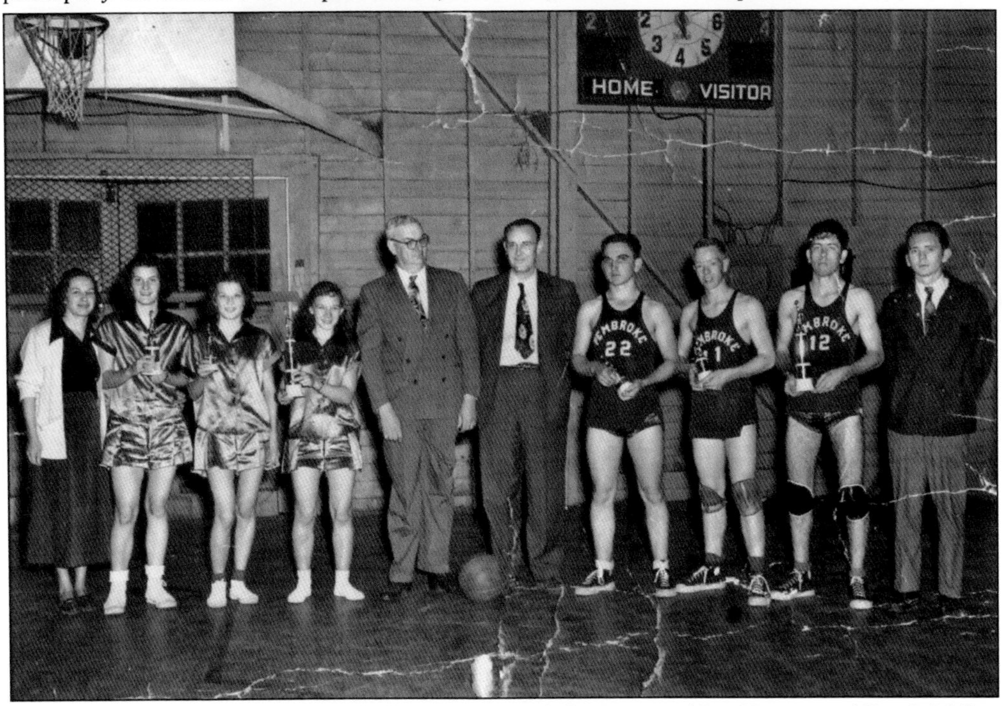

A presentation to the 1948 basketball team was made by Principal Jim Hussey and Frank Miller, editor of *Pembroke Journal*. The coaches were Sophie Smith and Rex Stubbs. The team won the regional championship. Pictured from left to right are Sophie Smith, Mary Ann Spinks, Betty Butler, Fay Wiggins, Mayor Frank Miller, principal Jim Hussey, Thomas Bacon, Marion Porterfield, Shelby Strickland, and Rex Stubbs.

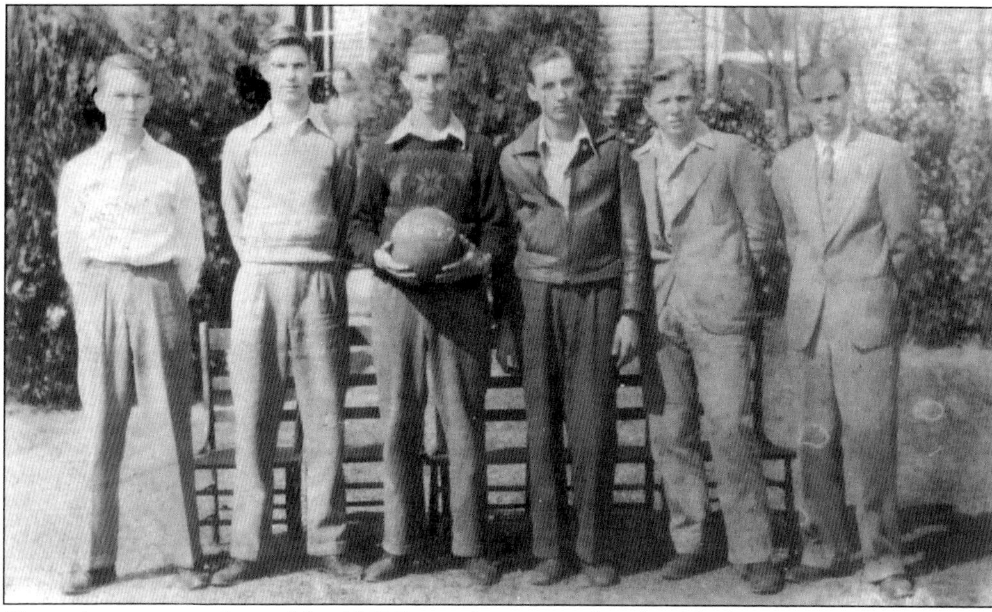

Shown here are members of the 1947 Bryan County High School basketball team. From left to right are unidentified, Ellison Lanier, Donald Johnson, Robert Williamson, unidentified, and principal Thomas Edwards.

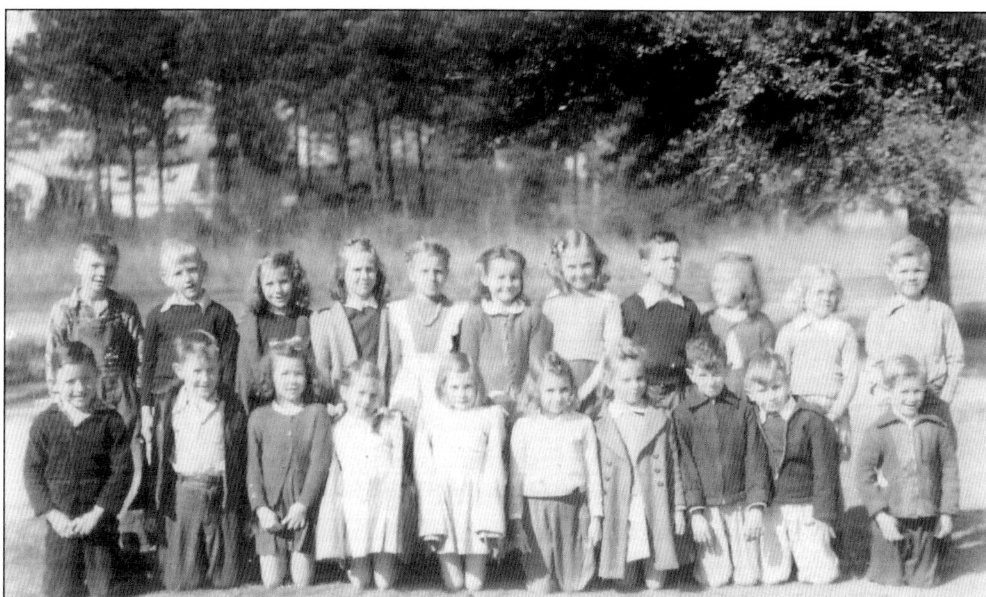

A second-grade class of 1945–1946 included, from left to right, (first row) Ernest Williams, Marion Hope, Lila Miles, unidentified, Cleo Bacon, Annette Parrish, Rose Buckner, Jimmy Cook, Freddie Cook, and Roy White; (second row) Curtis Blitch, Noel Osteen, Jane Purvis, Jan Deal, Montene Smith, Gloria Harvey, Ann Miles, JoJo Brewton, Ella Miles, Jane Lanier, and Vernon Jernigan.

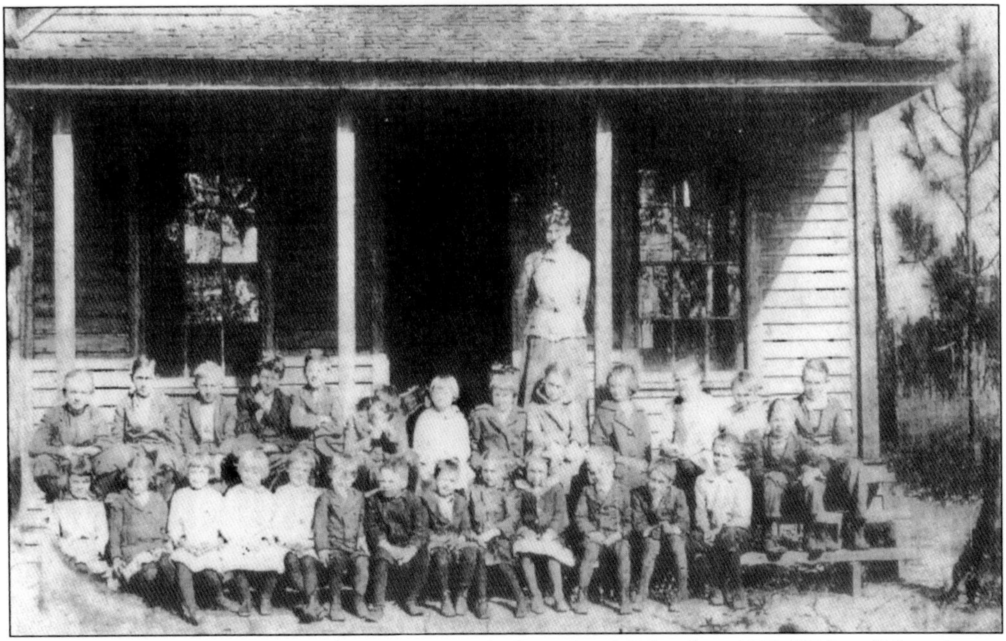

This photograph depicts a nearby community's Groveland School in 1912. Wilma Edwards was the teacher.

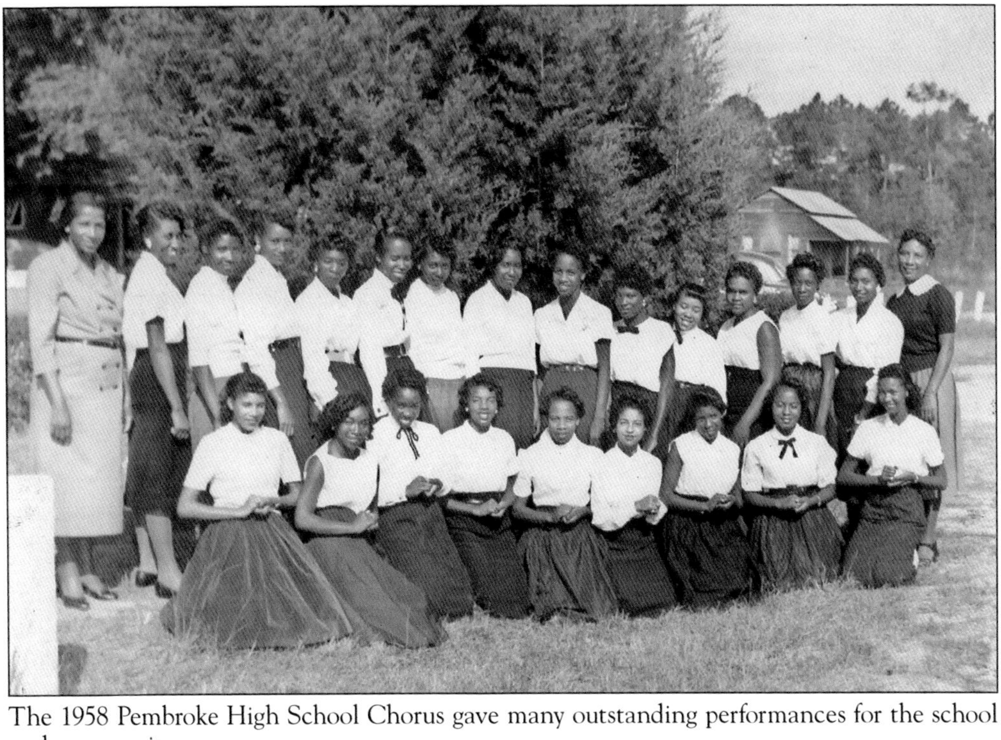

The 1958 Pembroke High School Chorus gave many outstanding performances for the school and community.

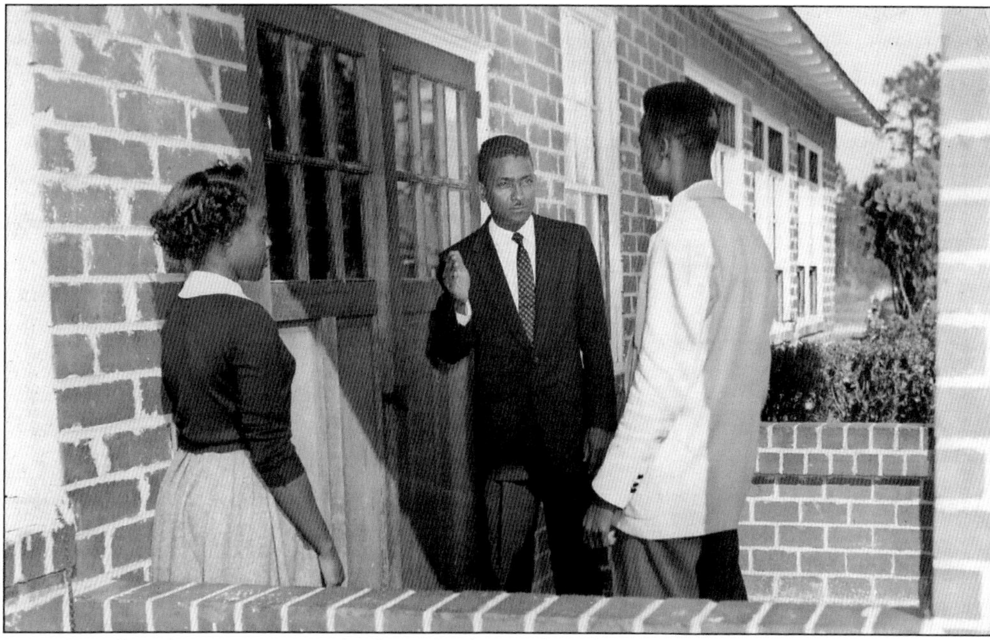

Leon Dingle, who was principal of Pembroke High School, is shown advising students. He graduated from Savannah State College with a bachelor's degree and obtained his masters degree from New York University.

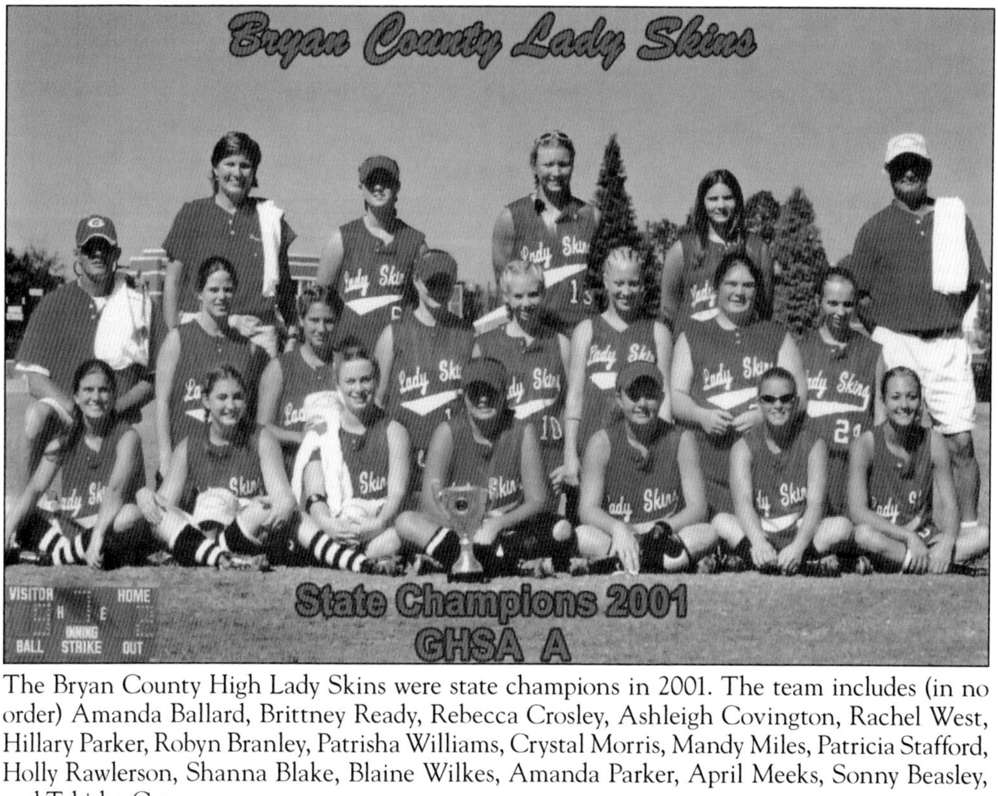

The Bryan County High Lady Skins were state champions in 2001. The team includes (in no order) Amanda Ballard, Brittney Ready, Rebecca Crosley, Ashleigh Covington, Rachel West, Hillary Parker, Robyn Branley, Patrisha Williams, Crystal Morris, Mandy Miles, Patricia Stafford, Holly Rawlerson, Shanna Blake, Blaine Wilkes, Amanda Parker, April Meeks, Sonny Beasley, and Tabitha Guy.

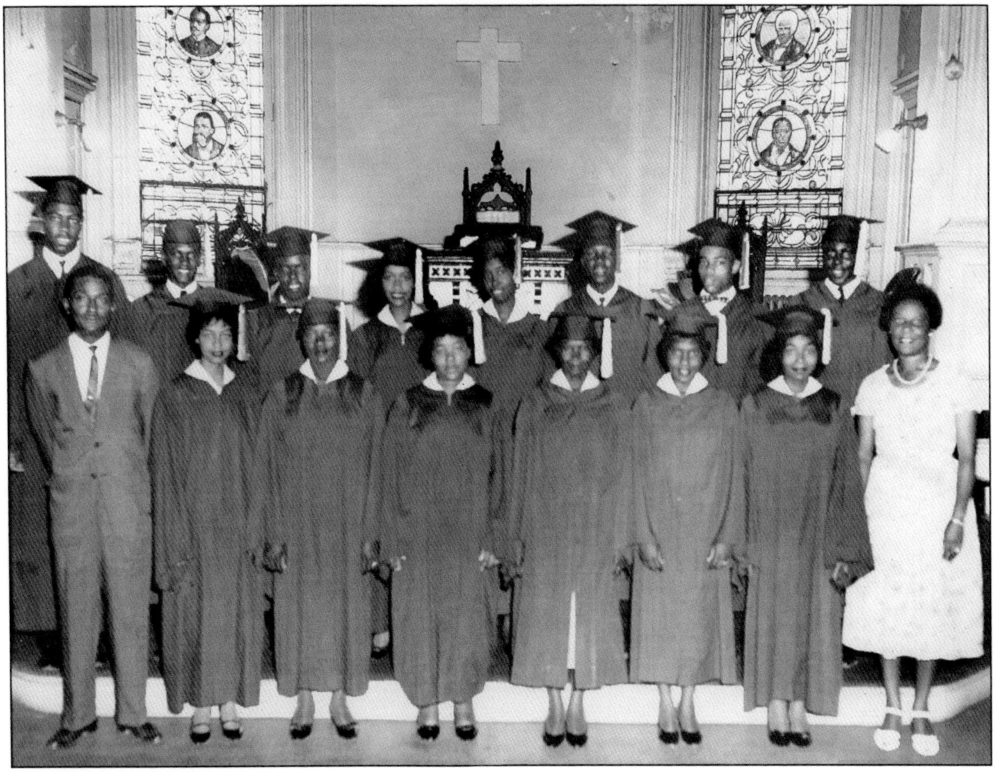

Pictured here is the 1959 Pembroke High School graduating class; Leon Dingle was the principal.

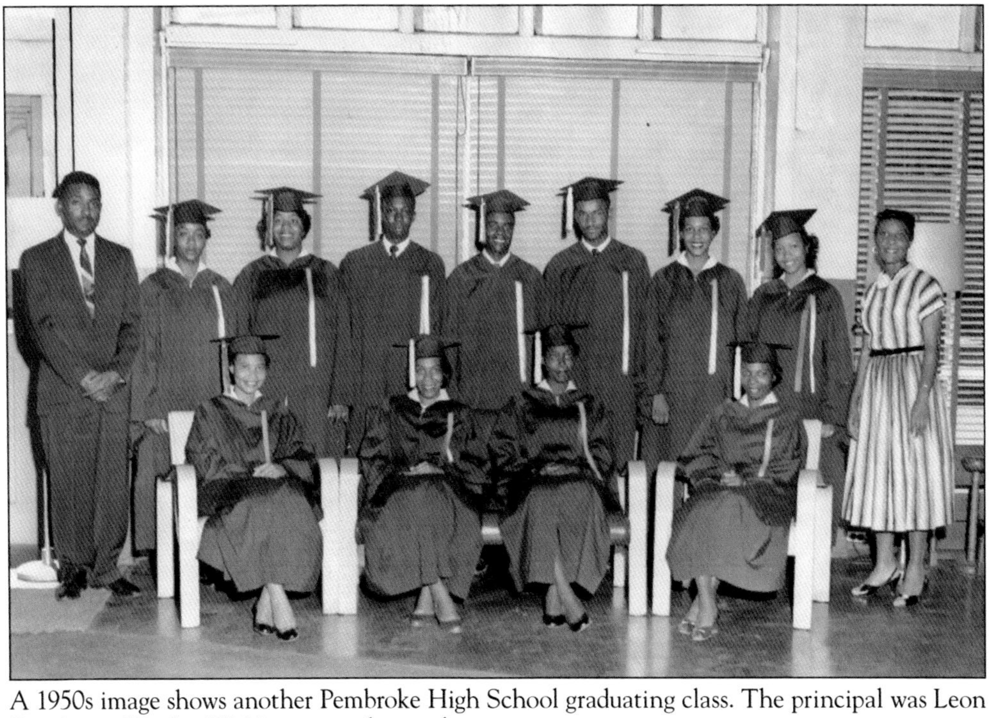

A 1950s image shows another Pembroke High School graduating class. The principal was Leon Dingle, and Pinkie W. Henry was the teacher.

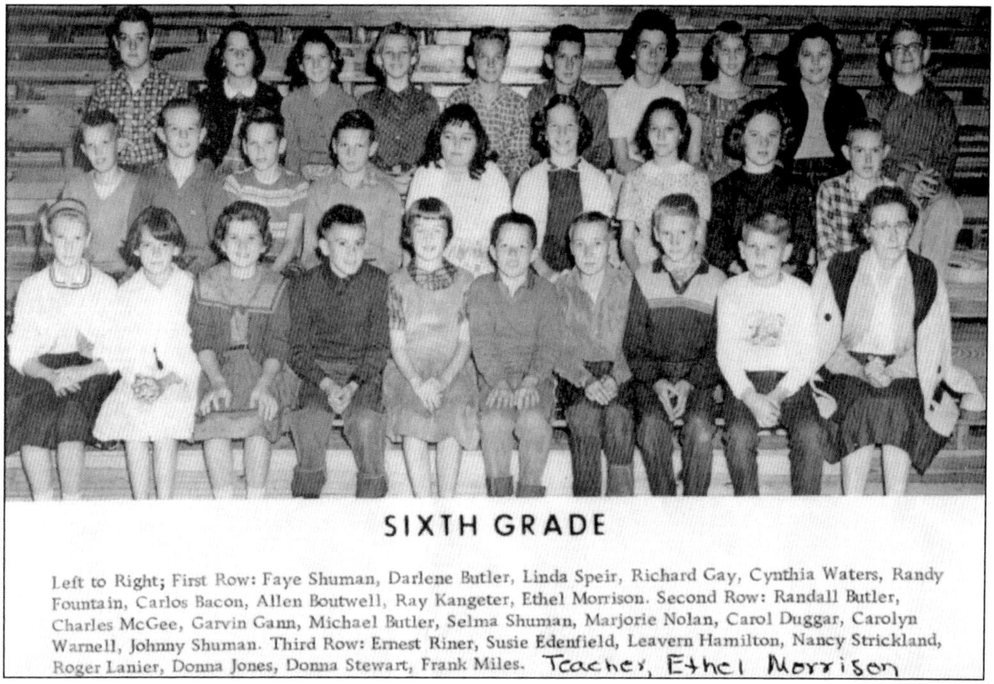

Ethel Morrison taught this 1963 first-grade class at Bryan County Elementary School in Pembroke.

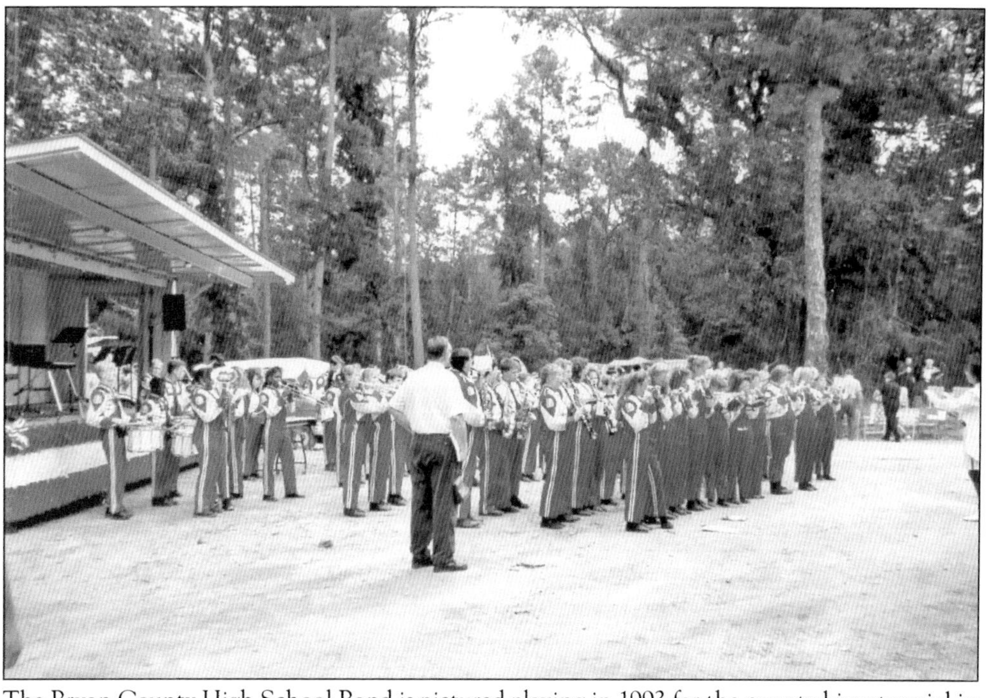

The Bryan County High School Band is pictured playing in 1993 for the county bicentennial in the former county seat, Clyde, on Fort Stewart.

Four

CHURCHES

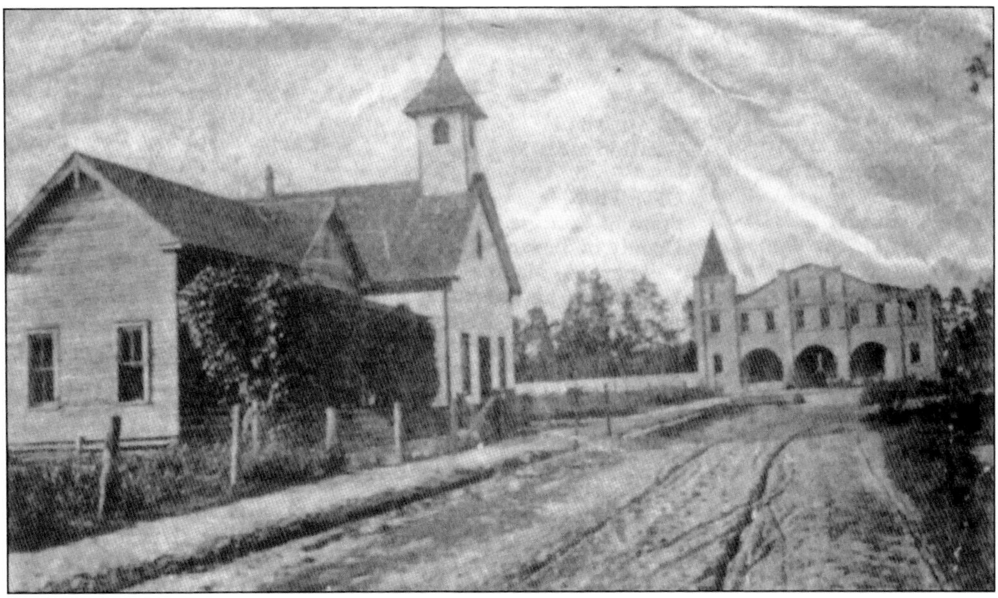

Bryan County's first Methodists arrived in 1880. The first Methodist services were held in Pembroke in 1896 in the Pembroke Baptist Church by invitation, since the Methodists did not have a church building. In 1903, one acre of land was purchased from Mr. J. W. Strickland, and later that year, the construction of the Pembroke Methodist Church began. This is a view of the Methodist church in the early 20th century. In the foreground is Pembroke Normal School.

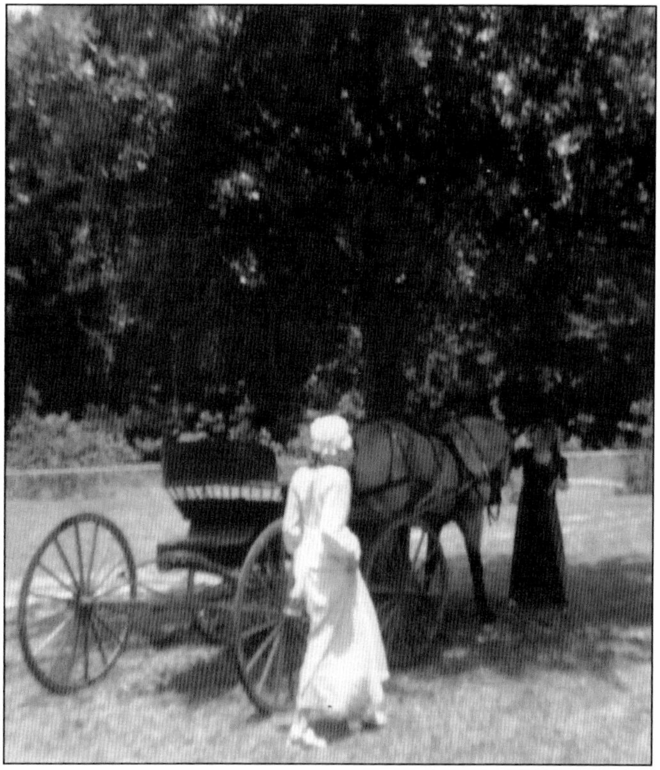

A 1976 centennial took place at Lawrence Baptist Church, with Mrs. Marcia Owens McCoy seen in period dress. The transportation of the period was the horse and buggy, seen under the shade of the tree.

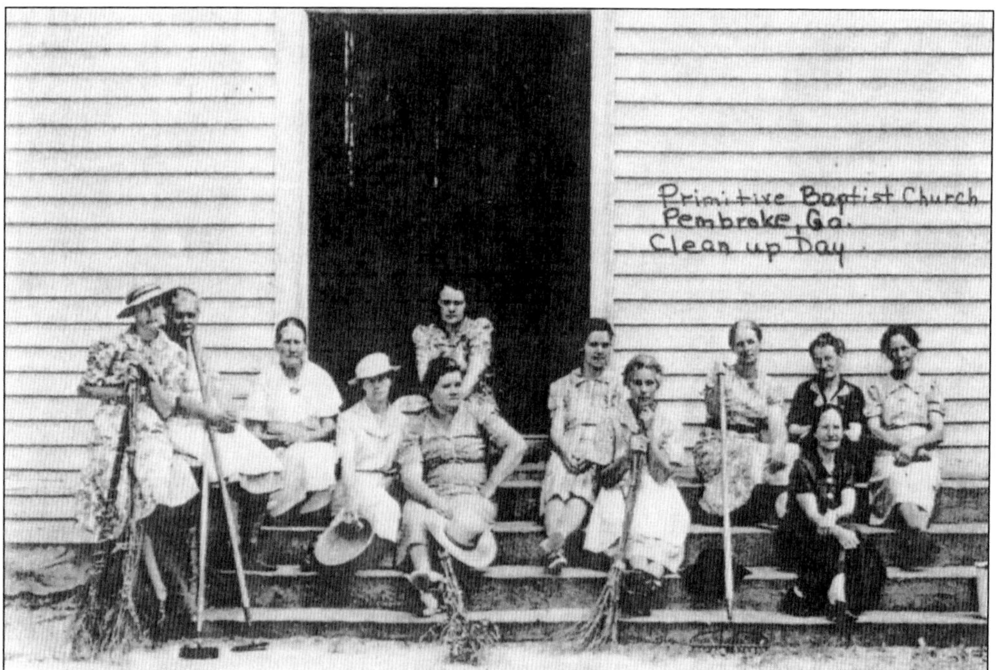

This was clean-up day at Pembroke Primitive Baptist Church. The ladies cannot be identified. They were cleaning the yards around the church c. 1940. There is no longer a Primitive Baptist church within the city of Pembroke.

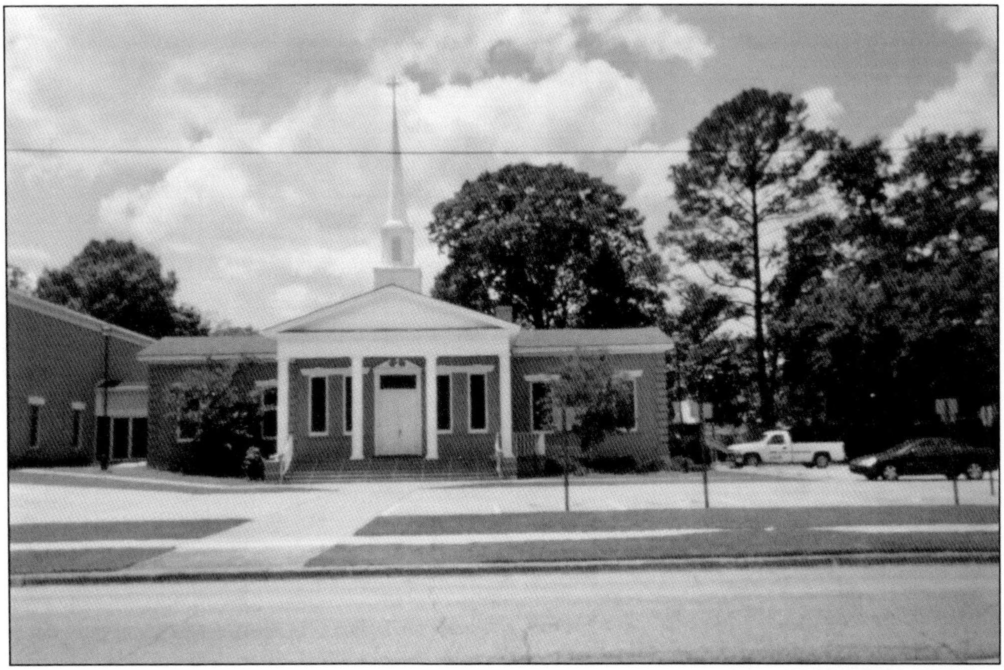

The Pembroke Baptist Church had its beginnings in the Hopeful Baptist Church. Hopeful was constituted in 1852 and in 1890 was represented by J. A. Murrow and R. C. McMillan as clerk. In 1892, Hopeful came to Pembroke and was named the Pembroke Baptist Church. In 1965, the name was changed to the First Baptist Church. There have been 28 pastors to serve Hopeful-First Baptist Church of Pembroke.

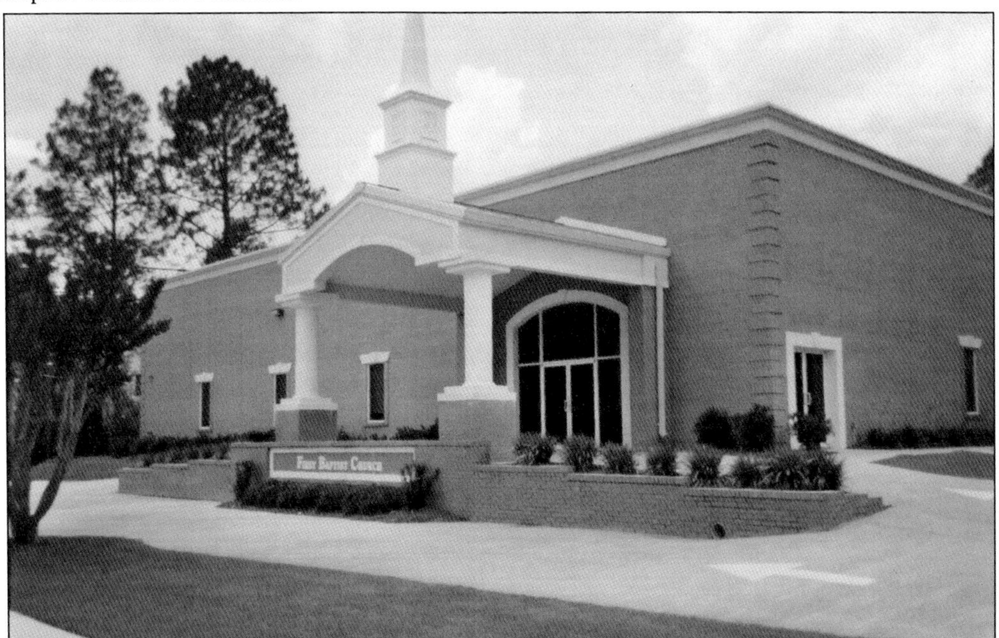

The First Baptist Church of Pembroke has gone through many renovations. Pictured here is the new church, dedicated in 2003.

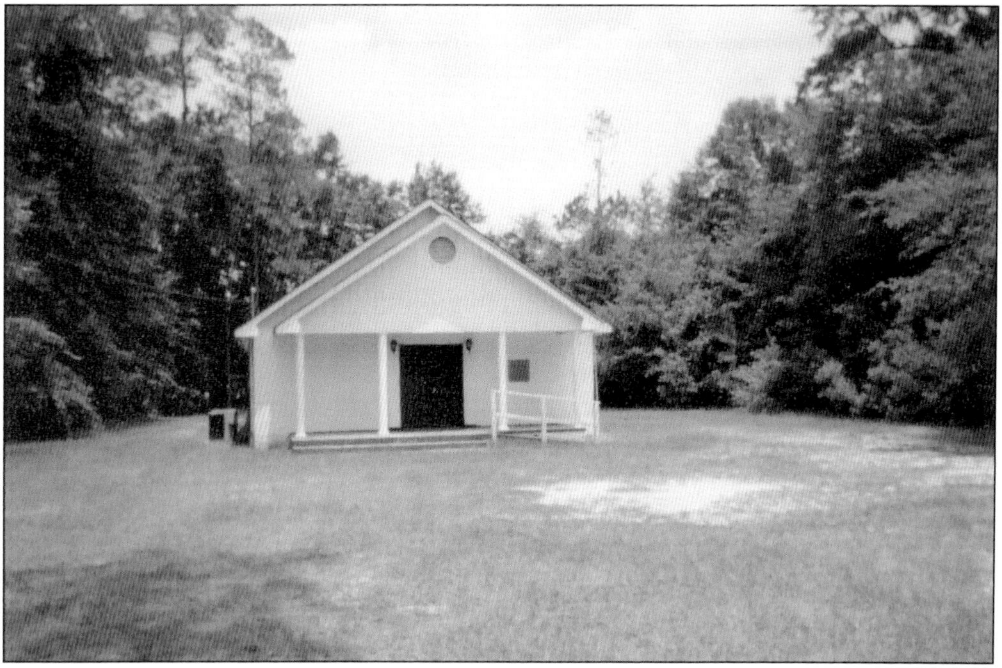

Byrd's Temple Baptist Church, in Pembroke, was built in 1925 and renovated in 1993. It is located on Bird Temple Road. Rev. Andrew Mincy is the current pastor.

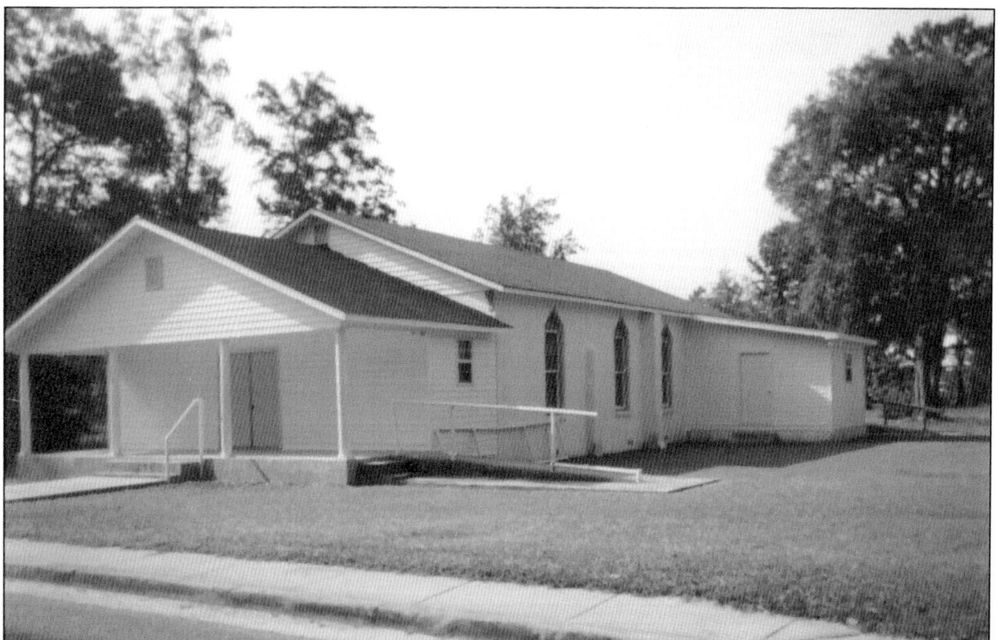

St. John AME Church was founded by a group of concerned citizens in the latter part of the 19th century. The first church was built on what is now known as East Railroad Street; it also included a cemetery on that property. The second site was on Old Clyde Road and was later destroyed by fire. In the 1940s, under the leadership of Rev. H. C. Wicker, a block church building was constructed, and it was dedicated on July 16, 1950.

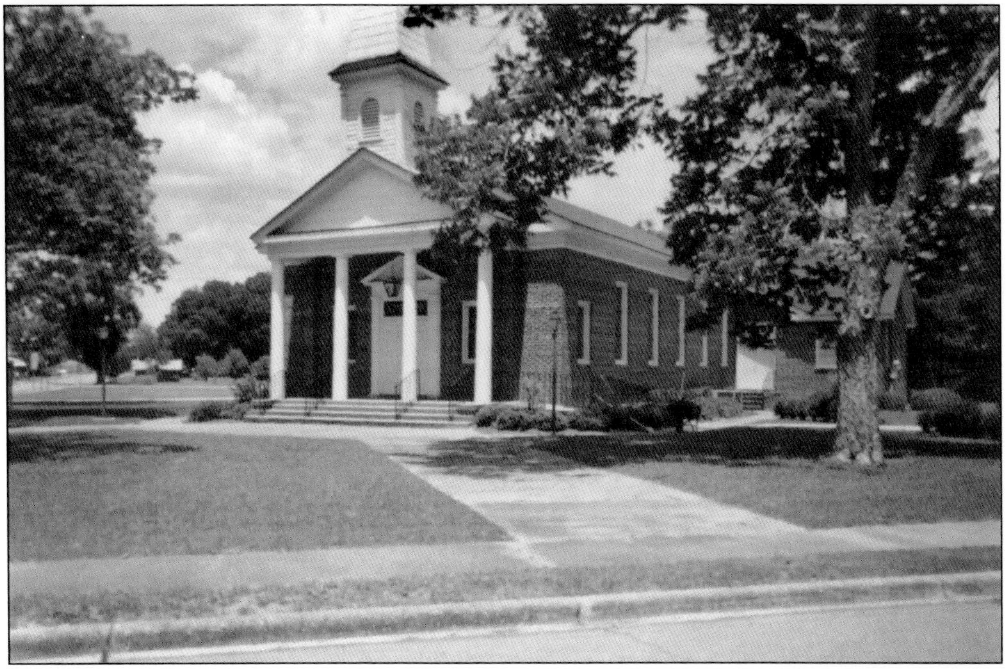

In 1947, groundbreaking services were held for a new Pembroke United Methodist Church building to be constructed on the corner of College and Burkhalter Streets. On October 2, 1950, the church was completed, debt free and with new furnishings.

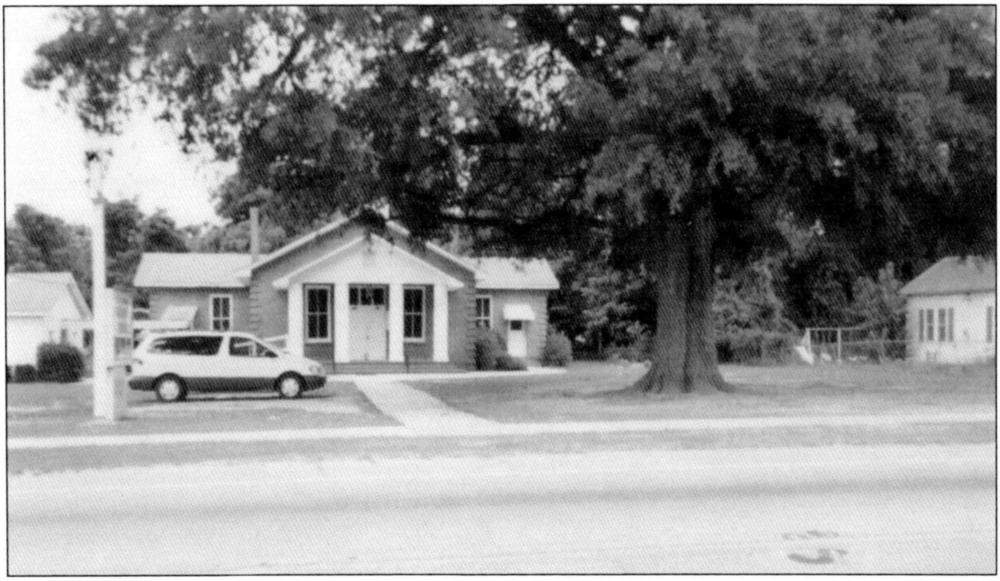

The original records of the Pembroke Christian Church were destroyed in a fire in December 1944. The story goes that a Mr. Polk, who worked for the railroad, met Rev. V. P. Bowers while riding the train. Reverend Bowers was district evangelist at the time, serving Guyton, Rocky Ford, and Meldrim. Mr. Polk asked Reverend Bowers to come to Pembroke and establish a congregation of the Christian Church. A revival was held at the old Pembroke School, and regular services were held at the school house. Mr. L. G. Manley and Mr. J. M. Smith were instrumental in establishing the new church.

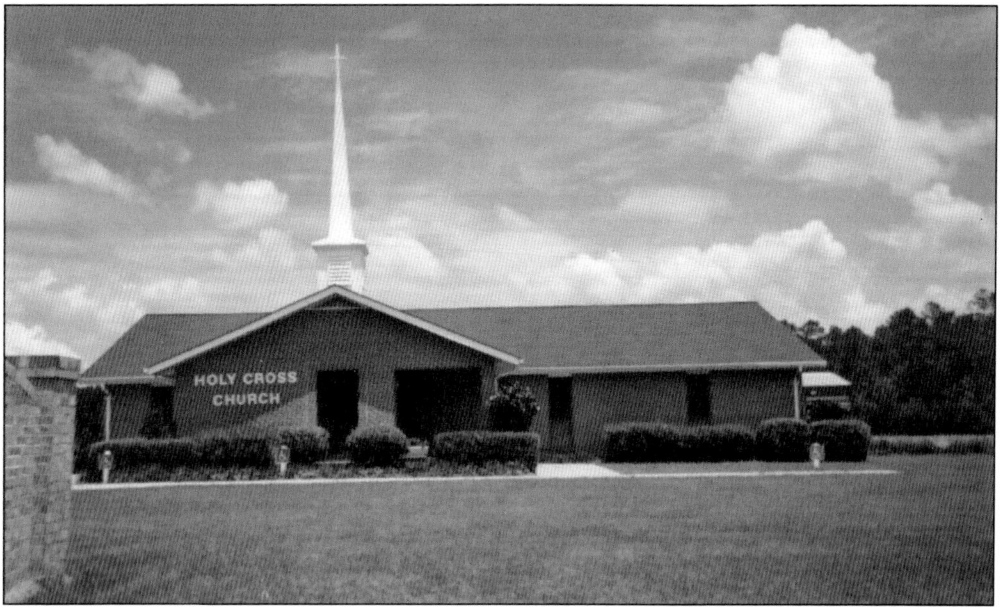

The Holy Cross Catholic Church of Pembroke was established in April or May 1974. Bishop Raymond Lessard of the Diocese of Savannah asked Father James Wilmes, the pastor of the Claxton congregation, to try to organize the beginning of a new congregation in Pembroke. They began their services in the old Tos Theatre in Pembroke. That same year, they bought the Quattlebaum property at the west end of Pembroke, and today they have a beautiful new Holy Cross Church.

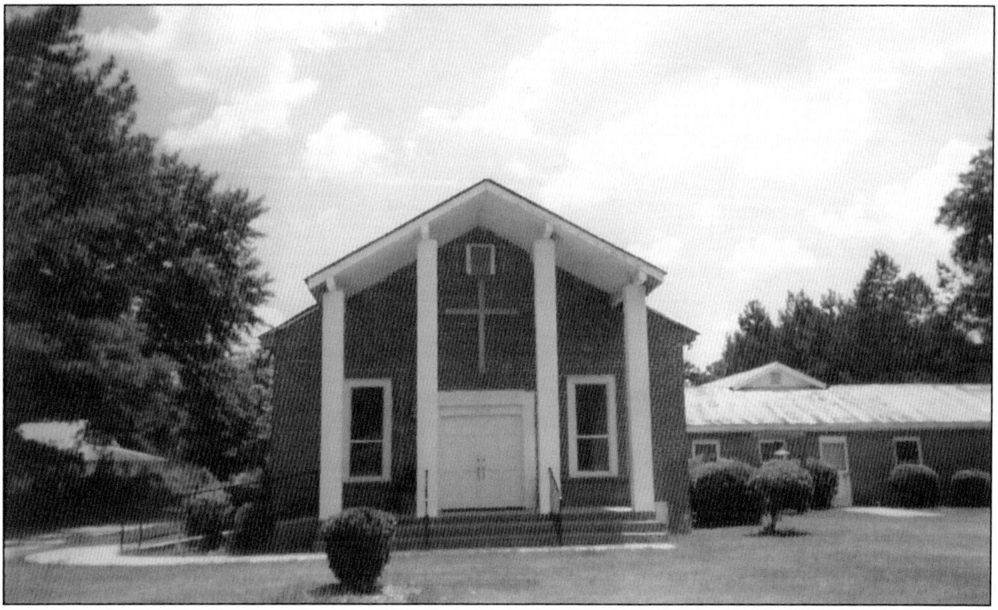

Mount Moriah Baptist Church was organized in March 1889. The founding members were Rev. Sampson Eason and Brothers J. D. McMoore, Frank Byrd, and Claudious Ealey. Rev. A. E. Hagins was called to pastor in 1939, and he was still serving in 1986. Through his leadership, the members of the church worked together and paid all expenses as they constructed the building. The church building was dedicated on April 28, 1985.

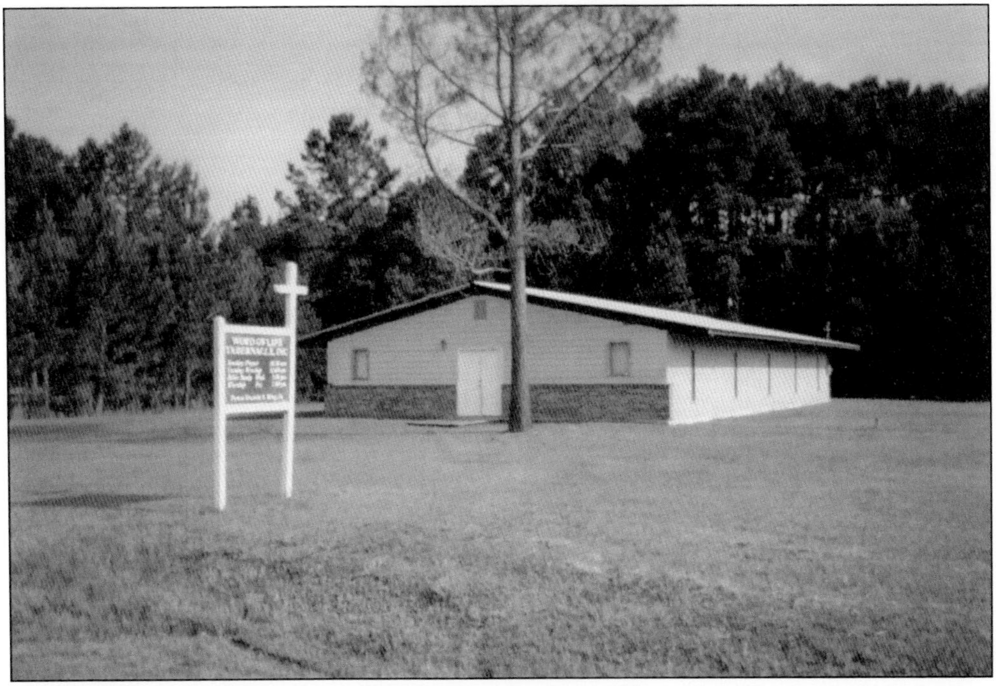

Pictured here is the Word of Love Tabernacle in Pembroke. This a newly formed church that has been in Pembroke since 2002. Its pastor is Rev. Donald Bing.

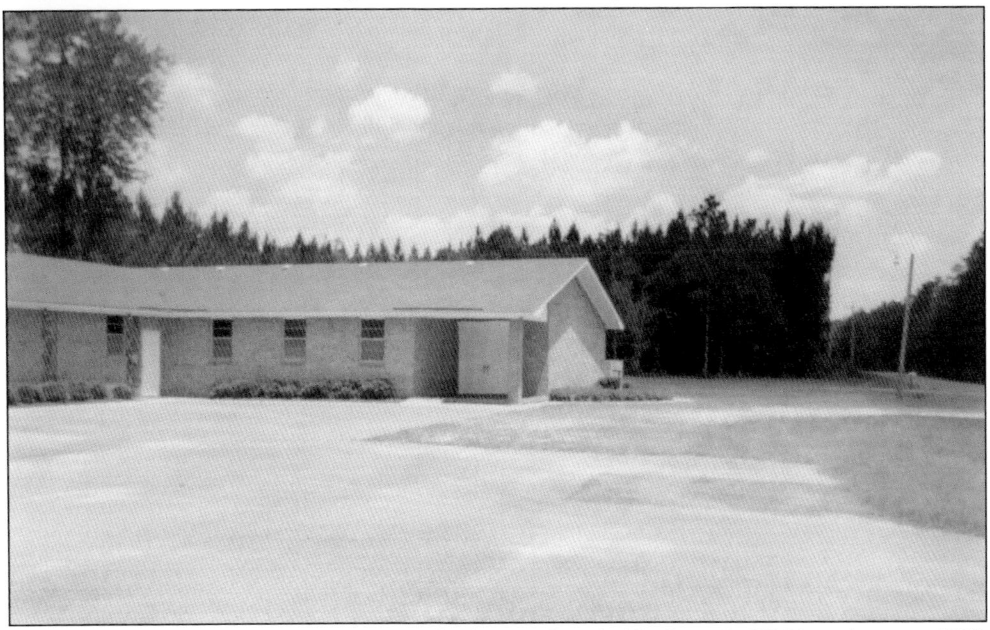

The Holy Church of God Church in Pembroke was founded by Rev. G. W. Humphries in 1957. Reverend Humphries worked for the railroad, and he was instrumental in getting a building fund started to construct a church. Pastors who have served the Holy Church of God, in addition to Reverend Humphries, are Larry Thomas, Wendell Pittman, Joe Wiggins, and Donald Downs. Rev. Lawrence Butler, son of Rev. C. M. Butler, came to Pembroke in 1966 at the age of 24 to serve as pastor of the church; he still serves as the pastor today.

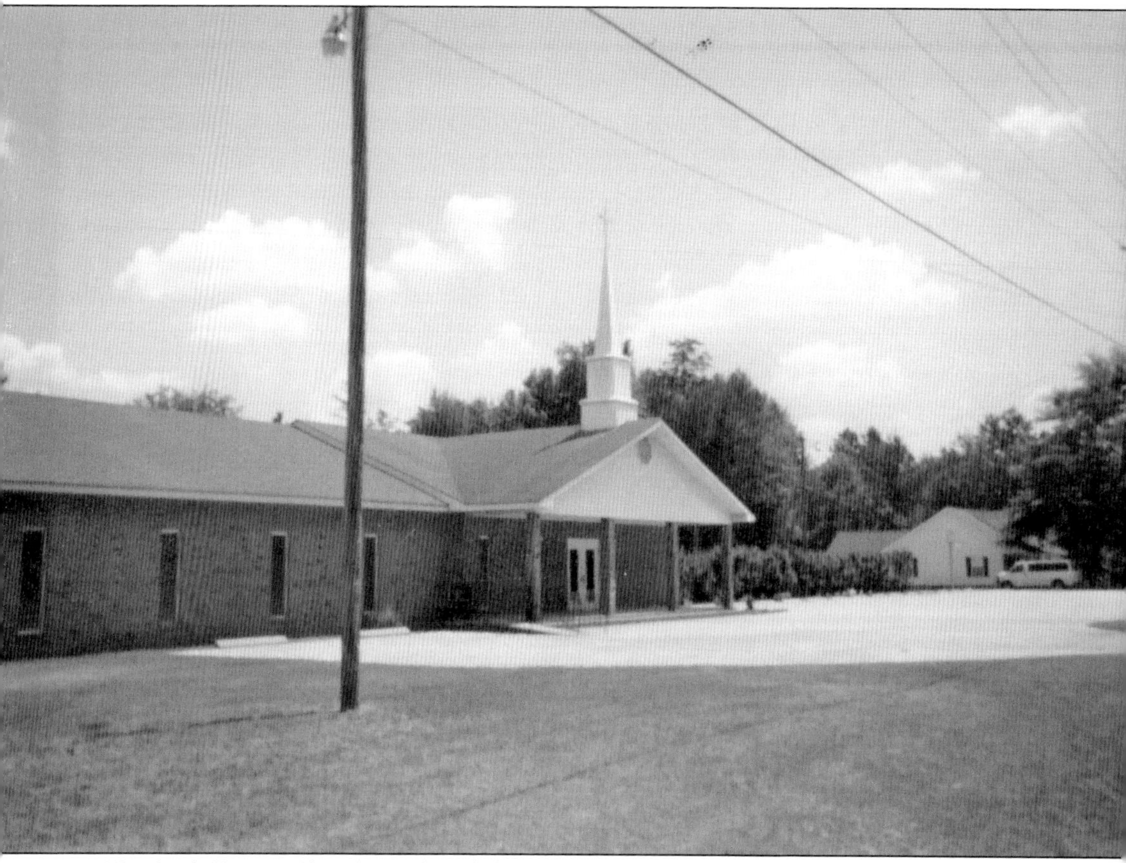

Northside Baptist Church was founded in 1969 by Rev. Hannie Burnsed, who was the first pastor. Mrs. Edra Burke is the only charter member who is still a member. The second pastor was Rev. James Dukes, and the third and present pastor is Rev. Ross Kight.

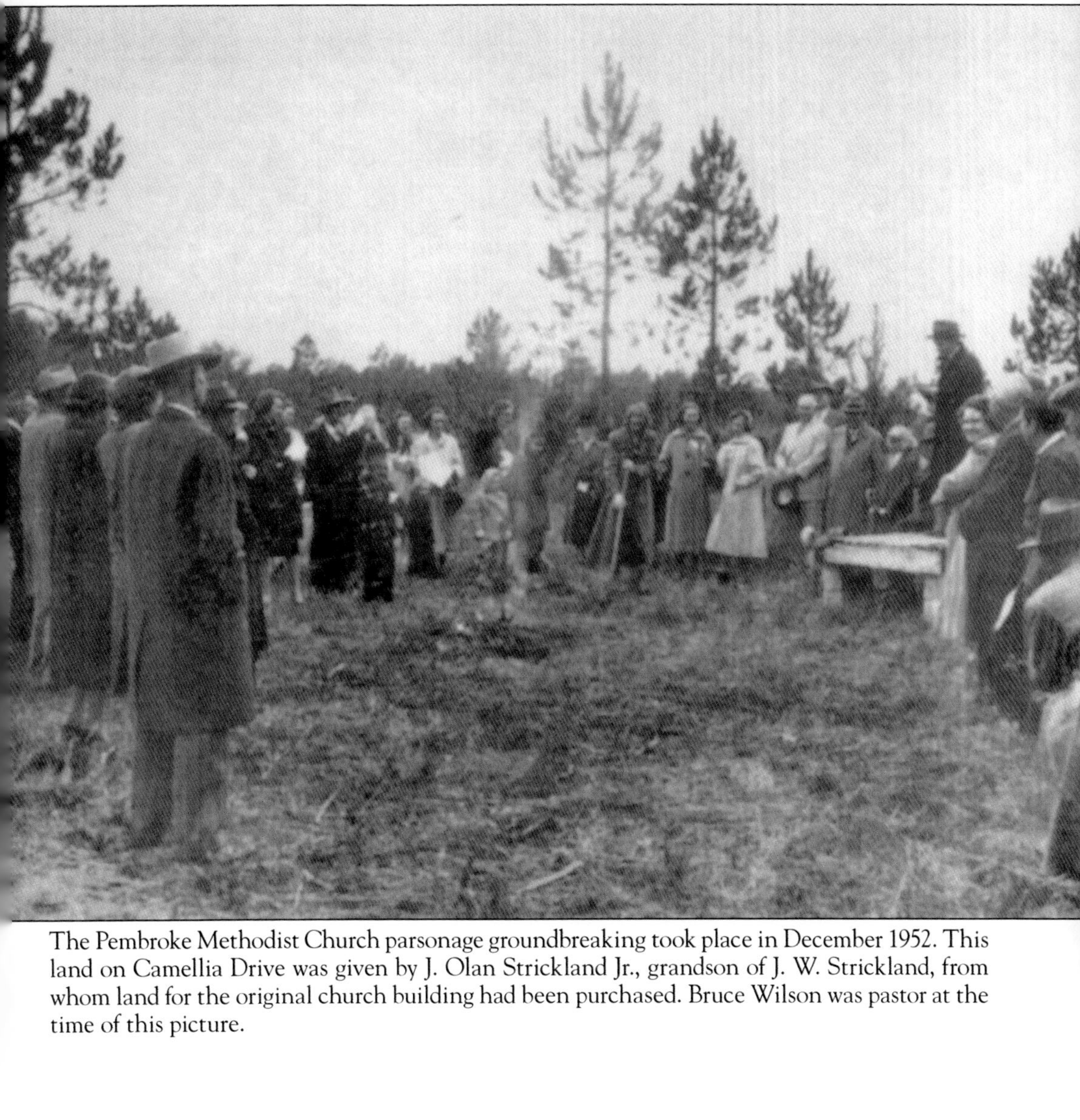

The Pembroke Methodist Church parsonage groundbreaking took place in December 1952. This land on Camellia Drive was given by J. Olan Strickland Jr., grandson of J. W. Strickland, from whom land for the original church building had been purchased. Bruce Wilson was pastor at the time of this picture.

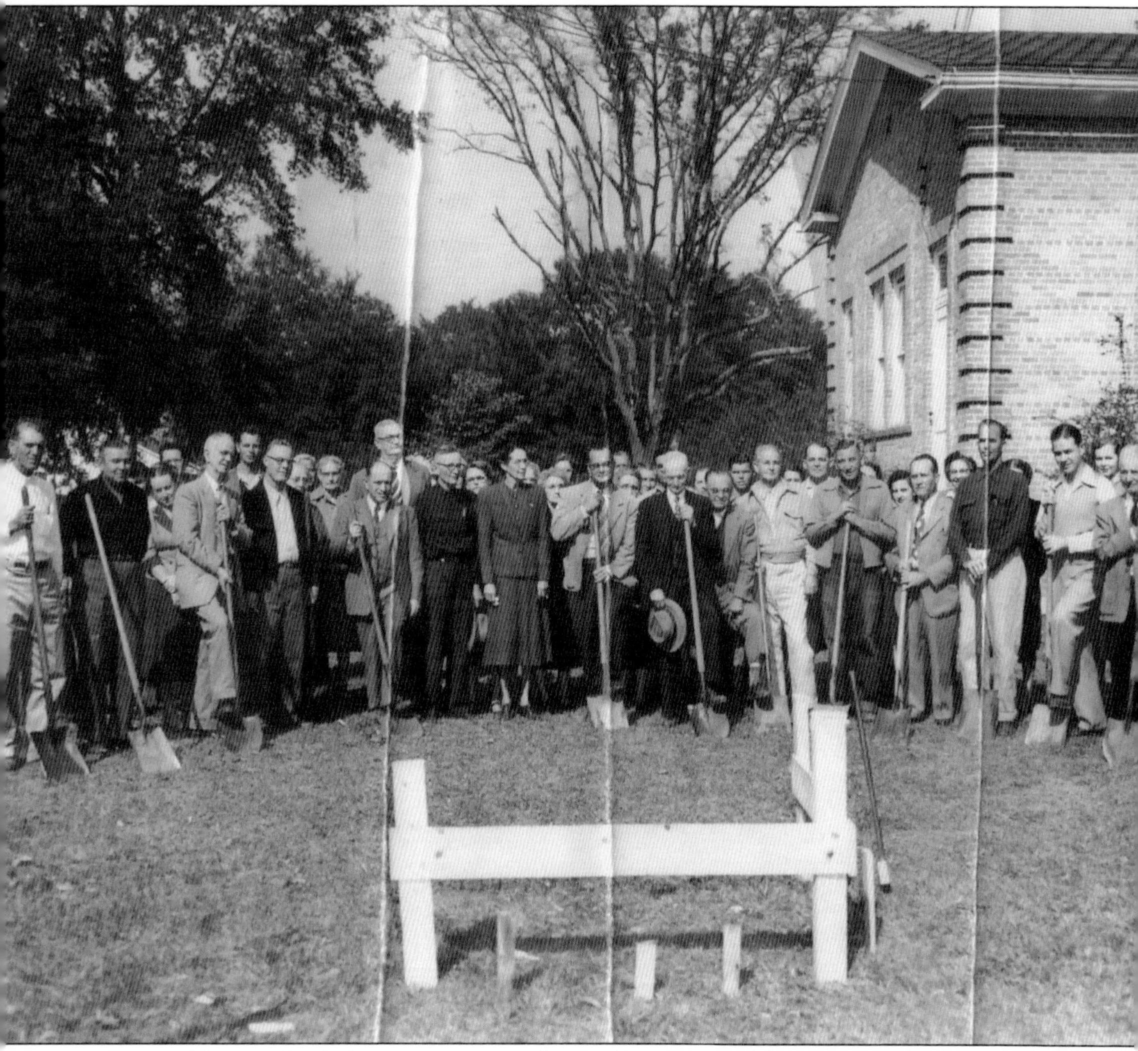

Pictured here is the dedication ceremony for the First Baptist Church in Pembroke.

Five

INDUSTRY AND BUSINESSES

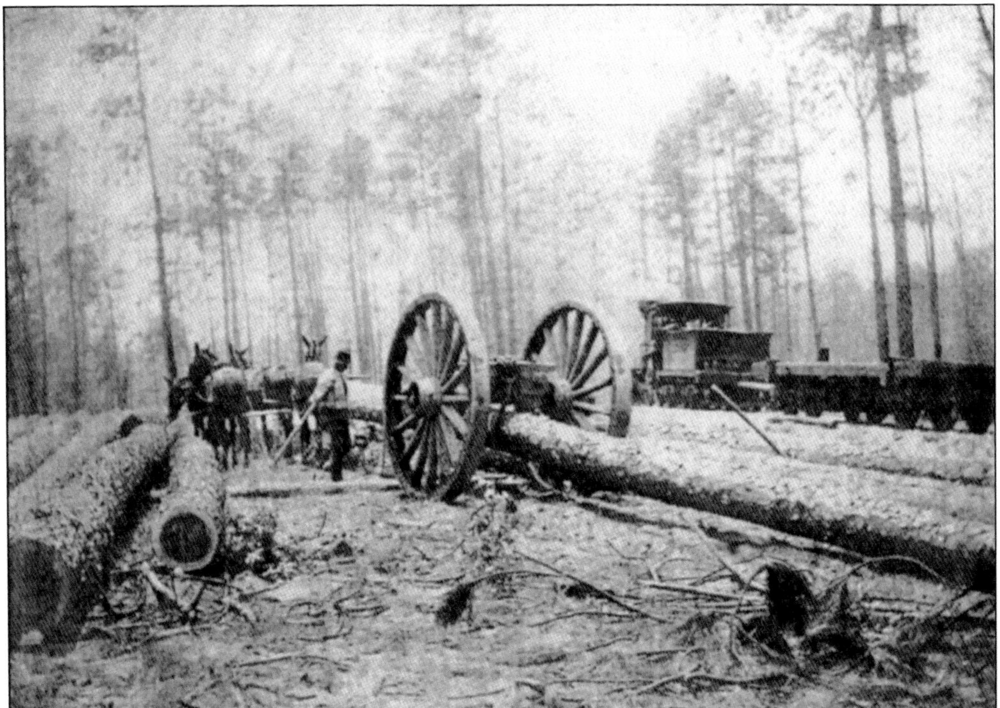

Logging in the late 19th and early 20th centuries was a lucrative business in Pembroke. This is a photograph of a typical timber operation. With all of the sawmills that sprang up in and around Pembroke, houses were quickly built and lumber was a necessity.

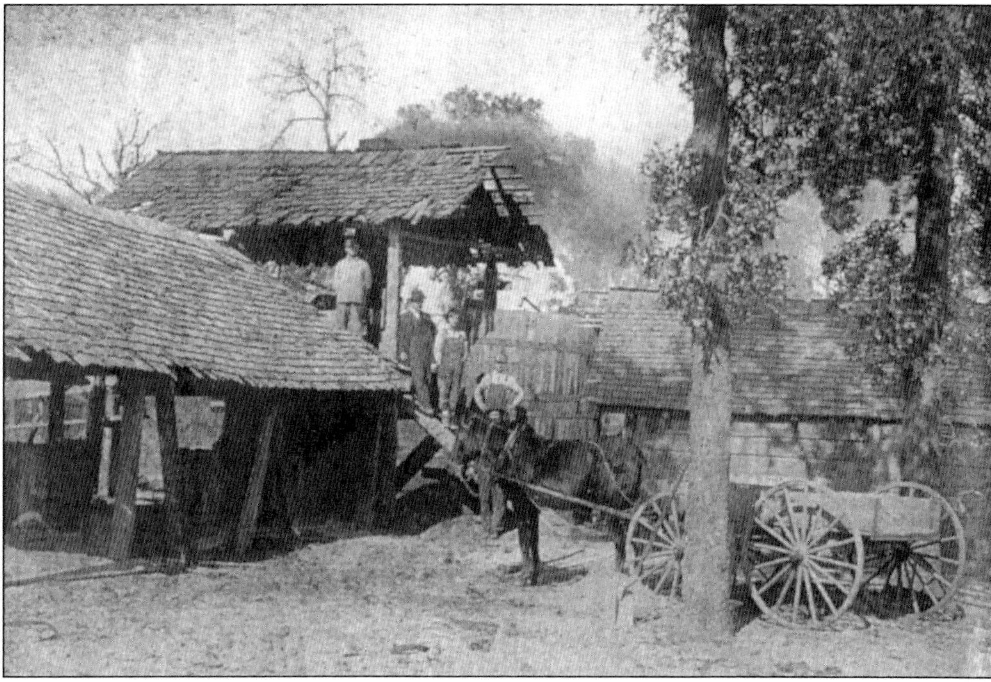

From 1880 through 1890, Bryan County turpentine farms and distillers employed anywhere from 50 to 200 laborers. The naval stores industry had its origin in Colonial Georgia. This is a photograph of an early turpentine still in North Bryan County near Pembroke. The growth of the turpentine and lumber business attracted increasing numbers of new settlers to this area.

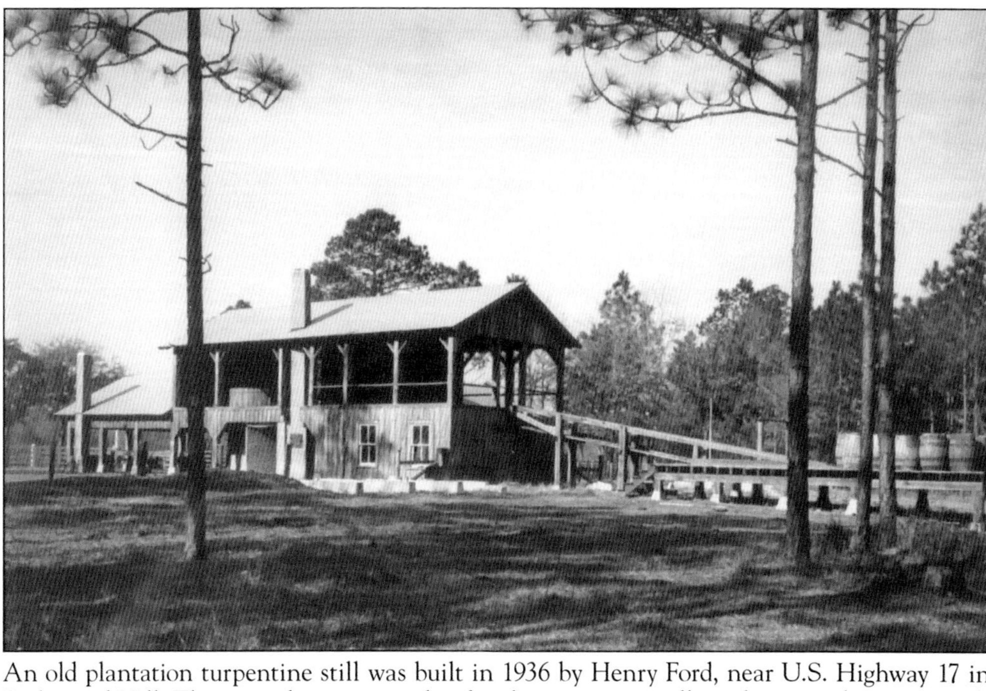

An old plantation turpentine still was built in 1936 by Henry Ford, near U.S. Highway 17 in Richmond Hill. This provides an example of early turpentine stills and was used as a research project for utilization of timber waste.

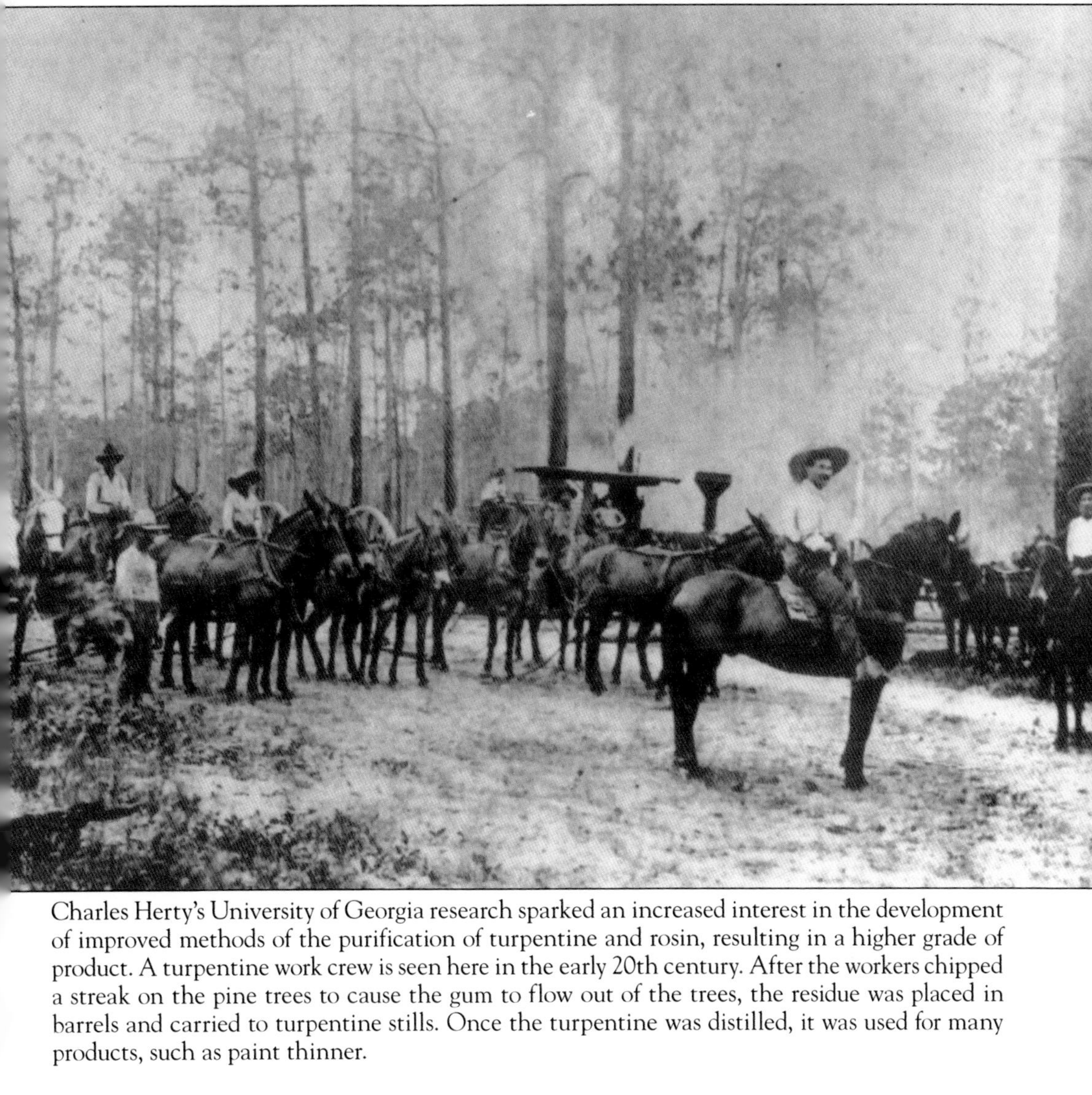

Charles Herty's University of Georgia research sparked an increased interest in the development of improved methods of the purification of turpentine and rosin, resulting in a higher grade of product. A turpentine work crew is seen here in the early 20th century. After the workers chipped a streak on the pine trees to cause the gum to flow out of the trees, the residue was placed in barrels and carried to turpentine stills. Once the turpentine was distilled, it was used for many products, such as paint thinner.

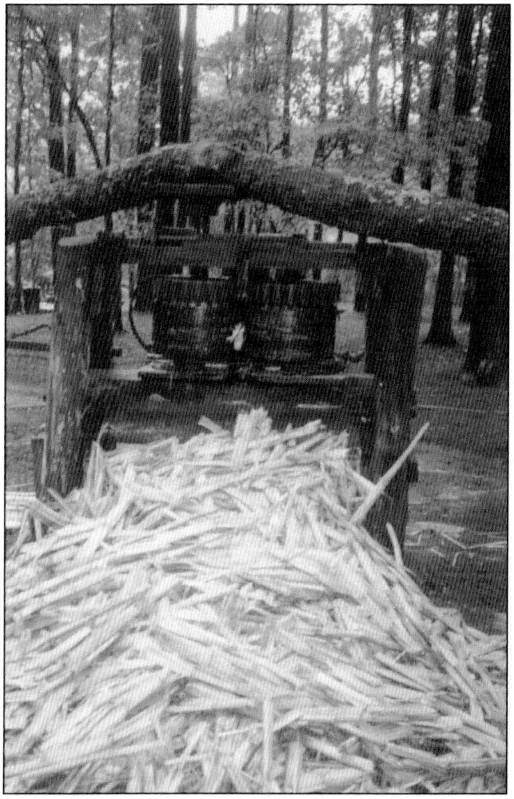

The cane grinding exhibition at Pickett Park was sponsored by the Home Town Task Force about 1990. Cane grinding was the process of taking the juice of sugar cane and boiling it down to syrup. This process was widely used in Bryan County up until the early 1950s. The Home Town Task Force is an organization that keeps the city clean and provides different events for the people of Pembroke. Its annual exhibit takes place in December, on the day of Pembroke's Christmas parade.

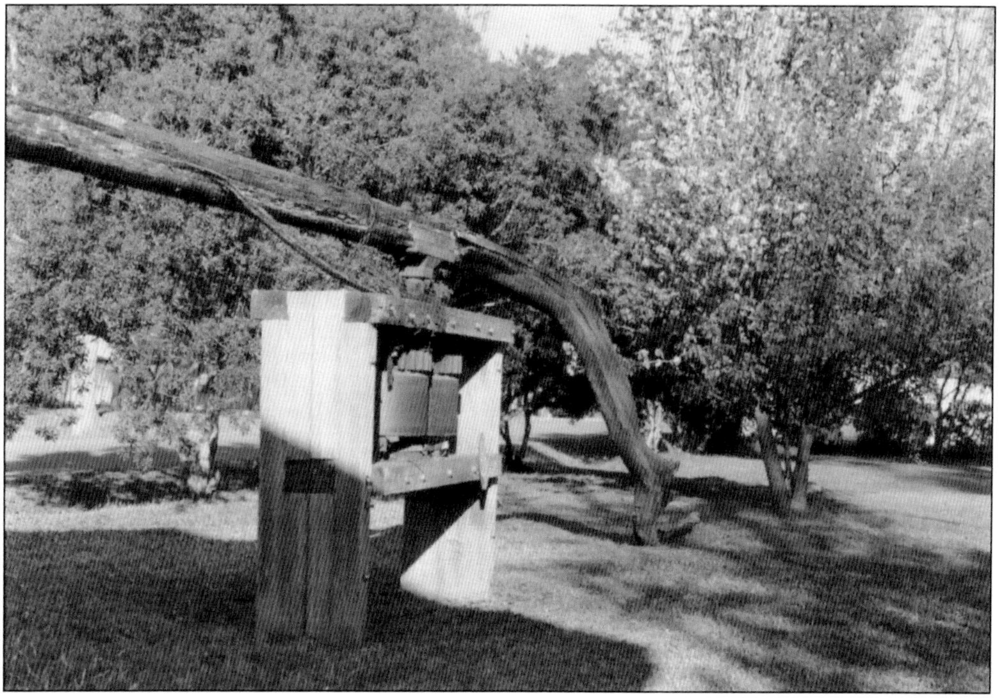

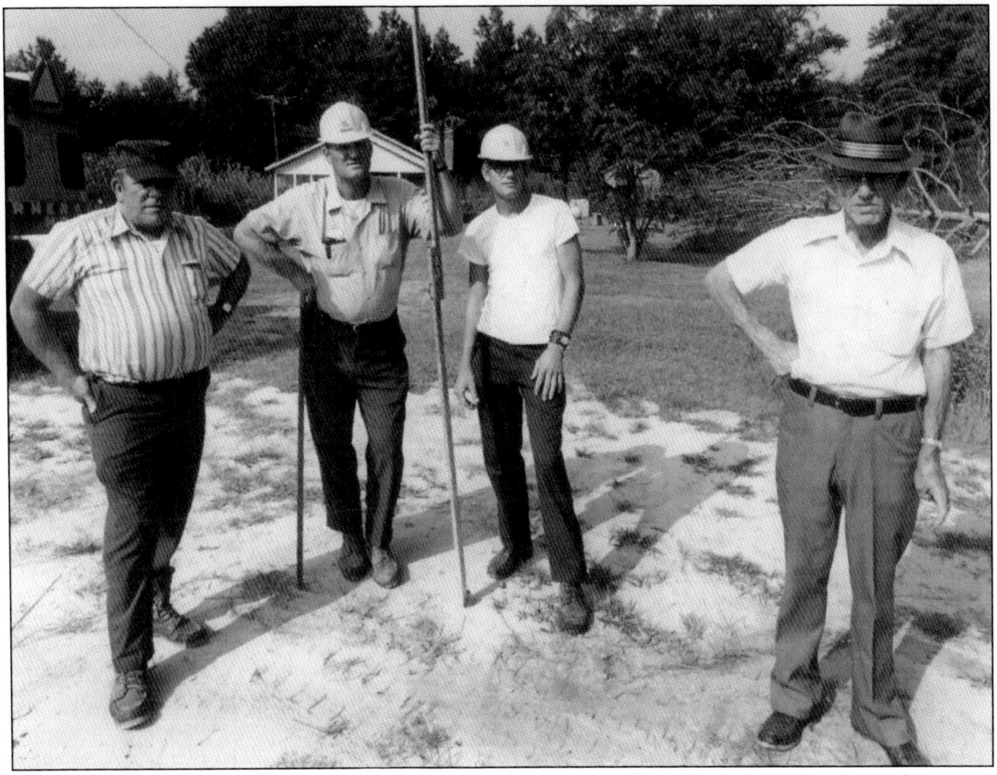

A highway crew is pictured preparing to do a survey on one of Pembroke's roads. The only person in this picture who has been identified is Ivey Kennedy (far right).

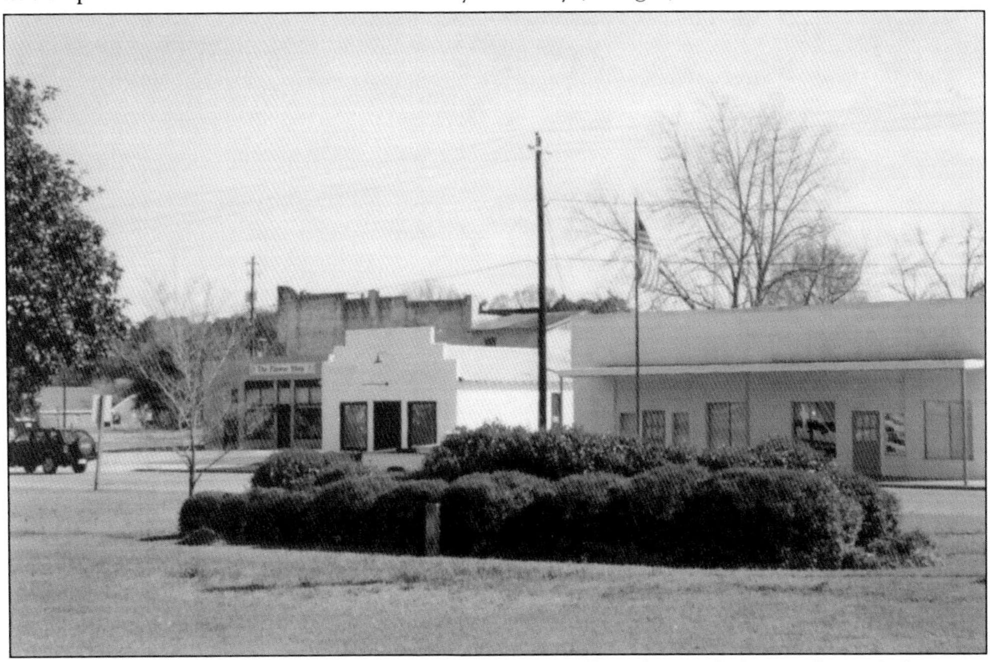

Little Rascals Day Care was founded by Marie Ennis Polk and provided a much needed service for the community.

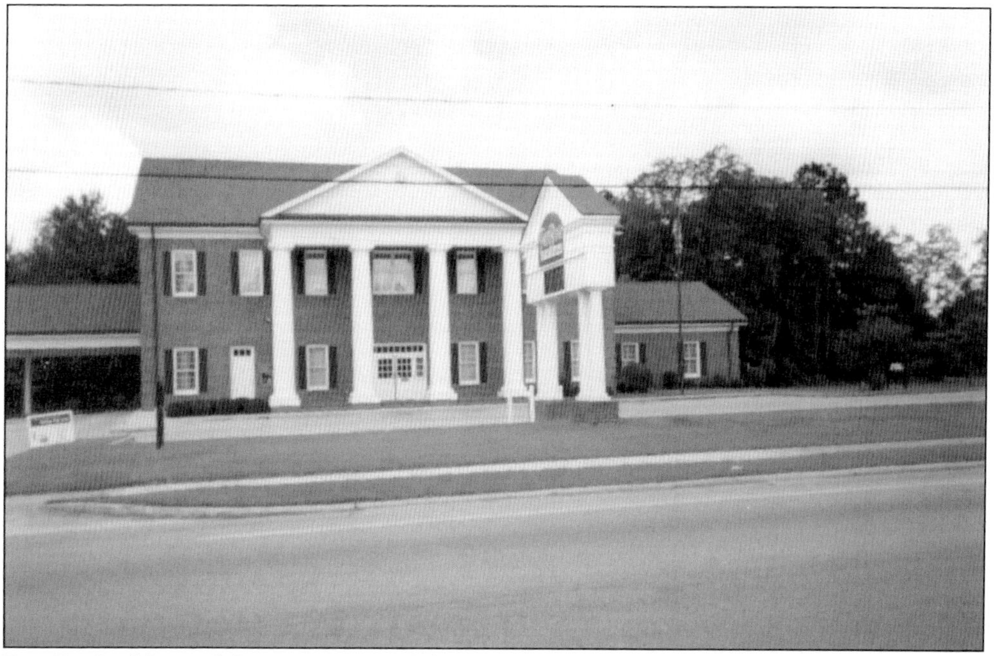

First Bank of Coastal Georgia, previously known as the Pembroke State Bank, was organized in 1907. Julius Morgan was the third president of the bank, which was known at the time as the Pembroke National Bank. In 1933, the bank failed, but Julius Morgan, by mortgaging everything he owned, paid his depositors in full. The Pembroke National Bank was one of only two Georgia banks that fully satisfied their obligations to depositors.

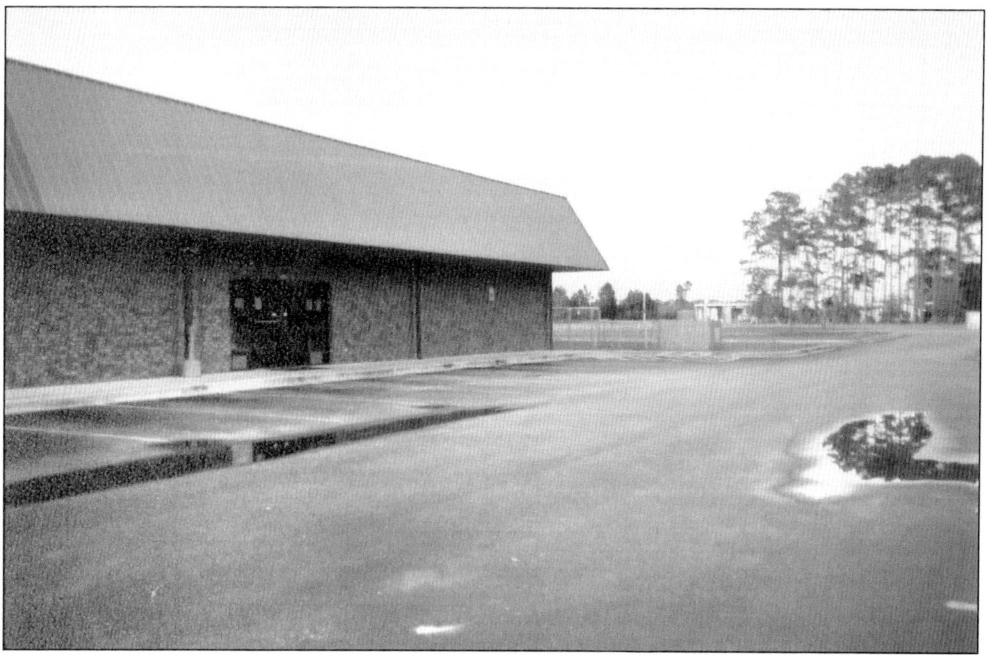

Owens Supply Company was formerly known as Shuman Supply, then Shuman-Owens Supply. It is now owned by the Owens family. Shuman Supply was owned and operated by Jack W. Shuman, a local businessman. It is a building supply company. Mr. Shuman sold out to the Owens *c.* 1990.

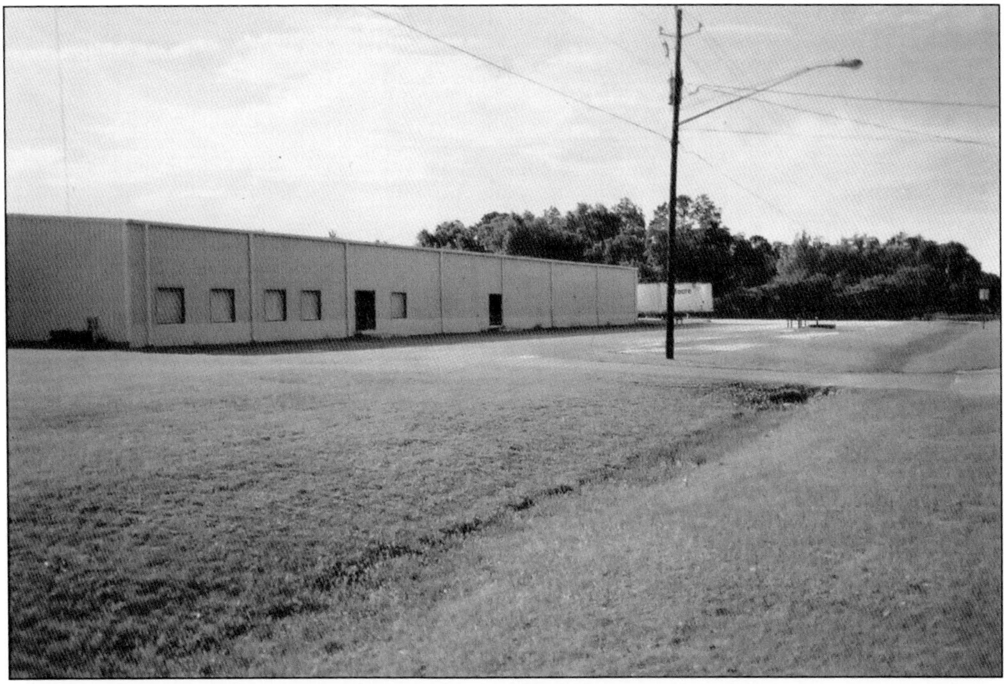

The Express Packing Inc., commonly known as "the box plant," manufacturers cardboard boxes and provides employment for many Pembroke citizens.

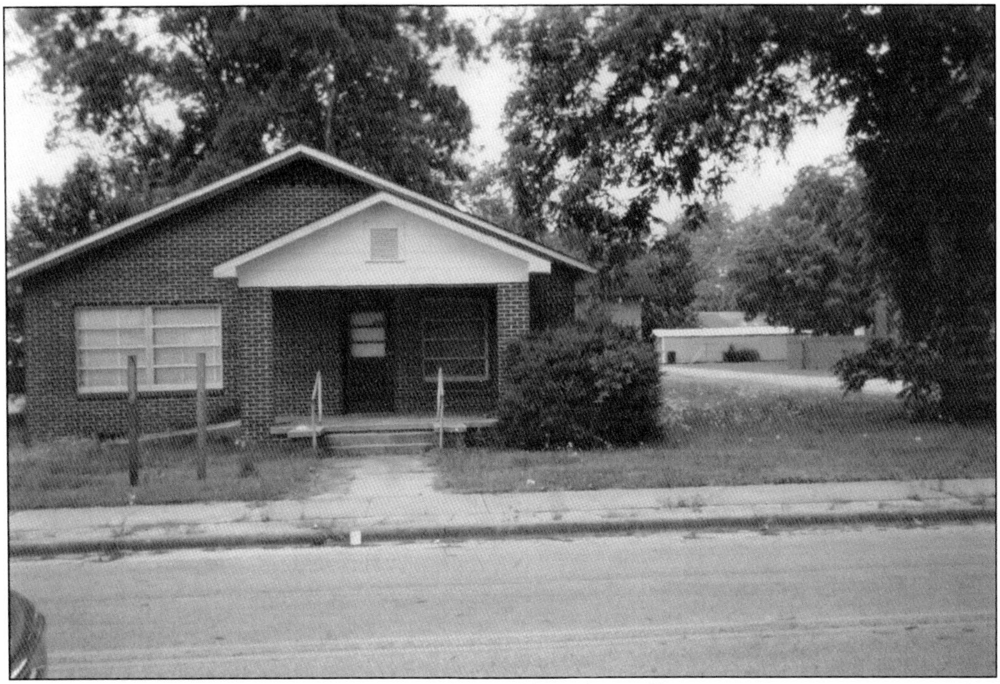

The old Morrison Funeral Home was established by John Kelly Morrison in 1938. Prior to his operation of the funeral home, Mr. Morrison was a farmer and carpenter. He served in World War I and was a captain in the Georgia Home Guard during World War II.

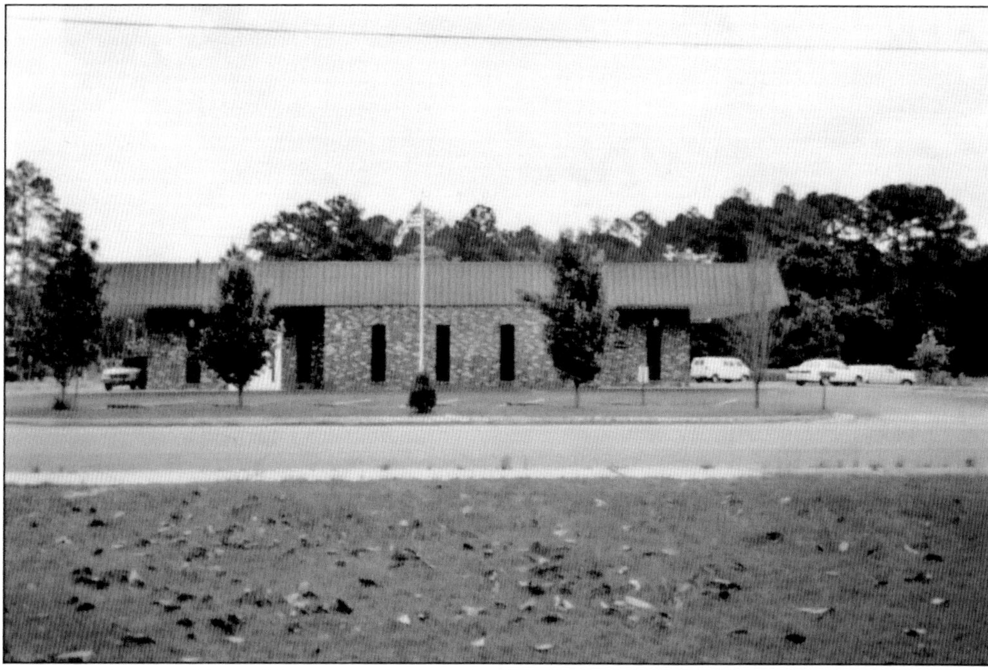

The new Morrison Funeral Home was built on College Street and opened for business in November 1976. It is located next door to the Bryan County Courthouse. Caldwell Morrison (the son of John Kelly Morrison) and his wife Clara provided many years of comforting services to the citizens of Pembroke and surrounding areas. In May 1996, they sold the funeral home to Loewen Group, and it is still operating today as Morrison Funeral Home.

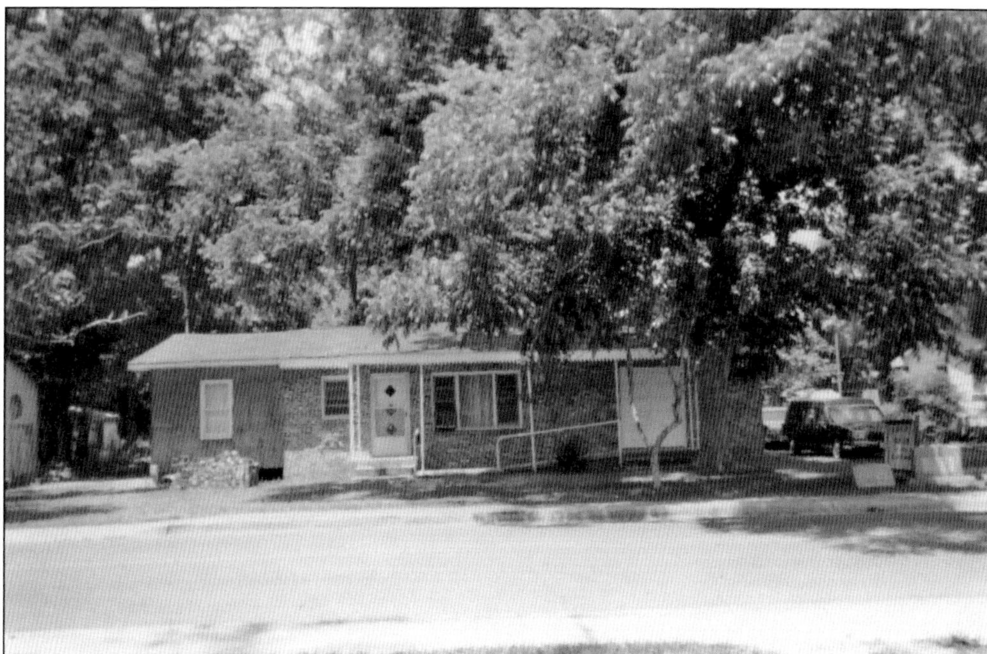

Crawley's Funeral Home was found in 1975 by James and Harriett Crawley. They have owned and operated the funeral home, serving the African American community, for the past 30 years.

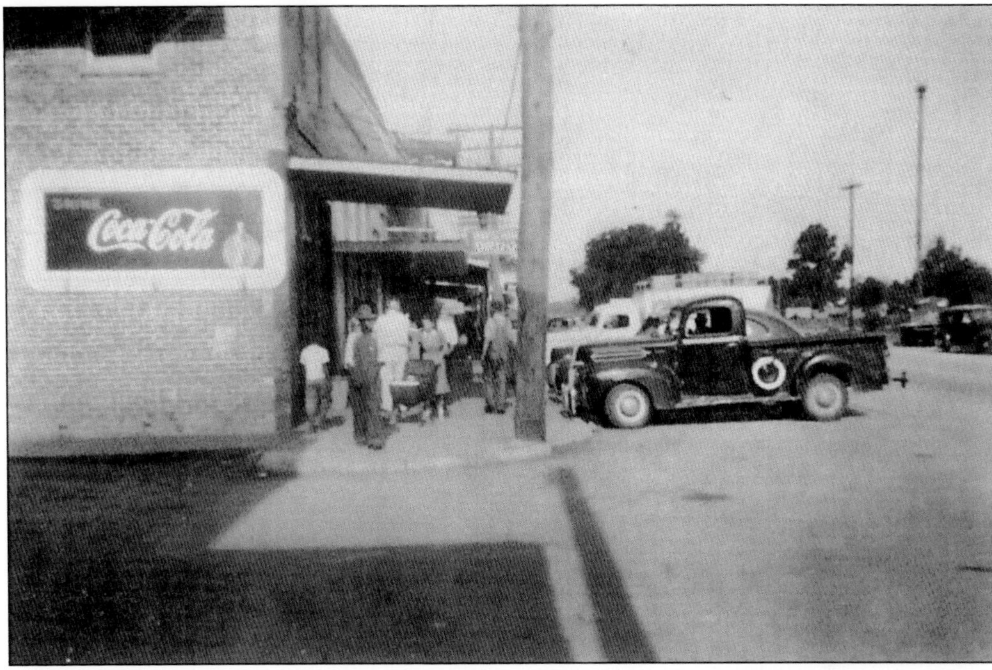

A photograph of old downtown Pembroke in the 1930s shows that much has changed today.

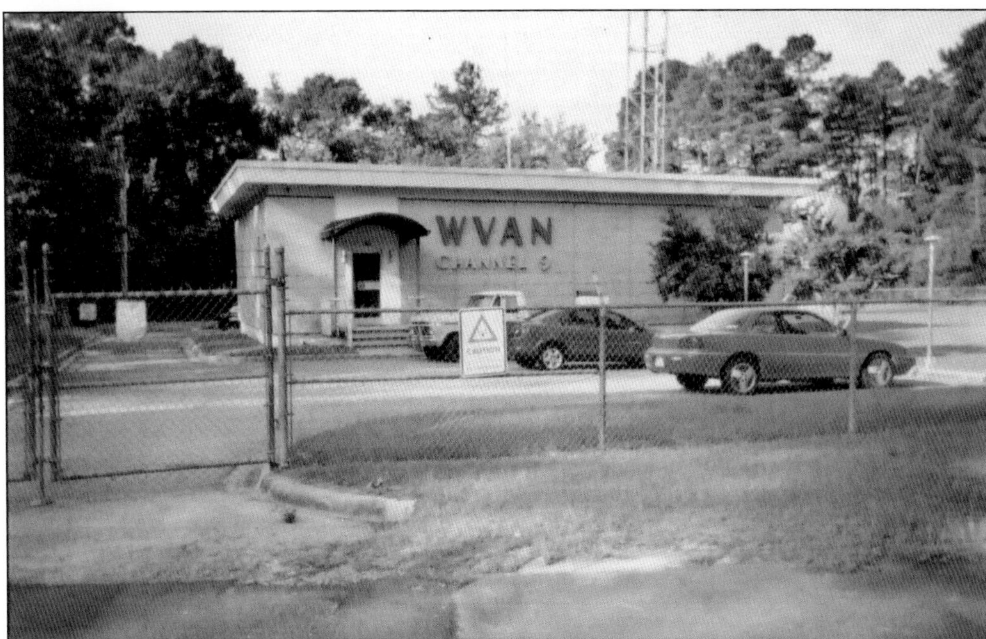

In 1963, a 1,086-foot television tower was constructed in Pembroke by the Georgia Department of Education as part of the developing state network for the telecast of classroom and educational programming. The station was designated as WVAN-TV in honor of former Georgia governor Ernest Vandiver. It was dedicated on September 19, 1963, and Ernest Vandiver was present, along with Gov. Carl Sanders.

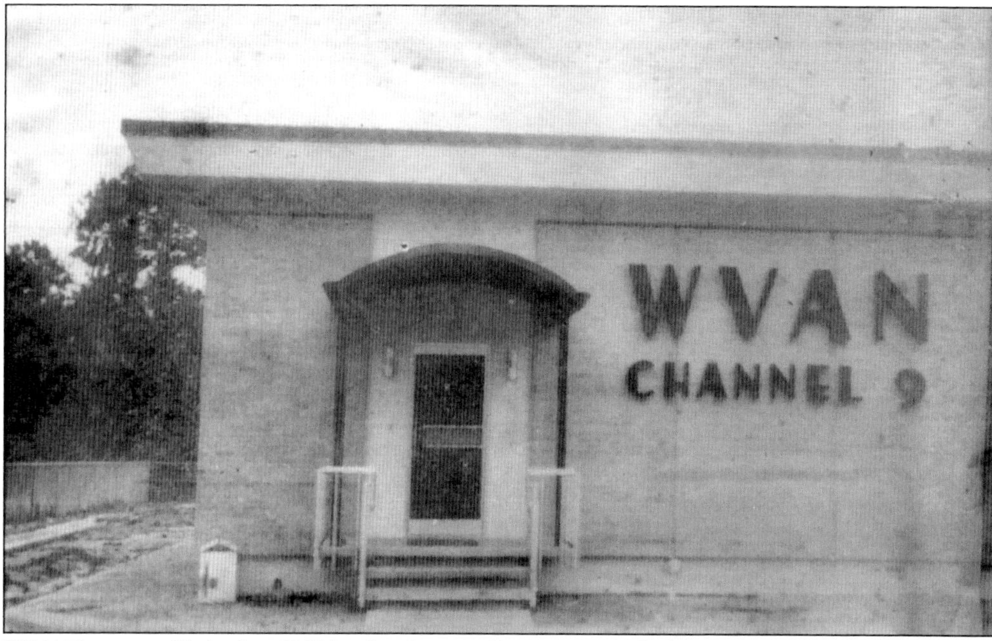

WVAN was established in 1963 by the Georgia Department of Education. It was named in honor of Georgia's former governor, Ernest Vandiver, and dedicated on September 19, 1963.

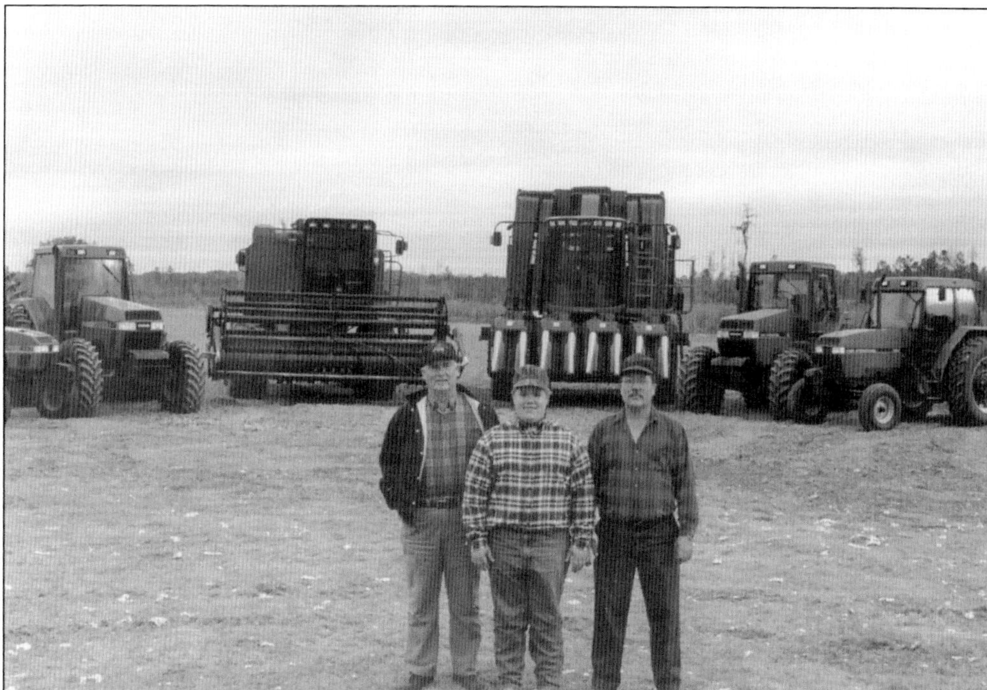
Three generations of farming are represented in this photograph from a nearby community. Pictured from left to right are Hughlyn Page, Danny Page, and Shaun Page. This is the only large farm still operating in the community. The Page Farm grows cotton, soybeans, tobacco, strawberries, and tomatoes. The farm is located six miles northeast of Pembroke.

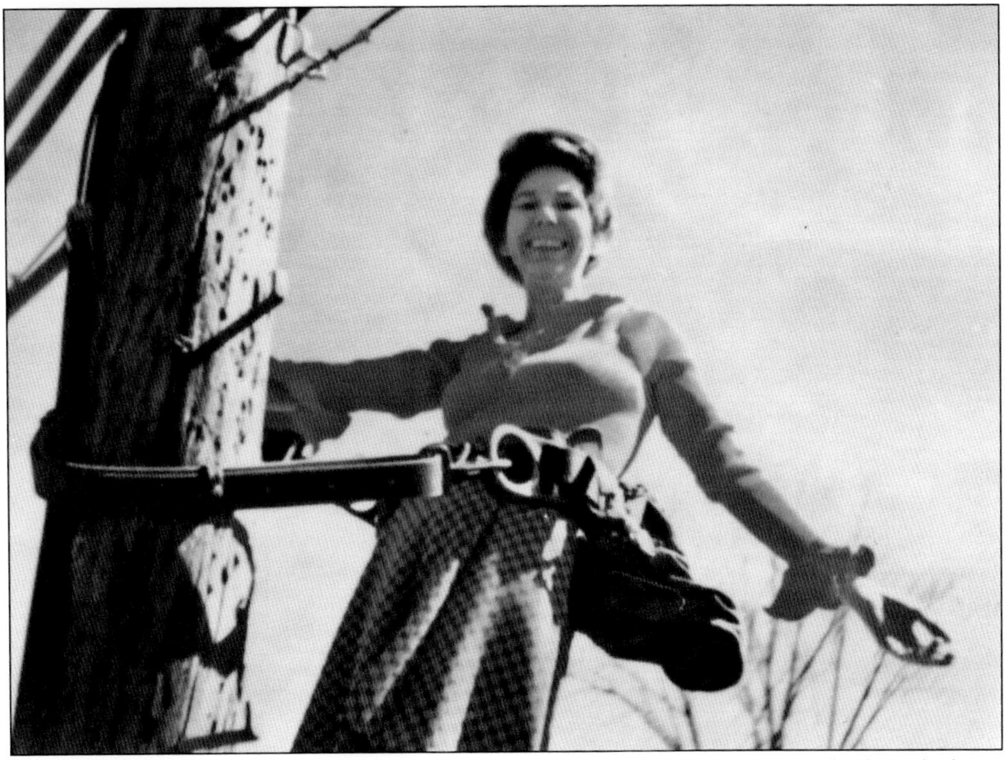

Mrs. Ivey Beardslee is pictured working on one of the telephone poles for Pembroke Telephone Company. The company had its beginnings in 1898. In 1946, it was acquired by Paul and Ivey Beardslee, son-in-law and daughter of Mr. U. J. Bacon. After Mr. Beardslee's untimely death in 1951, the telephone company was managed by his widow, Ivey Beardslee, with assistance from her father and brother Gerald Bacon. She is still the president of the phone company as of 2005.

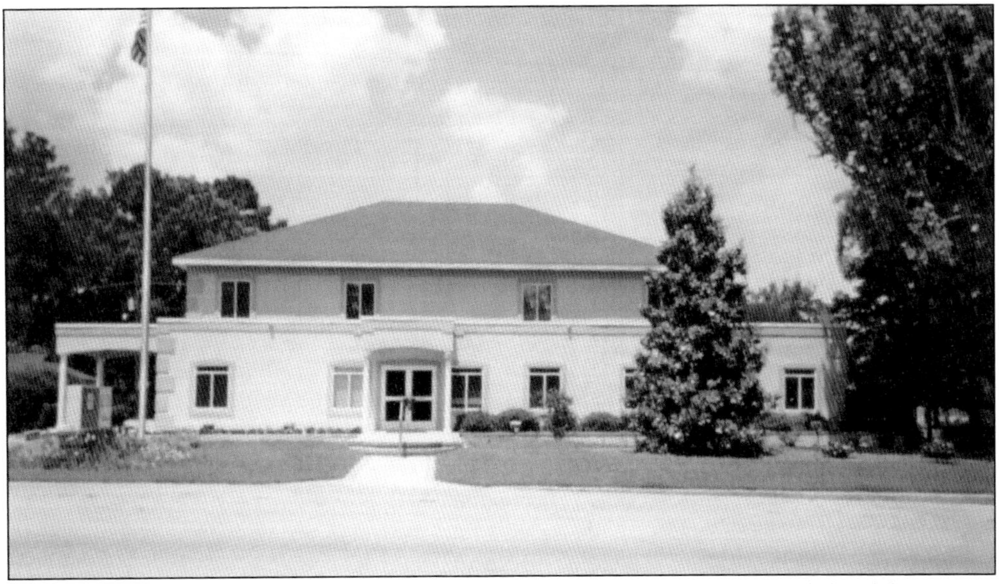

By 1988, the new Pembroke Telephone Company had developed from a small local firm into a high-tech company.

This Was The Makings Of New Bank

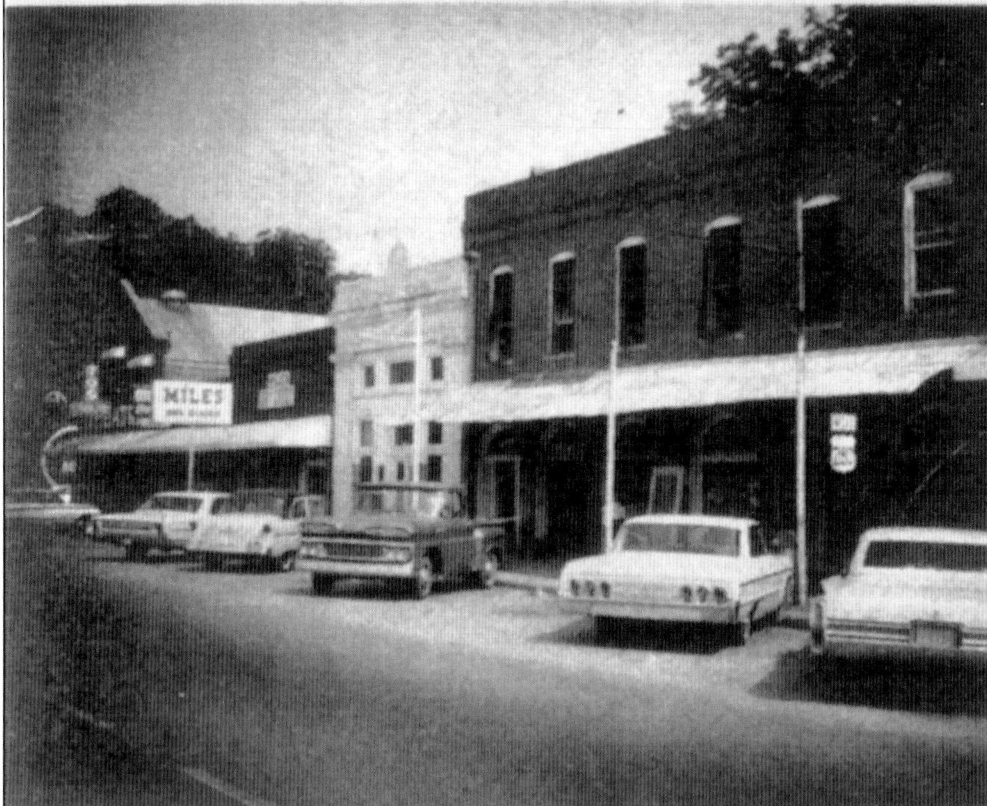

Shown above is the old set up of the bank, the marble front building was the home of the bank and the two stores to the right with the doors being taken out was added to the original bank building, and upper story took off, a new roof installed and an entirely new front put on, as well as a modern lay out for the banks use. This we believe to be the most complete and modern set up of any small town bank in Georgia

Shown above is the old setup of the Pembroke State Bank. It was extensively remodeled in late 1965; the marble front building was the home of the bank and the two stores to the right (with the doors being taken out) were added to the original bank building. The upper story was removed, a new roof was installed, and an entirely new front put on, as well as a modern layout for the bank's use. On February 27, 1966, an open house was held, and it was viewed with great pride.

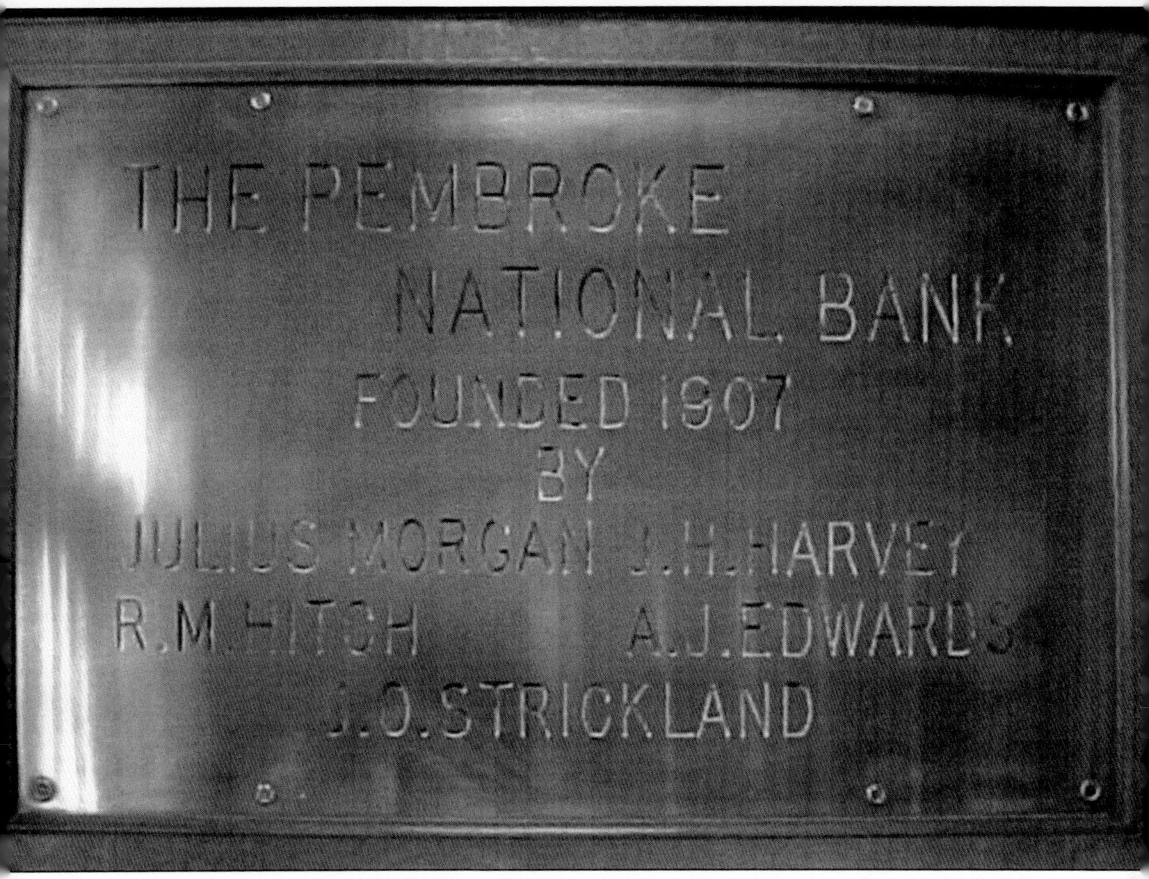

The cornerstone plaque of Pembroke State Bank is representative of the time during which Billy Miles served as president. The plaque reads "The Pembroke National Bank, founded 1907 by Julius Morgan, J. H. Harvey, R. M. Hitch, A. J. Edward, and J. O. Strickland."

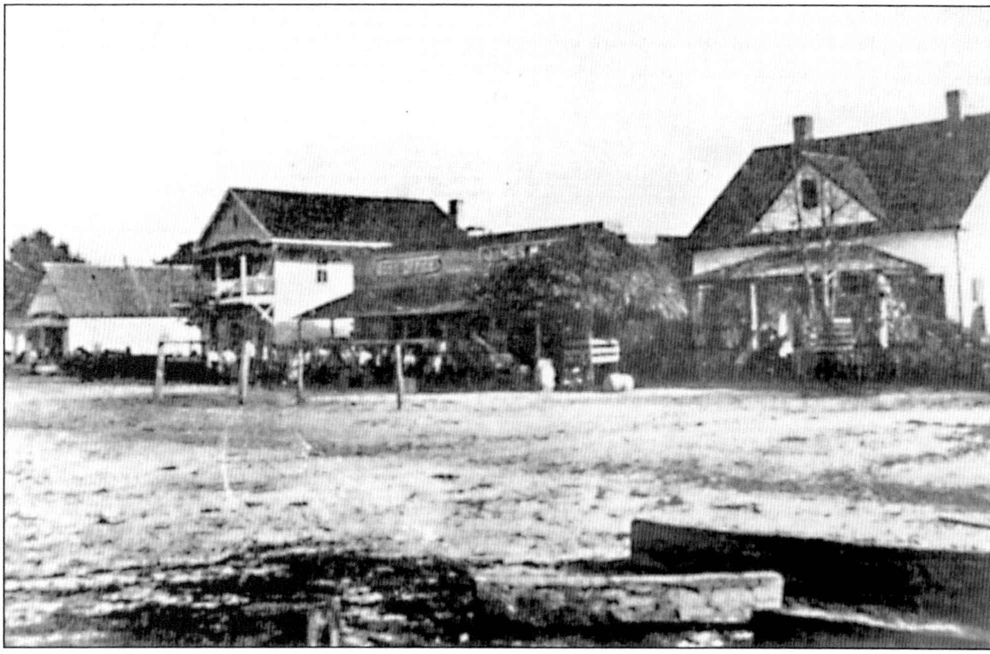

This view of Railroad Street, looking east, shows the old post office. This picture was taken c. 1897.

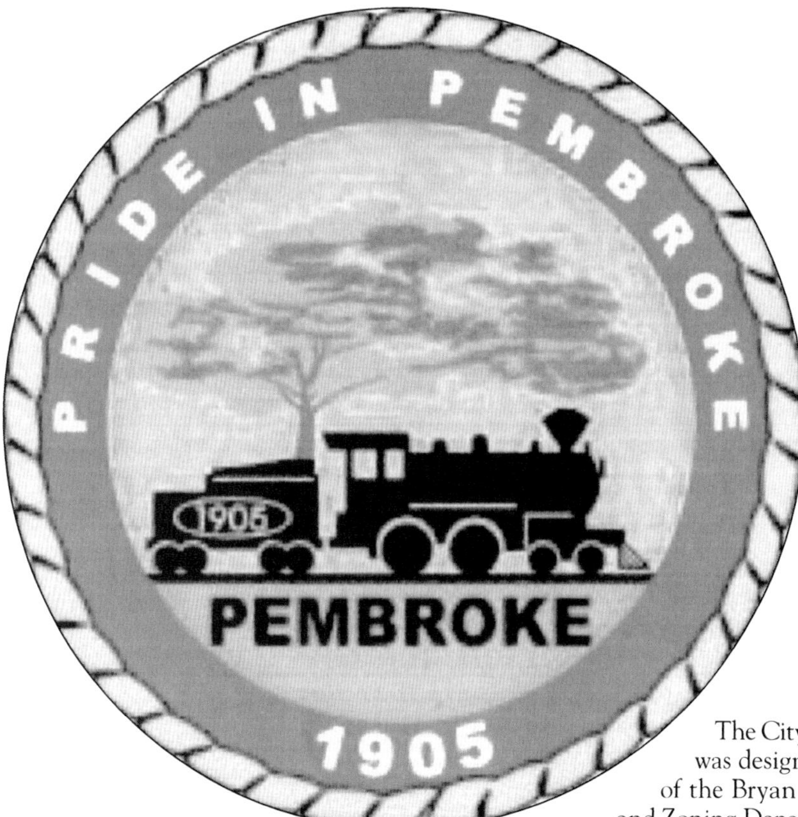

The City of Pembroke's logo was designed by John Butler of the Bryan County Planning and Zoning Department.

Six

HOMES

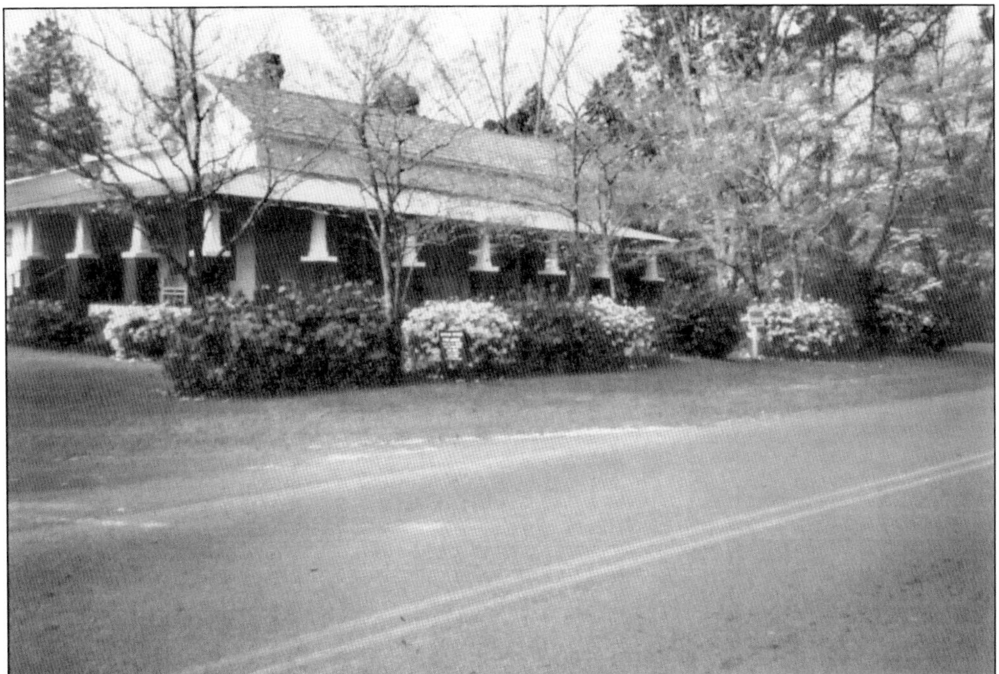

The original home of Dr. W. K. Smith was built in 1897 and moved from Clyde, Georgia, to Pembroke in 1927.

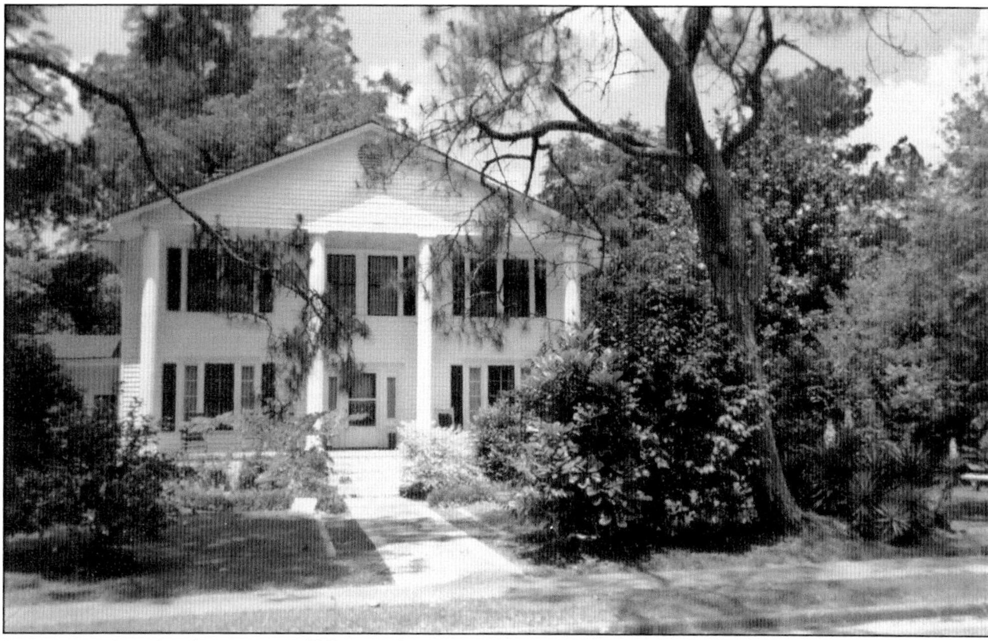

Dr. Gene Smith's home is still located on Strickland Street. Dr. Smith graduated from Bryan County High School in 1932 and attended Emory at Oxford and the University of Georgia; he later attended the University School of Medicine. He began practicing medicine in 1946. In 1942, Dr. Smith married Bernice Hooks of Bulloch County. They had two children, William Kelly and Janice Jean.

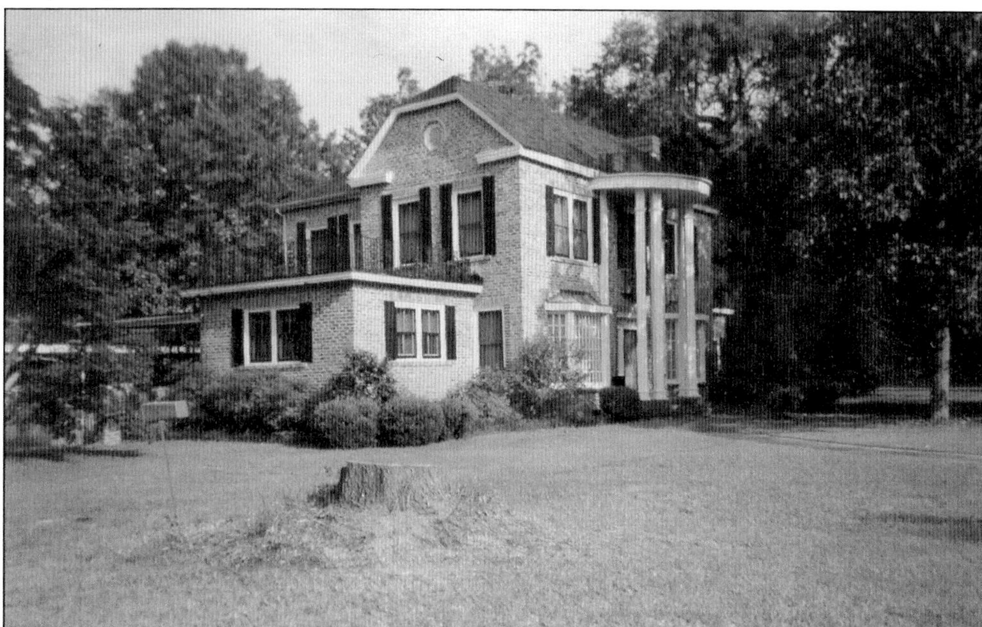

The home of Mrs. J. O. Bacon was built in 1890 by Mr. W. J. Strickland, father of Dr. J. O. Strickland. Mr. Strickland lived in the home with his two daughters, Ophelia and Ruby. In 1927, the home was sold to Mrs. Ella Hughes. In 1994, J. O. and Imogene Bacon purchased the property and began a renovation.

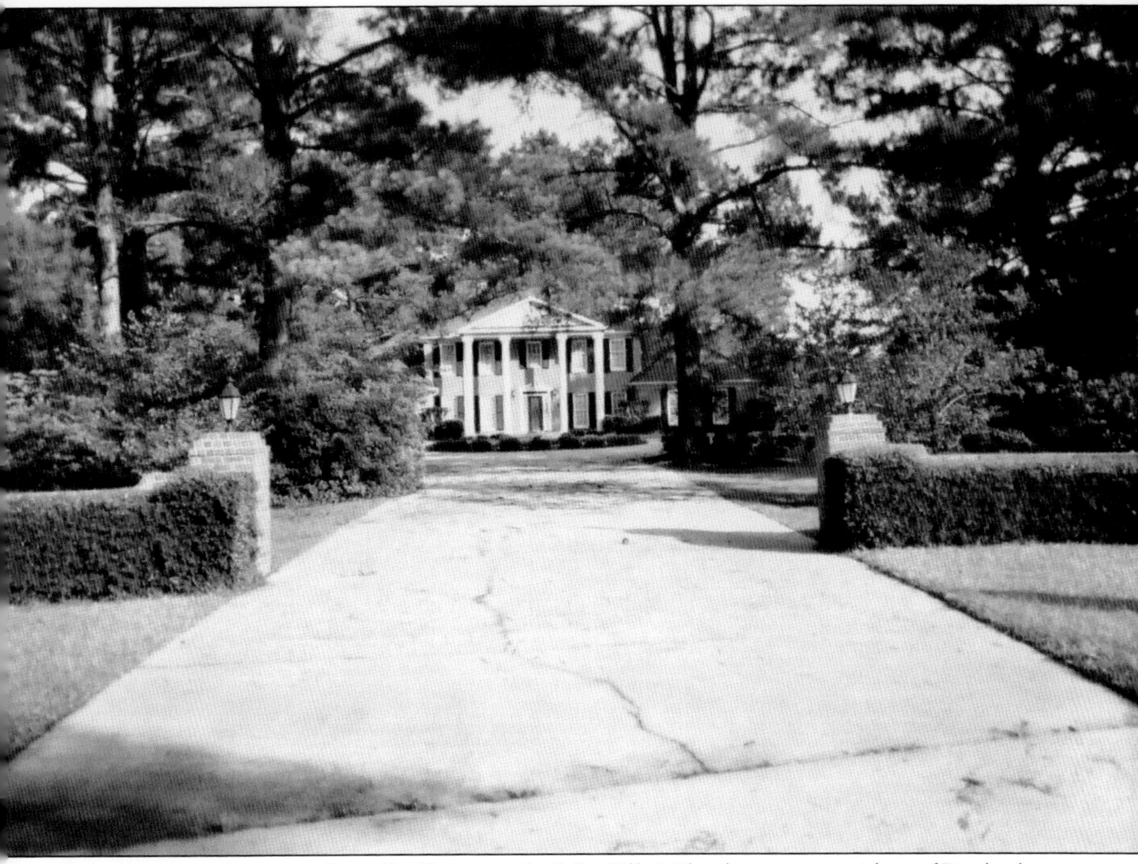

This magnificent house on Camellia Drive was built by Billy Miles, longtime president of Pembroke State Bank. Mr. Miles's tenure with the bank ran from 1946 until his retirement in 1984.

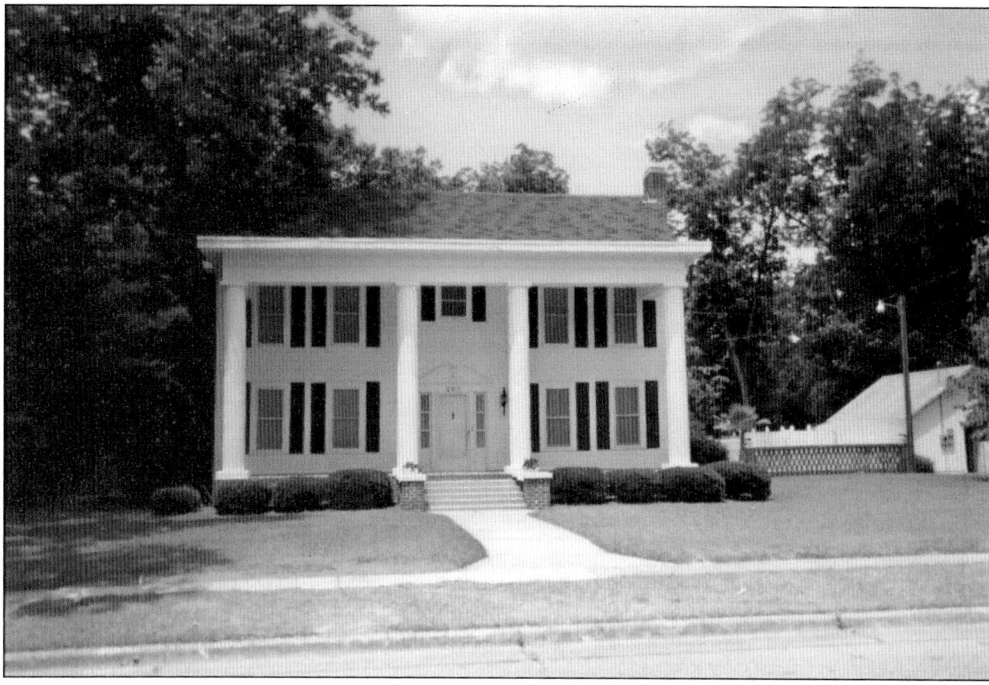

The Warnell home on Strickland Street was owned by William Alvin Warnell and Brightie Blue Warnell. The Warnells had one son, William Daniel. Mr. William Alvin Warnell died in 1950.

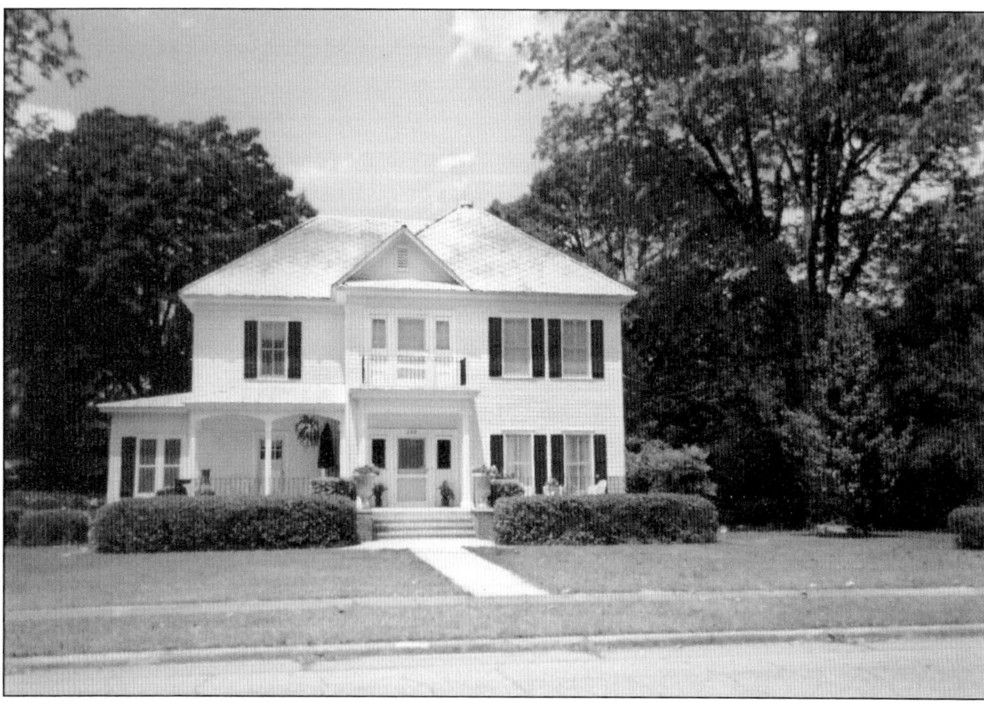

This home was built in 1906 for Dr. J. O. Strickland and Rosa Averitt, his bride of three years. It remained in the Strickland family until it was sold to Paul and Mindy Boyette.

Seven

ORGANIZATIONS

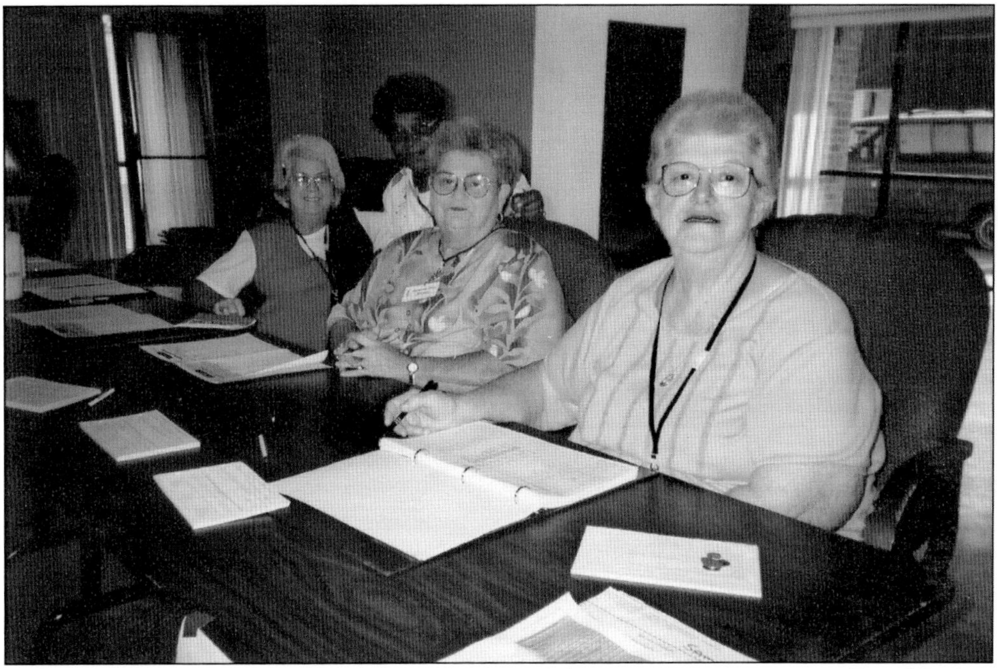

Pictured on election day in 2004 are (from left to right) Lavern Scott, Betty Powell, and Earline Geiger. The election was held in Pembroke, and only 26 people voted. It was an nonpartisan runoff election.

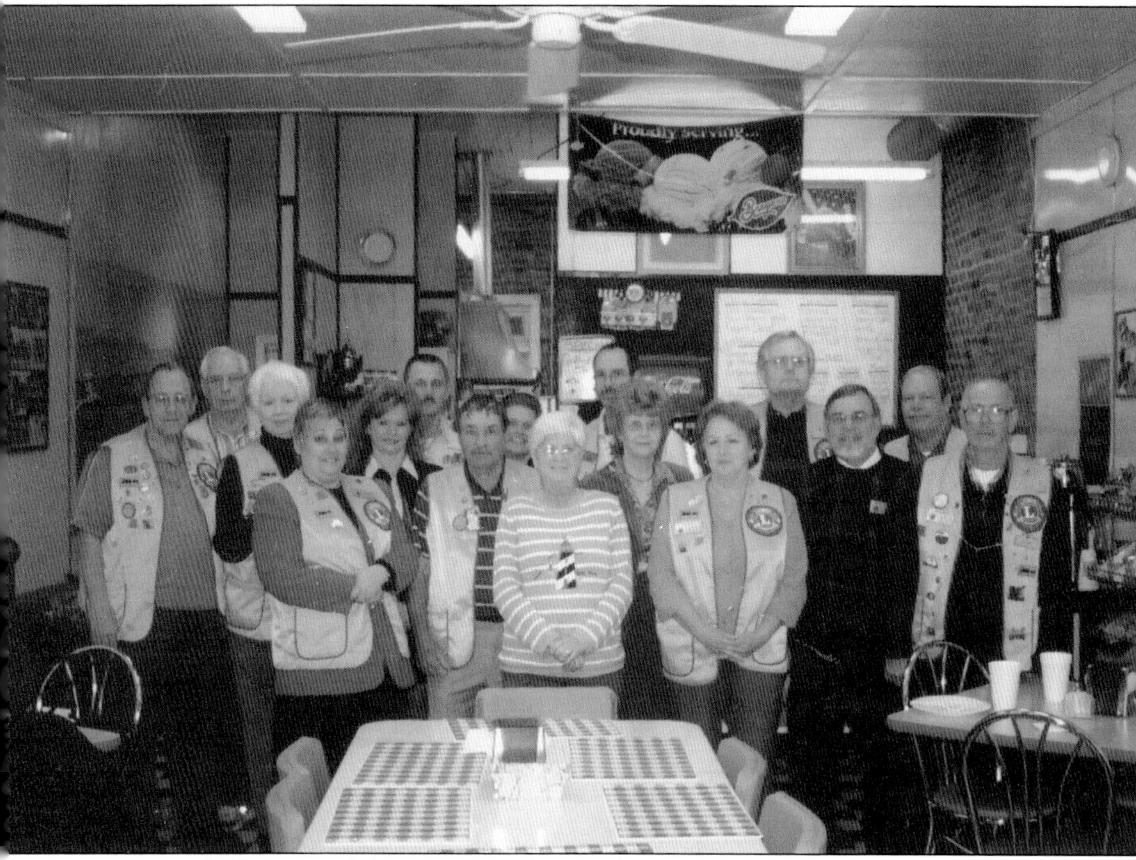

The Pembroke Lions Club was organized May 6, 1975. The club functions today, with the Sight Program as one of its main activities. Other activities include the Leader Dog Program, Lighthouse Foundation, and Georgia Lions Camp for the Blind. Meetings are held once a month at the Coffee Hop in Pembroke.

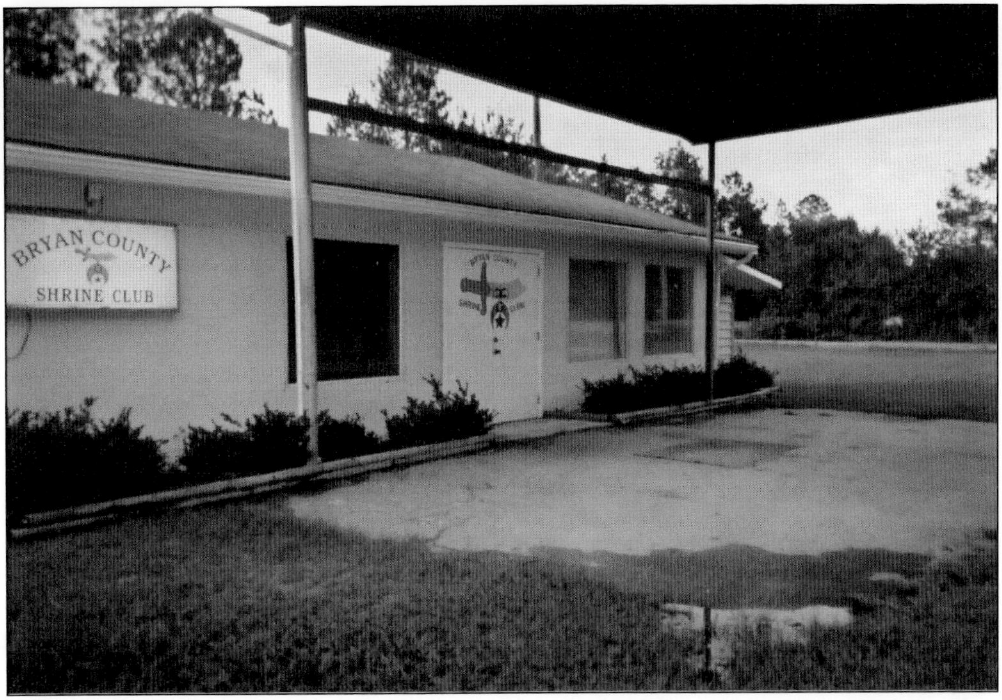

The Bryan County Shrine Club holds meetings at their clubhouse located on Highway 280, east of Pembroke. Shriners are always dedicated to helping burn victims and crippled and handicapped children.

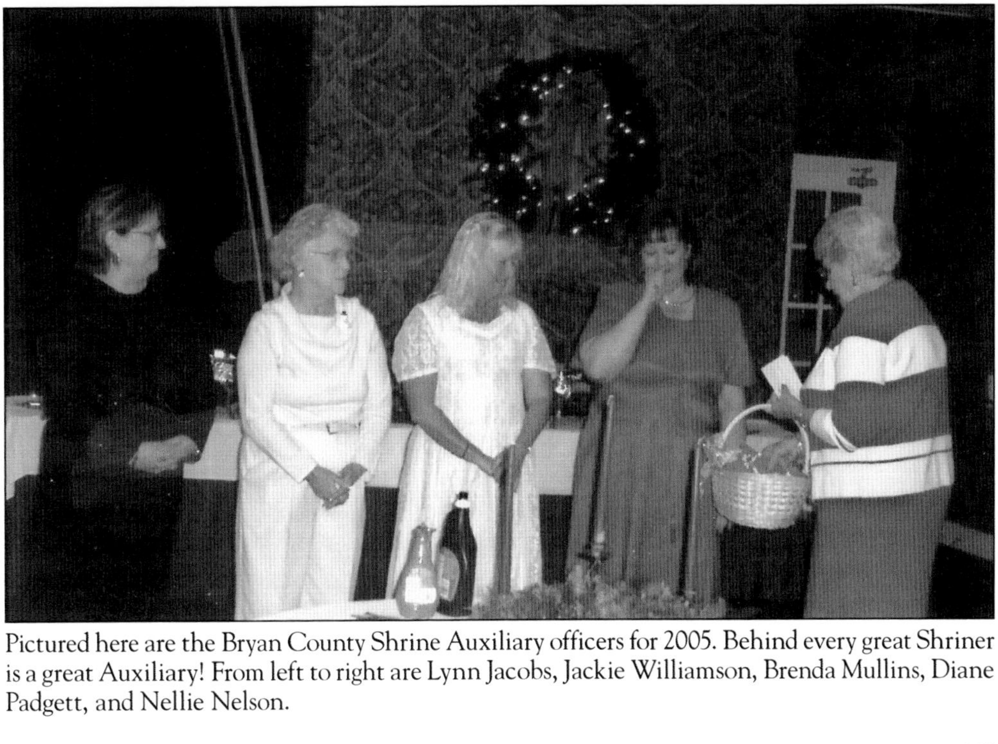

Pictured here are the Bryan County Shrine Auxiliary officers for 2005. Behind every great Shriner is a great Auxiliary! From left to right are Lynn Jacobs, Jackie Williamson, Brenda Mullins, Diane Padgett, and Nellie Nelson.

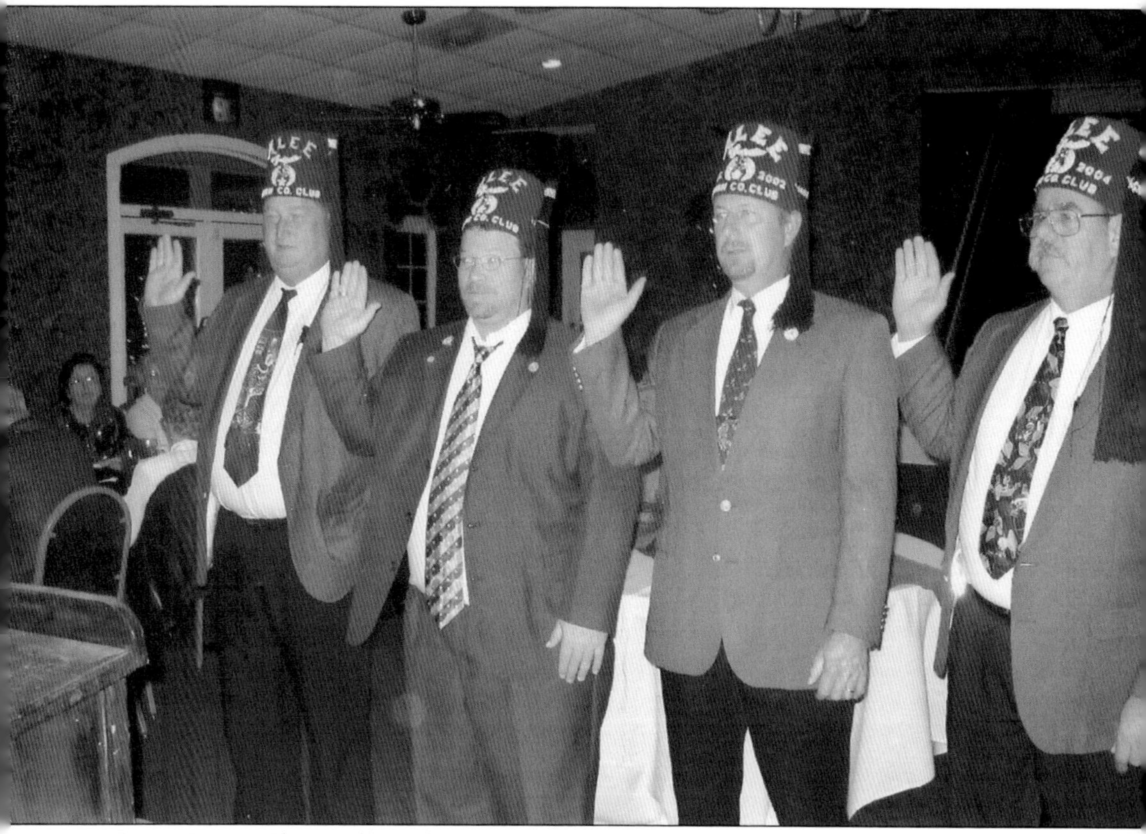

Bryan County Shrine officers for 2005 are sworn in. From left to right are Oscar Padgett, Ronnie Mullins, Aaron Williamson, and Larry Jacobs.

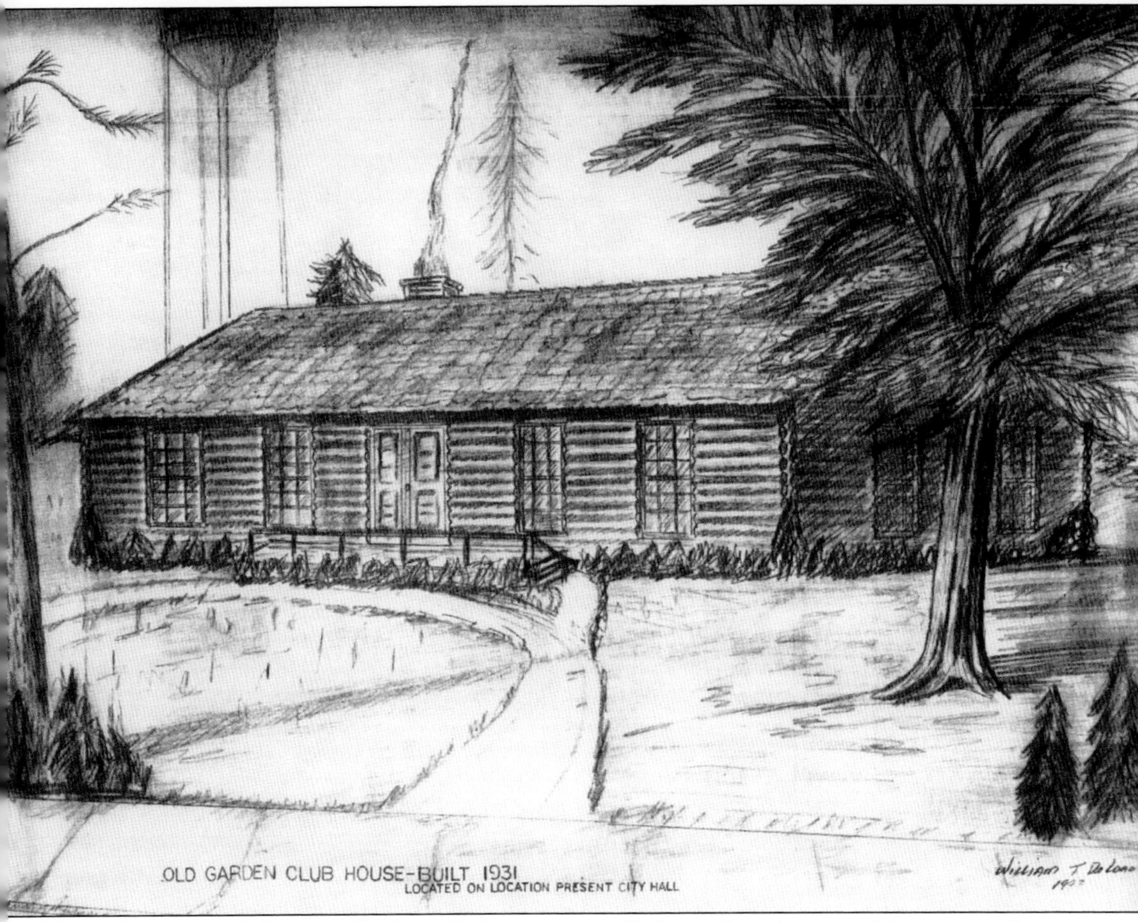

The old Garden Club House, built in 1931, was originally located on the site of the present-day Pembroke City Hall. Members of the building committee were Mrs. C. C. DeLoach, chairperson;, Mrs. R. M. Surles, secretary; Mrs. N. O. Morrison; Mrs. R. L. Adams; Mrs. H. M. Sanders; Mrs. T. H. Edwards; and Mrs. C. M. Sims.

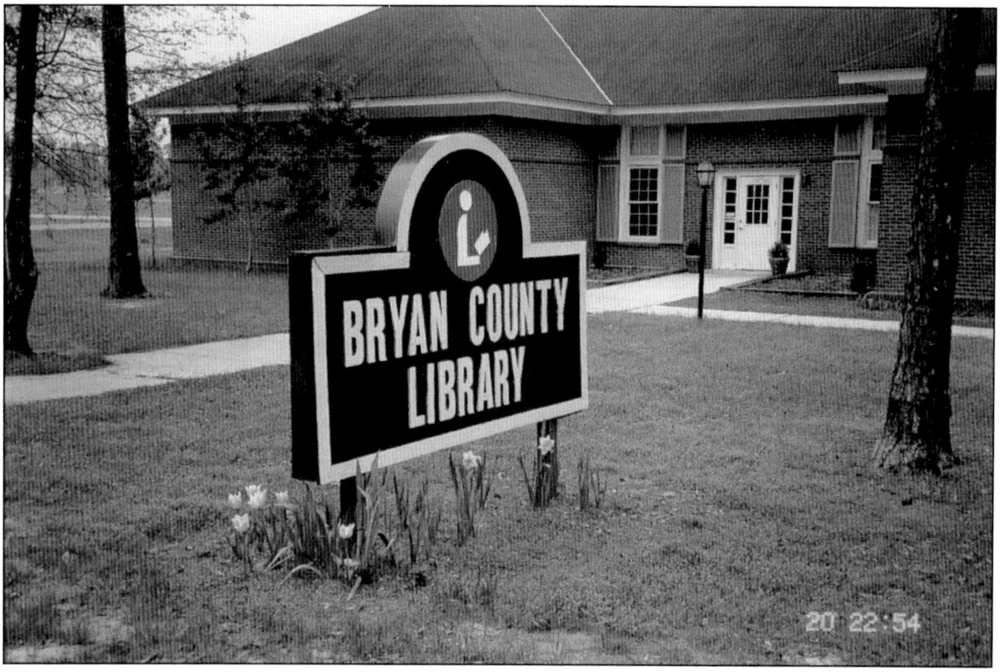

The Bryan County Library sign is located on Camellia Drive within walking distance of Bryan County High School. The sign is a beautification project of the Garden Club, as are the grounds. The landscape design installation and the maintenance of the grounds were accomplished by the Garden Club in 1996.

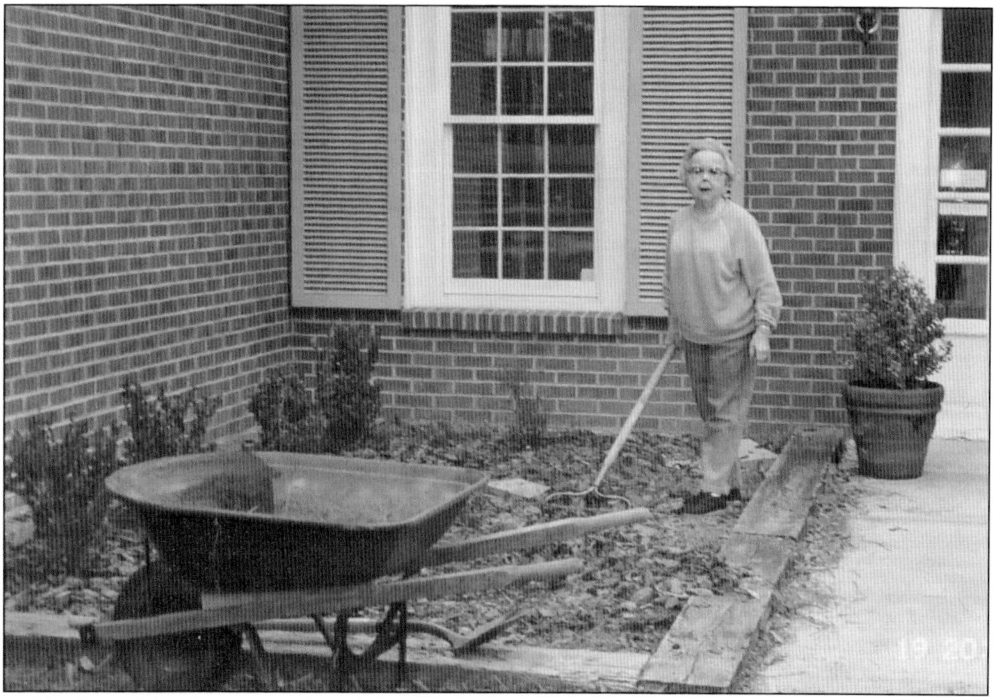
Mildred Strickland is pictured working on landscaping project at the library. Ms. Strickland is a longtime officer and member of the Pembroke Garden Club.

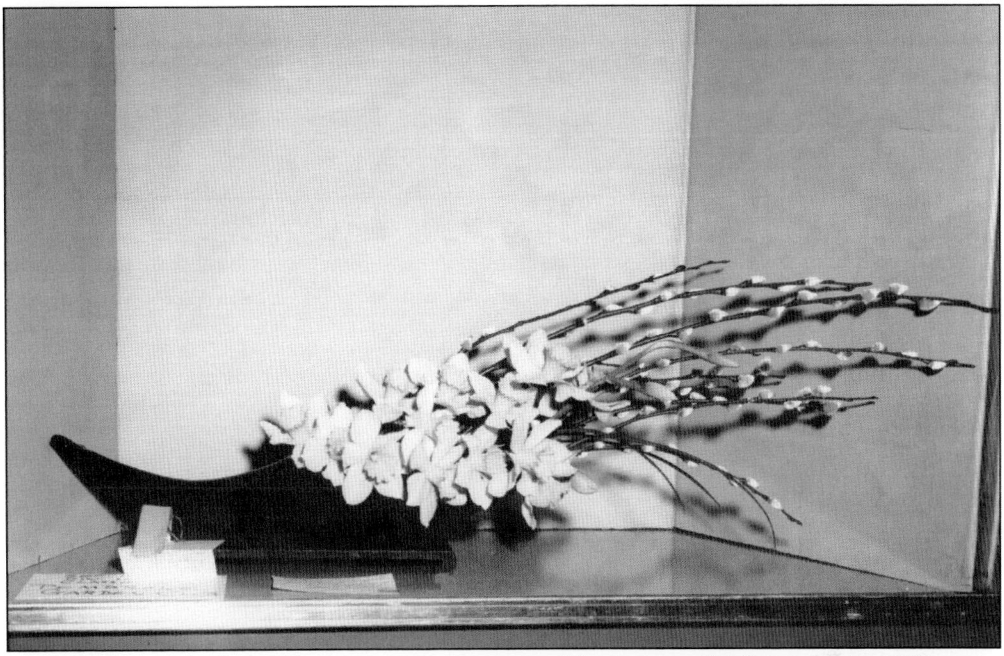

This Garden Club Flower Show winner was presented by Imogene W. Bacon in the 1950s.

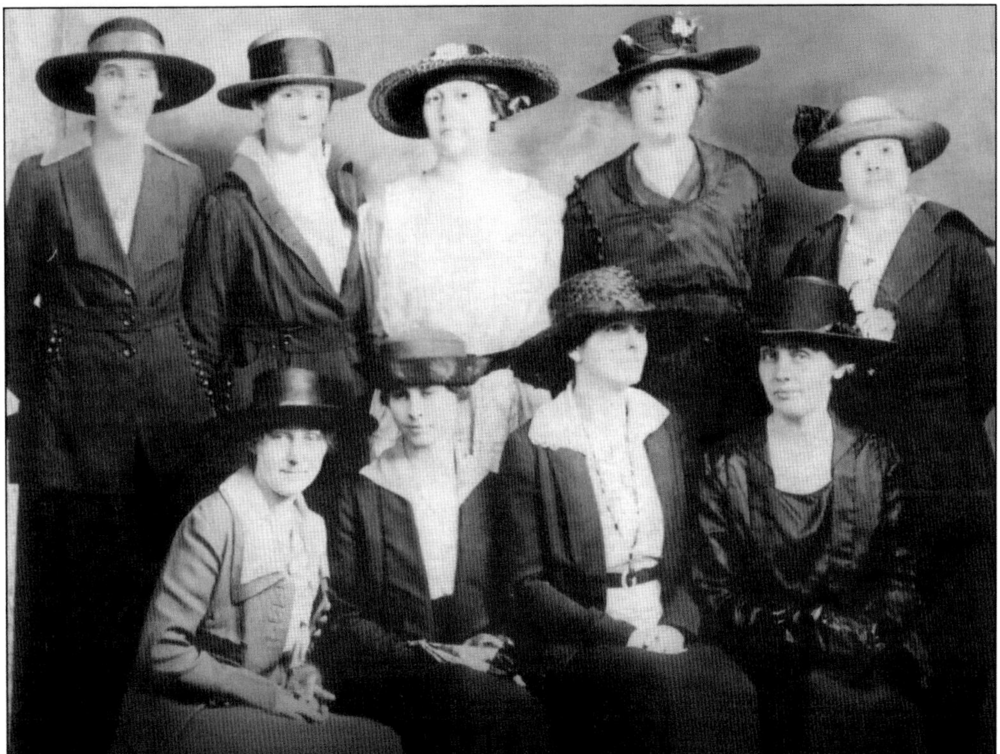

In this 1930 photograph, the original Garden Club members, pictured in alphabetical order, are Mrs. L. R. Adams, president; Mrs. Benton; Mrs. H. H. Dukes; Mrs. Perry Dukes; Mrs. Stella Lanier; Mrs. Eloie Mikell; Mrs. Ethel Morrison; Mrs. W. K. Smith; and Mrs. J. O. Strickland.

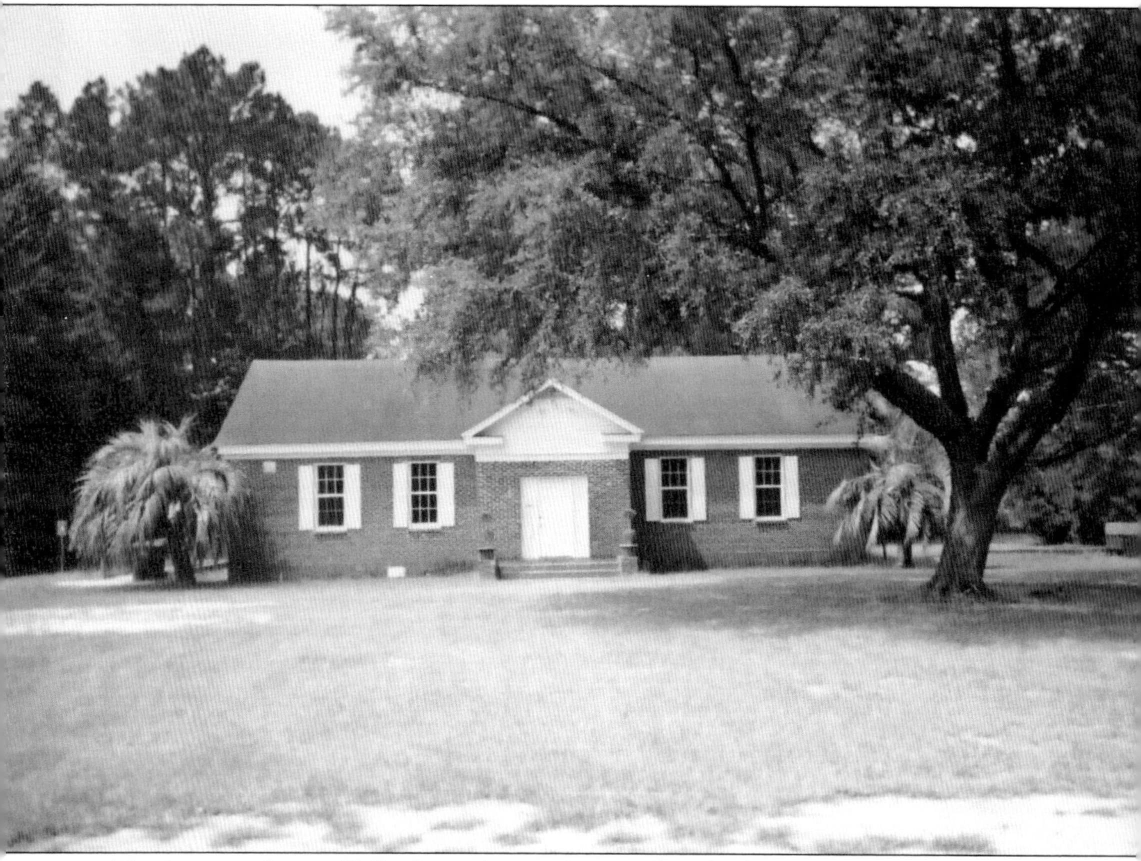

The American Legion Hall is located one mile west of Pembroke on Highway 280. It was founded in 1943 and is known as the John Duggar Post 164. The permanent charter was not obtained until 1947. The American Legion originally began in 1918 after World War I, and it is the only patriotic organization sanctioned by Congress. The purpose of this organization is to help veterans and their families.

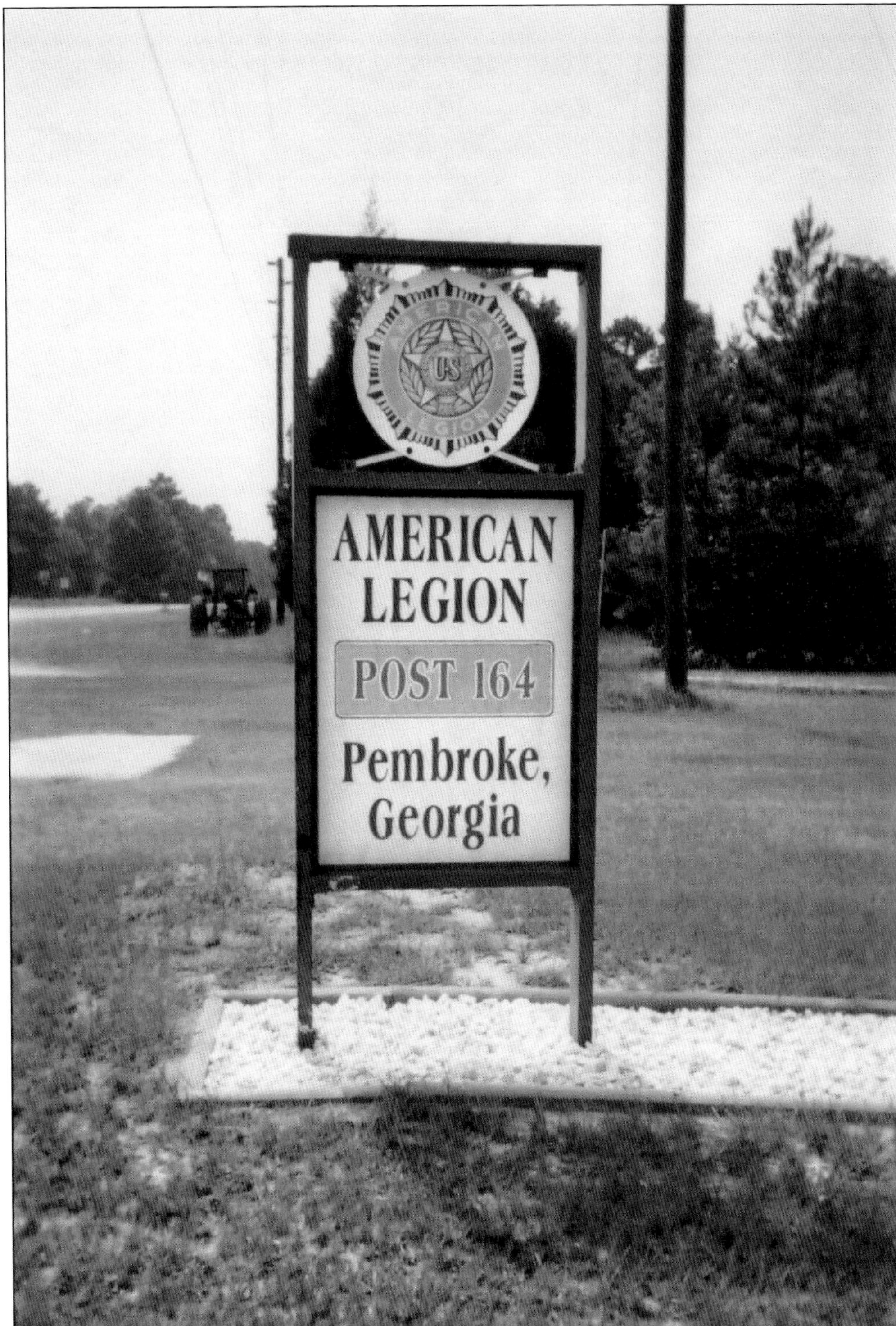

This American Legion sign designates the location of the American Legion Hall building on the west side of Pembroke on Highway 280.

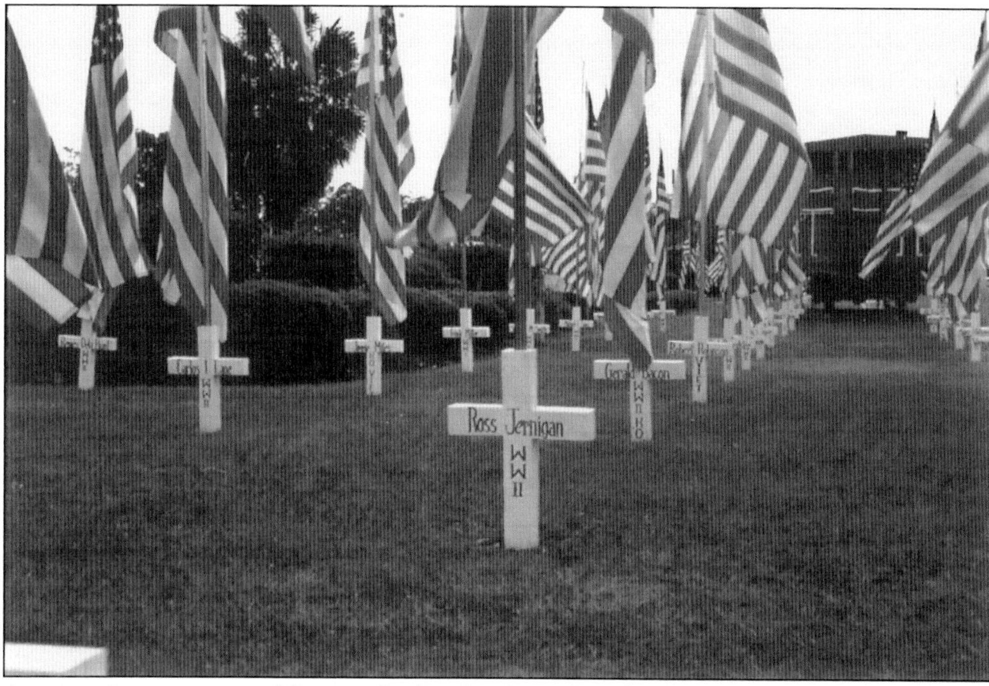

American Legion memorial flags are displayed at the park in downtown Pembroke. The displaying of the flags began on Memorial Day, 1995.

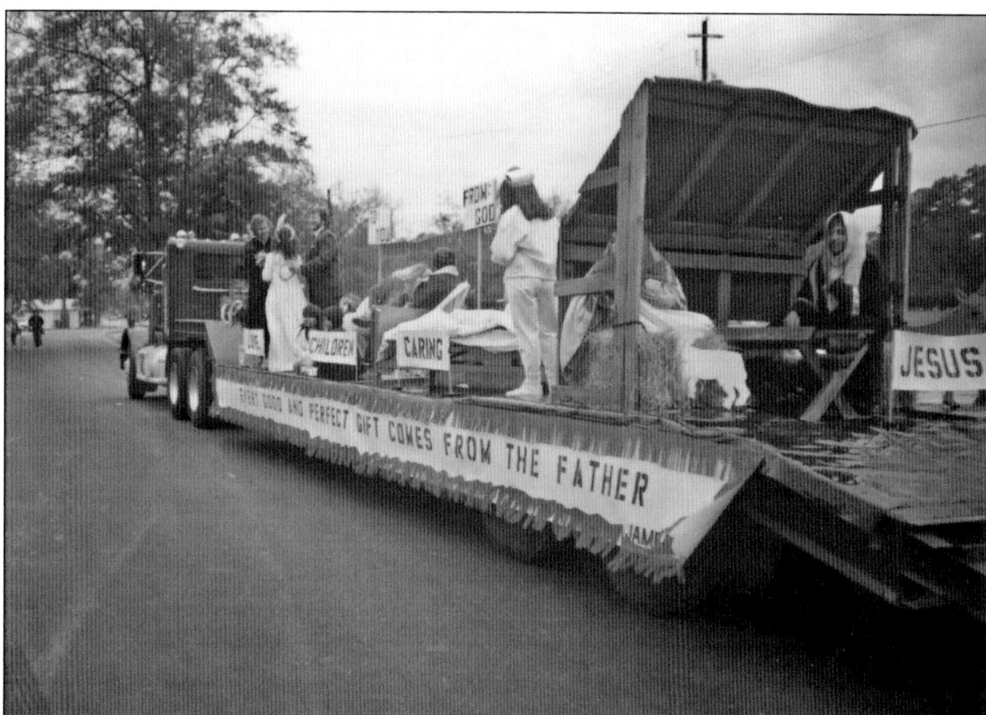

A beautiful rendition of the Christmas season was created by Beulah Baptist Church for this Pembroke Christmas parade in the mid-1990s.

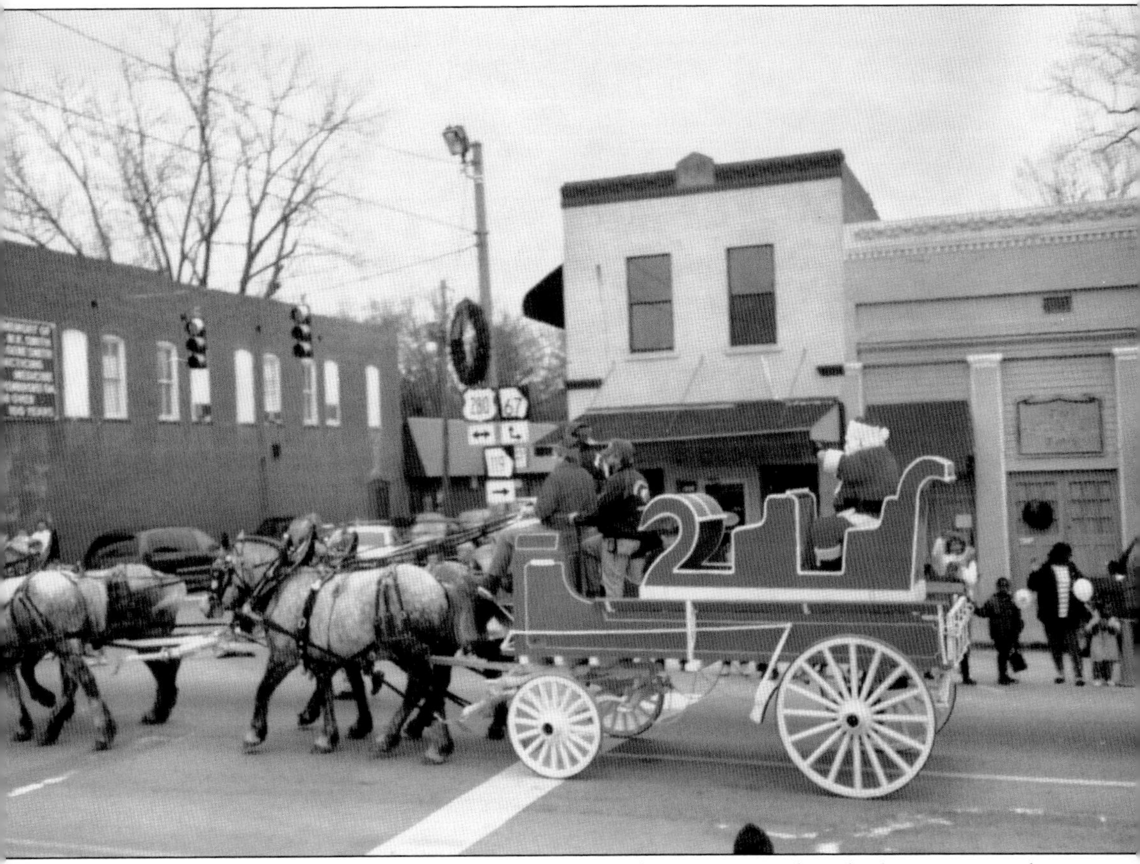

A mule-drawn wagon was another attraction in the Christmas parade, which is sponsored annually by the 4-H Club.

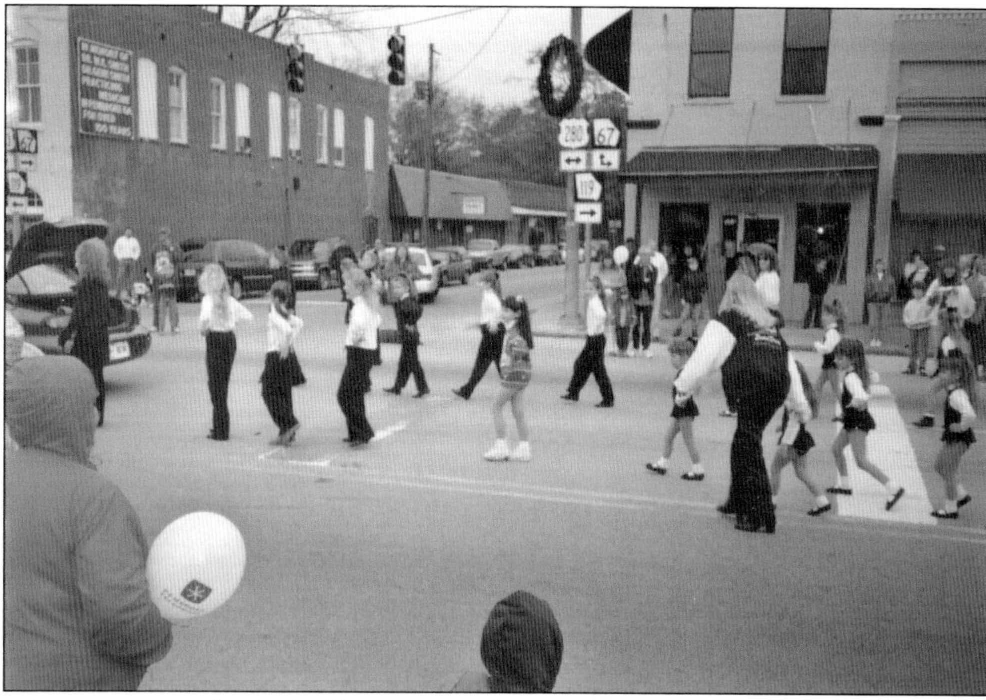

A dance group marches in the Christmas parade.

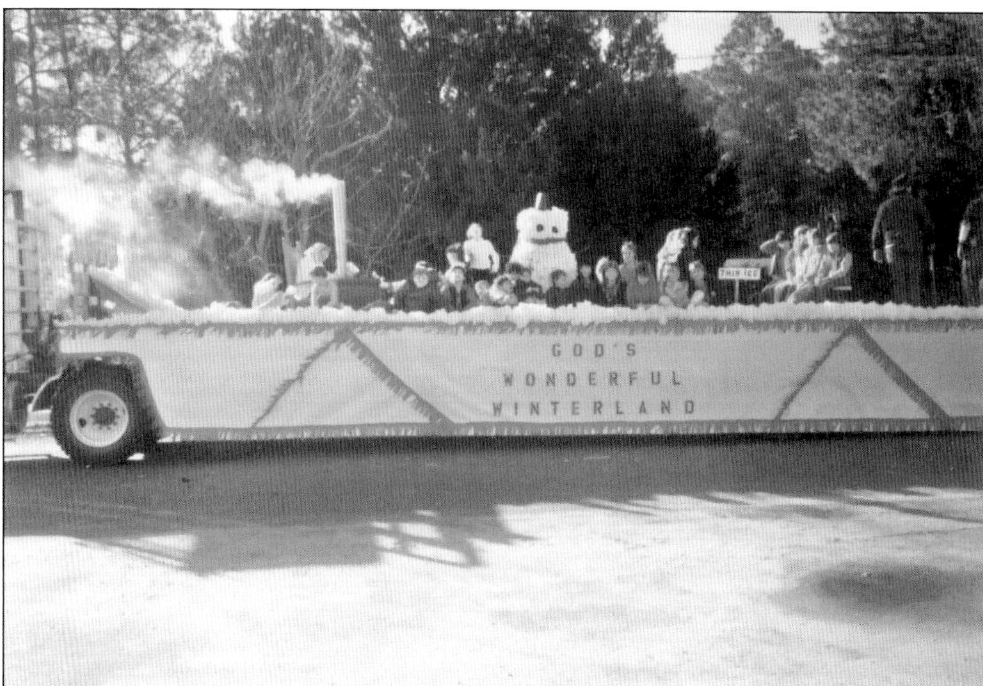

The Winterland float was another beautiful float created by Beulah Baptist Church.

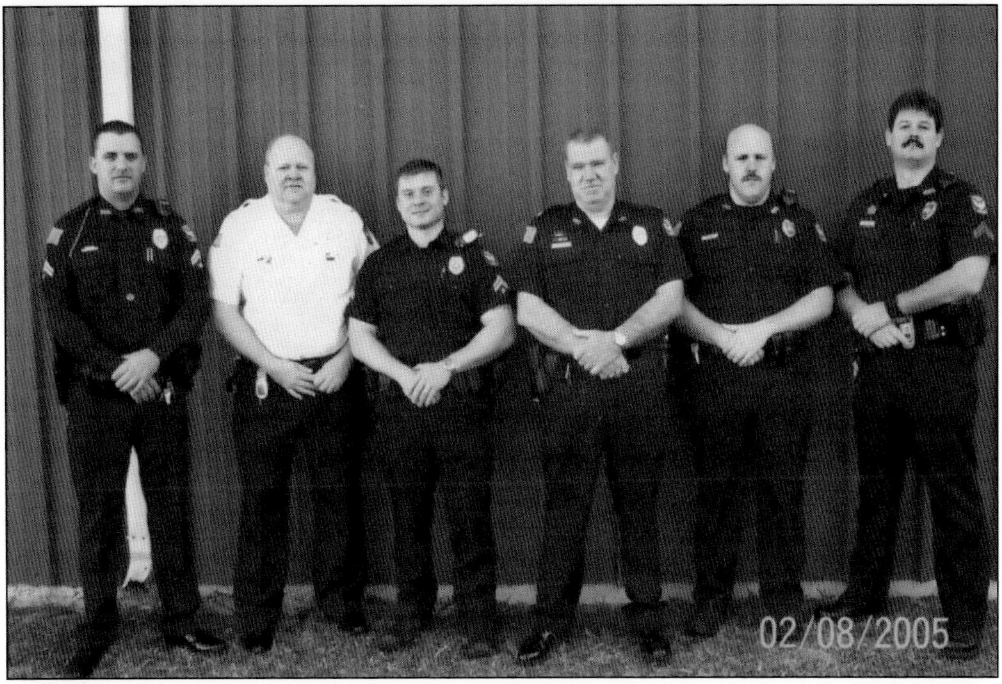

Pembroke police officers pictured here are, from left to right, James Doyle, Chief Bill Collins, Billy Jack Grey, Pat Kyle, Richard Taylor, and Jim Jefferies.

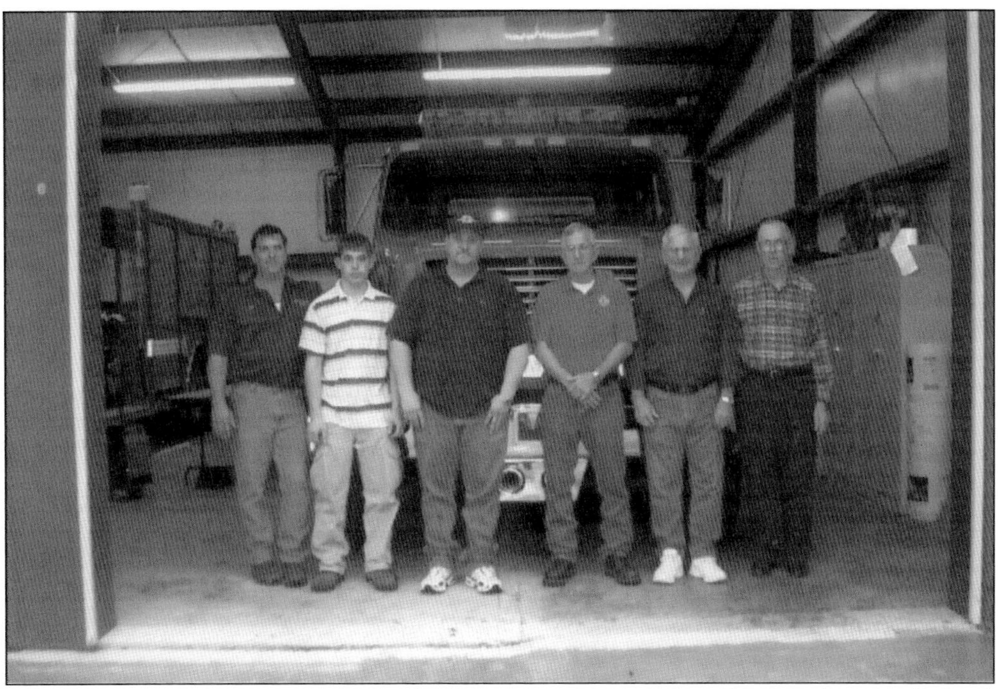

Jimmy Cook is the fire chief of the Pembroke Fire Department. From left to right are Bob Floyd, Peter Waters, David Shuman, Jimmy Cook, Freddie Cook, and Rex Smith.

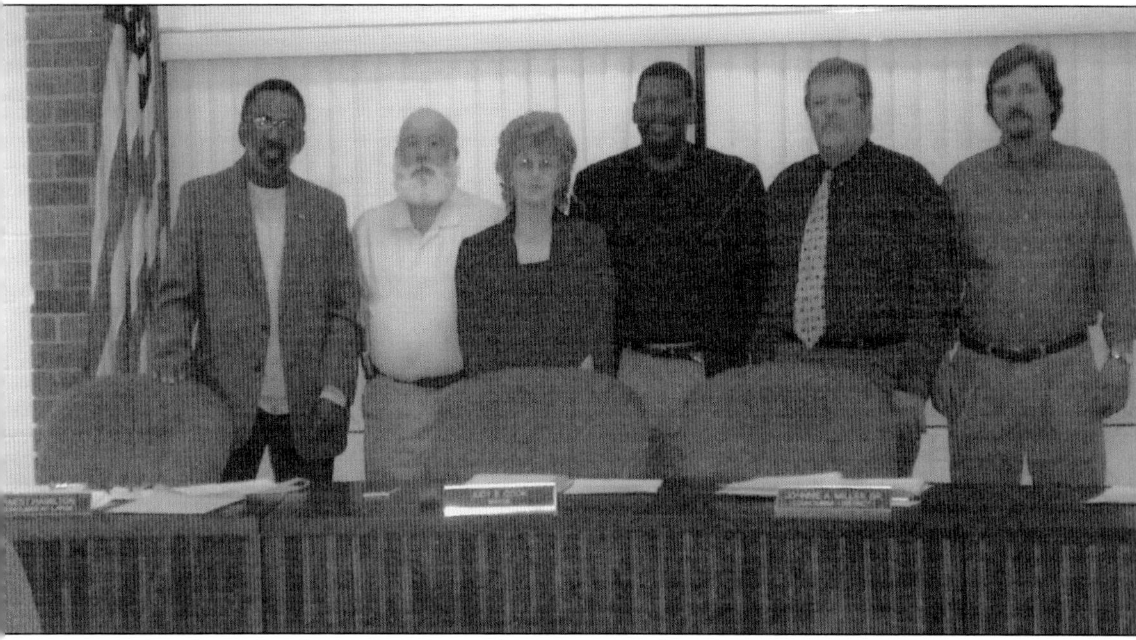

Pictured at a Pembroke City Council meeting are, from left to right, council members Elijah Lewis and Ernest Hamilton, Mayor Judy Cook, and council members Johnnie Miller, Randall Butler, and Joey Burnsed.